ECONOMETRICS OF CLIMATE, ENERGY, AND GREEN TRANSITION

ADVANCES IN ECONOMETRICS

Recent Volumes:

Volume 38:	Regression Discontinuity Designs: Theory and Applications – Edited by Matias D. Cattaneo and Juan Carlos Escanciano
Volume 39:	The Econometrics of Complex Survey Data: Theory and Applications – Edited by Kim P. Huynh, David T. Jacho-Chávez and Guatam Tripathi
Volume 40A:	Topics in Identification, Limited Dependent Variables, Partial Observability, Experimentation, and Flexible Modelling Part A – Edited by Ivan Jeliazkov and Justin L. Tobias
Volume 40B:	Topics in Identification, Limited Dependent Variables, Partial Observability, Experimentation, and Flexible Modelling Part B – Edited by Ivan Jeliazkov and Justin L. Tobias
Volume 41:	Essays in Honor of Cheng Hsiao – Edited by Tong Li, M. Hashem Pesaran and Dek Terrell
Volume 42:	The Econometrics of Networks – Edited by Áureo de Paula, Elie Tamer and Marcel-Cristian Voia
Volume 43A:	Essays in Honor of M. Hashem Pesaran – Edited by Alexander Chudik, Cheng Hsiao and Allan Timmermann
Volume 43B:	Essays in Honor of M. Hashem Pesaran – Edited by Alexander Chudik, Cheng Hsiao and Allan Timmermann
Volume 44A:	Essays in Honour of Fabio Canova – Edited by Juan J. Dolado, Luca Gambetti and Christian Matthes
Volume 44B:	Essays in Honour of Fabio Canova – Edited by Juan J. Dolado, Luca Gambetti and Christian Matthes
Volume 45A:	Essays in Honor of Joon Y. Park – Edited by Yoosoon Chang, Sokbae Lee and J. Isaac Miller
Volume 45B:	Essays in Honor of Joon Y. Park – Edited by Yoosoon Chang, Sokbae Lee and J. Isaac Miller
Volume 46:	Essays in Honor of Subal Kumbhakar – Edited by Christopher F. Parmeter, Mike G. Tsionas, and Hung-Jen Wang

ADVANCES IN ECONOMETRICS VOLUME 47A

ECONOMETRICS OF CLIMATE, ENERGY, AND GREEN TRANSITION

EDITED BY

THOMAS B. FOMBY
Southern Methodist University, USA

MARINA FRIEDRICH
Vrije Universiteit Amsterdam, The Netherlands

AND

ERIC HILLEBRAND
Aarhus University, Denmark

emerald PUBLISHING

United Kingdom – North America – Japan
India – Malaysia – China

Emerald Publishing Limited
Emerald Publishing, Floor 5, Northspring, 21-23 Wellington Street, Leeds LS1 4DL.

First edition 2026

British Library Cataloguing in Publication Data
A catalogue record for this book is available from the British Library

ISBN: 978-1-80686-480-5 (Print)
ISBN: 978-1-80686-479-9 (Online)
ISBN: 978-1-80686-481-2 (Epub)

ISSN: 0731-9053 (Series)

An electronic copy of the supplementary material can be downloaded for free at any time from Emerald's website, www.emerald.com. This additional content includes computer programs, data sets, and mathematical appendices related to chapters in the published volumes.

Printed and bound by CPI Group (UK) Ltd, Croydon, CR0 4YY

INVESTOR IN PEOPLE

CONTENTS

Introduction
Thomas B. Fomby, Marina Friedrich, and Eric Hillebrand 1

Chapter 1 Understanding Vulnerability to Poverty and Natural Disasters in Latin America and the Caribbean
Gustavo Canavire-Bacarreza, Sergio Olivieri, Monserrat Serio, and Adriana Conconi 7

Chapter 2 The Effect of US Climate Policy on Financial Markets: An Event Study of the Inflation Reduction Act
Michael D. Bauer, Eric A. Offner, and Glenn D. Rudebusch 57

Chapter 3 Nighttime Light Pollution and Economic Activities: A Spatio-Temporal Model with Common Factors in US Counties
Georges Bresson, Jean-Michel Etienne, and Guy Lacroix 91

Chapter 4 Wind Energy, CO_2 Abatement, and the Environmental Kuznets Curve in Denmark
Federico Carlini, Bent Jesper Christensen, Nabanita Datta Gupta, and Paolo Santucci de Magistris 119

Chapter 5 Persistent Cycles and Long-Run Covariability in Paleoclimate Time Series
Vasco J. Gabriel, Luis F. Martins, and Anthoulla Phella 147

INTRODUCTION

Thomas B. Fomby[a], Marina Friedrich[b], and Eric Hillebrand[c]

[a]*Southern Methodist University, USA*
[b]*Vrije Universiteit Amsterdam, The Netherlands*
[c]*Aarhus University, Denmark*

The field of climate econometrics has undergone rapid development in recent years, shaped by the growing demand for empirical methods that can rigorously assess the multifaceted interactions between the economy and the climate system. Situated at the intersection of climate science and econometric methodology, this field responds to the urgent need for tools that quantify the economic impacts of climate variability and long-term climate change. Rising policy interest, data availability, and the increasing frequency of extreme events have collectively motivated the expansion of climate econometrics as a recognized and distinct research area.

This volume appears at a particularly timely juncture. The contributions assembled here reflect the current momentum in climate econometric research, both in theoretical development and empirical application. The methodological approaches span reduced-form time series models, structural identification strategies, spatial econometrics, and long-memory estimation techniques. Thematically, the volume addresses a wide spectrum of questions: from the dynamic response of financial markets to climate policy announcements, to the co-evolution of greenhouse gas concentrations and global temperatures over paleoclimatic timescales. Several contributions are directly concerned with the effects of the Paris Agreement, the COVID-19 pandemic, or natural disaster exposure, showing how economic inference can be brought to bear on recent and salient global phenomena.

The increasing scholarly attention to these topics is evidenced not only by the quantity and quality of research output but also by institutional developments. Among these, the **Econometric Models of Climate Change (EMCC)** network has

Econometrics of Climate, Energy, and Green Transition
Advances in Econometrics, Volume 47A, 1–6

ISSN: 0731-9053/doi:10.1108/S0731-90532026000047A001

played a central role in creating a forum for exchange and collaboration. As board members of EMCC and co-organizers of its conferences, we have observed how the network has contributed to consolidating this field. Since its inception in 2016, the annual EMCC conference series has brought together econometricians, statisticians, and climate scientists to present work at the frontier of model-based climate-economic analysis. The upcoming 9th EMCC conference in Victoria, Canada, in August 2025 continues this tradition, reaffirming the role of econometrics in shaping the empirical foundations of climate-related policy.

In parallel, leading journals have increasingly dedicated space to this research area. Notably, the *Journal of Econometrics* published a special issue in 2020 (Volume 214, Issue 1) focused entirely on EMCC, highlighting advances in identification, trend-cycle decomposition, and cointegration techniques in climate applications. Similarly, a special issue in *Energy Economics* (2023, Volume 121) compiled recent research on climate risk and transition pathways, further underscoring the centrality of econometric tools to the analysis of climate policy and its economic repercussions. This was followed by a second themed issue in *Journal of Econometrics*, published in 2024 (Volume 239), devoted to econometric models of the socio-economic impacts of climate change, climate policy evaluation, and econometric models of climate finance. These editorial decisions reflect the broad recognition of the methodological and applied contributions that climate econometrics now offers to both economics and climate science.

The present volume is situated within this broader research agenda. Each chapter included here contributes new empirical insights or methodological strategies, advancing the understanding of climate-related economic processes. By emphasizing rigor, replicability, and the integration of domain-specific knowledge, the contributions demonstrate the potential of econometric models to inform debates on mitigation, adaptation, and financial resilience in a changing climate.

We hope that this volume serves as a resource for researchers working in climate econometrics and as a bridge for scholars in related domains – energy economics, finance, environmental policy – who seek to engage with this growing literature. The diversity of questions addressed and the analytical clarity of the approaches taken exemplify the intellectual vibrancy of the field and the continuing relevance of econometrics to the climate challenge.

SUMMARY OF ARTICLES – VOLUME 47A

Canavire-Bacarreza, Olivieri, Serio, and Conconi develop a method to assess household-level vulnerability to poverty due to natural disasters in seven Latin American and Caribbean countries. Using cross-sectional household survey data (SEDLAC) and disaster risk information (ThinkHazard! and EM-DAT), the authors estimate the probability of a household falling into poverty, conditional on exposure to hazards (e.g., floods, droughts, and earthquakes) and coping capacities. The core method is a multilevel mixed-effects probit model incorporating spatial and demographic heterogeneity. Results indicate strong geographic variation in vulnerability, with Honduras exhibiting the highest rates. Key risk factors include reliance on informal employment, agricultural income, and inadequate housing. Conversely, salaried employment, asset ownership, and social protection reduce vulnerability. The model also reveals that disaster exposure and adaptive capacity jointly shape poverty risks. The study provides spatially disaggregated outputs to guide local policymaking.

Bauer, Offner, and Rudebusch examine how US equity markets responded to major legislative developments surrounding the Inflation Reduction Act (IRA) of 2022, the most significant US climate policy to date. Using event study methodology, they identify two pivotal announcements in July 2022 – first, when climate legislation appeared dead ("brown event"), and second, when the IRA was unexpectedly revived ("green event"). Stock market responses were heterogeneous: green firms, with low emissions or high ESG scores, declined after the brown event but rose sharply after the green event, while brown firms responded oppositely. Industry-level analyses revealed similar patterns, though standard industry greenness measures poorly predicted firm-level responses. The findings underscore that transition risk from climate policy – while economically significant – did not trigger instability, suggesting that even ambitious policies like the IRA can be absorbed smoothly by financial markets. The authors argue for more granular transition risk assessments beyond traditional sectoral classifications.

Bresson, Etienne, and Lacroix develop a spatial econometric model to analyze how nighttime light pollution in US counties responds to economic activity, urban density, and air pollution. Building on a spatial urban framework, they specify a dynamic general nesting spatial panel model with common factors (DGNSP-CCE), which accounts for both spatial spillovers and unobserved global shocks. Using county-level data for 2012–2019, they estimate the model via quasi-maximum likelihood. Their results indicate that radiance increases with GDP/km^2, urbanization, and PM2.5 levels, with significant heterogeneity across counties. Spillover effects are particularly strong – neighboring counties' characteristics exert measurable influence on local light pollution. High-radiance counties show saturation effects, while peri-urban and mid-density areas exhibit higher marginal sensitivities. The model outperforms simpler spatial specifications and underlines the necessity of accounting for spatial dependence and latent factors in environmental-economic modeling. Policy implications include targeting pollution control in counties with the highest marginal responsiveness.

Carlini, Christensen, Gupta, and Santucci de Magistris analyze the impact of wind energy on CO_2 emissions from Danish electricity production using data from 2005–2019. They estimate a series of regression models, including dynamic specifications and two-stage least squares (2SLS), where wind speed serves as an instrument for wind energy. Their findings indicate that wind energy has a statistically significant and causal negative effect on emissions. Moreover, the traditionally observed Environmental Kuznets Curve (EKC) – a concave relationship between emissions and output – disappears once wind energy is included in the model, implying that emissions reductions associated with economic growth are actually attributable to clean energy adoption. Temperature also influences emissions primarily through reduced heating demand. The analysis is robust to fractional cointegration methods that allow for long memory in the data. Their results support wind adoption as a key driver of decarbonization in Denmark and question the explanatory role of the EKC.

Gabriel, Martins, and Phella investigate the statistical implications of persistent cycles in paleoclimate time series – particularly for estimating long-run relationships between atmospheric CO_2 concentration and temperature. They demonstrate analytically and through Monte Carlo simulations that standard cointegration tests become invalid in the presence of large, cyclical components characteristic of glacial-interglacial dynamics. To address this, the authors adopt and extend the low-frequency covariability framework of Müller and Watson (2018), which enables robust inference on long-term comovement without requiring assumptions on the order of integration. Applying this method to 800,000 years of Antarctic ice-core data, they find that a 100 ppm increase in atmospheric CO_2 corresponds to a ~1°C rise in temperature over long horizons. Their results confirm a strong, statistically significant long-run correlation between CO_2 and temperature, robust to orbital forcing controls. The paper advances empirical paleoclimatology by offering tools better suited for paleoclimate analysis.

SUMMARY OF ARTICLES – VOLUME 47B

Gadea and Gonzalo develop a methodology for analyzing climate change in the polar regions by transforming distributional temperature characteristics – such as quantiles and interquartile range – into time series. Applying this framework to Arctic and Antarctic land-based station data, they test for warming, its acceleration, and amplification. In the Arctic (1950–2019), all quantiles show statistically significant warming, particularly in the lower quantiles, indicating intensified winter warming. Amplification is concentrated in cold extremes, consistent with climate models but lower than some observational studies. The upper quantiles, by contrast, show stabilization. No significant warming, acceleration, or amplification is detected in the Antarctic, reflecting sparse and uneven data as well as different geophysical dynamics. The authors argue for distributional approaches in climate analysis, as focusing solely on averages masks crucial heterogeneity. Their regression-based amplification method offers improved inference over common ratio-based techniques.

Gronwald and Jin analyze the long-run relationship between global temperature anomalies and radiative forcing from greenhouse gases using two methods: Müller and Watson's (2018) long-run covariability framework and the Thick Pen Measure of Association (TPMA). The former estimates a long-run linear regression coefficient of 0.35 K/(W/m^2), indicating substantial climate sensitivity and a statistically significant relationship over multi-decade horizons. Long-run correlation estimates range between 0.64 and 0.89, depending on the temporal smoothing parameter. The TPMA and its multiscale extension (MTTPMA) confirm that co-movement increases with time scale, and suggest modest time-variation in the relationship, particularly post-1950. The study contributes to debates on temperature-forcing dynamics, addressing concerns about trend specification in traditional cointegration models. It also informs climate-economy modelers by providing robust empirical measures of temperature sensitivity to greenhouse gas forcing, highlighting that long-run associations are comparable in strength to key macroeconomic relationships.

Jackson, Juselius, Martinez, and Pretis apply multi-cointegration vector autoregression (CVAR) models to study the joint dynamics of Greenland and Antarctic ice mass loss from 1992 to 2010. They show that the ice sheets are best modeled as integrated of order two ($I(2)$), capturing persistent trends and equilibrium relationships missed by simpler $I(1)$ models. The analysis reveals a significant long-run relationship between Greenland and West Antarctica, and an intra-Antarctic link between West and East Antarctica. These connections align with climate drivers, especially ocean heat content, and suggest feedbacks indicative of tipping behavior in Greenland. Out-of-sample forecasts (2011–2023) and long-term projections to 2100 align with physical model estimates under high-emission scenarios. The results challenge static copula-based sea-level models and demonstrate that econometric methods can capture dynamic interdependence, nonlinearity, and potential instability. The study offers an empirical framework for improving probabilistic sea-level rise forecasts using observational ice sheet data.

Kivedal investigates the impact of natural disasters and extreme weather on regional housing markets in Norway, leveraging a unique dataset of insurance claims and housing transactions from 2000 to 2019. Given the near-universal and affordable coverage for natural disasters via fire insurance policies, Norway offers an ideal case to assess whether physical damage and perceived risk affect housing prices. Using local projection methods on municipality-level panel data, the study estimates dynamic effects of disaster-related claims – distinguishing between storm, flood, and avalanche impacts – on house prices. The findings reveal limited but occasionally significant negative effects, particularly in municipalities with historically severe damages. Water-related damages, however, show no consistent influence. The results suggest that while insurance mitigates direct financial loss, disasters can still alter subjective risk perceptions, modestly affecting housing demand. The study concludes that climate change-induced increases in disaster frequency may amplify these effects, warranting closer integration of risk assessments into housing market analyses.

Li and Cummins develop a Bayesian composite likelihood framework to estimate Equilibrium Climate Sensitivity (ECS) by pooling energy balance model fits to 31 Atmosphere-Ocean General Circulation Model (AOGCM) simulated datasets from CMIP5 and CMIP6 under a CO_2 quadrupling experiment. Their approach treats ECS as a common structural parameter, allowing model-specific heterogeneity in feedbacks and forcing. They derive composite posteriors using a curvature-adjusted MCMC sampler, addressing misspecification and dependence across AOGCMs. The resulting ECS estimate is 3.65K with a 95% credible interval of (2.5K, 5K), aligning with but narrowing the IPCC's "very likely" range. The posterior distribution is right-skewed, indicating upward risk. Their framework allows integration of observational data and emergent constraints through estimated model weights, and supports robust, data-driven ECS inference across climate models. The authors argue their method improves upon existing techniques by statistically combining evidence while retaining physical interpretability and econometric rigor.

O'Donnell proposes a theoretically grounded method for constructing a Sustainable Productivity Index (SPI) that integrates good outputs, bad outputs (e.g., greenhouse gases), and inputs. The author's framework uses volume indexes that satisfy six axioms from measurement theory – such as proportionality, commensurability, and transitivity – ensuring internal consistency. The SPI is defined as a composite index combining output and input volumes, parameterized by $\alpha \in [0,1]$, which determines the weight on bad outputs. The author demonstrates that many commonly used productivity indexes violate key axioms and yield misleading results. The paper offers both analytical and empirical tools to assess the sensitivity of SPI values to index choice and α, including regression-based estimation. An application to sixteen Australian economic sectors from 1995 to 2019 shows that incorporating bad outputs substantially lowers productivity growth estimates – most notably in mining. The study concludes with a strong normative claim: only "proper" indexes yield meaningful productivity comparisons across time and space.

Tol develops a stochastic frontier model to disentangle the distinct effects of climate and weather on economic output across 160 countries over 1950–2014. In this framework, climate – measured by 30-year averages of temperature and precipitation – shapes the production frontier, while weather anomalies – deviations from those averages – contribute to inefficiency. The model reveals that climate strongly influences potential output: cold countries benefit from warming, hot countries suffer. Weather shocks reduce efficiency in poor and hot countries but may increase output in rich countries, possibly due to recovery effects or measurement artifacts. The climate effect dominates the weather effect in magnitude. The model is robust to alternative specifications, distributions, and trends, and distinguishes permanent impacts from transient fluctuations. Tol's results challenge previous findings that downplay precipitation effects, revealing strong heterogeneity across countries. The paper concludes by advocating for climate-economy models that explicitly separate long-run climate impacts from short-run weather shocks using frontier-based approaches.

Vera-Valdés and Kvist analyze how the Paris Agreement (PA) and the COVID-19 pandemic affected the persistence of volatility in stocks associated with the climate crisis, particularly energy stocks. Using long-range dependence estimators and squared log-returns, they compare volatility persistence across three periods: before and after the PA (2016) and before and after the pandemic (2020). Results show that the PA reduced volatility persistence for energy stocks – both green and brown – while it increased persistence for general (non-energy) stocks. In contrast, the COVID-19 pandemic increased volatility persistence across the board. To ensure robustness, the study uses multiverse analysis across a wide range of bandwidths and estimators. The findings suggest that international agreements like the PA may stabilize climate-related financial assets by reducing uncertainty, whereas exogenous shocks like pandemics broadly increase volatility. The study also introduces multiverse analysis as a valuable tool in financial econometrics.

CHAPTER 1

UNDERSTANDING VULNERABILITY TO POVERTY AND NATURAL DISASTERS IN LATIN AMERICA AND THE CARIBBEAN*

Gustavo Canavire-Bacarreza[a], Sergio Olivieri[b], Monserrat Serio[c], and Adriana Conconi[d]

[a]*World Bank, Poverty and Equity Global Practice, USA and Universidad Privada Boliviana, Bolivia*
[b]*World Bank, Poverty and Equity Global Practice, USA*
[c]*Universidad Nacional de Cuyo, Argentina*
[d]*VR, Brazil*

ABSTRACT

The frequency and intensity of natural disasters have increased worldwide in recent years, representing a severe threat to the most vulnerable households in Latin America and the Caribbean. This chapter provides measures of vulnerability to poverty at the household level considering natural hazards such as floods, landslides, cyclones, earthquakes, and droughts for seven countries of the region (Brazil, the Dominican Republic, Ecuador, El Salvador, Honduras,

*The opinions expressed in this paper are those of the authors and do not necessarily reflect the views of the World Bank, its Board of Directors, or the countries it represents, or the authors' affiliations.

Econometrics of Climate, Energy, and Green Transition
Advances in Econometrics, Volume 47A, 7–56

Published under exclusive licence by Emerald Publishing Limited
ISSN: 0731-9053/doi:10.1108/S0731-90532026000047A002

Mexico, and Peru), using cross-sectional data of household surveys from the SEDLAC database and natural events from the ThinkHazard! and the EM-DAT databases. The analysis displays different rates of vulnerability to poverty by country. Results suggest that vulnerability to poverty is remarkably related to the households' coping and adaptation strategies, and there is great heterogeneity depending on the country. The evidence generated by this approach helps understand which coping mechanisms and adaptation strategies are missing among vulnerable households that would alleviate or help to face the effects of natural disasters better. In addition, the information can be presented in the most disaggregated representative unit that the data allows, so policymakers can build more efficient management policies in their location.

Keywords: Vulnerability; natural disasters; poverty; LAC; shocks

JEL Classifications: Q54; I32; D1

1. INTRODUCTION

Climate change is a threat to the objective of sustainably eradicating poverty. Poor people are more often and harshly affected by climate change, having fewer mechanisms to cope, more losses, and less support to recover. But even those not in poverty can suffer negative impacts that condition their future welfare prospects. Climate change may impact people's welfare through various channels and simultaneously influence natural disasters, affecting people's well-being too. The specific impact of climate change on natural disaster events such as floods, landslides, droughts, and storms is challenging and complex to estimate. However, as Hallegatte (2014) mentions, climate change has played an increasing role over time, dramatically escalating natural hazards and displaying heterogeneous effects on people's well-being depending on the type of hazard. In Latin America and the Caribbean (LAC), the acceleration of climate change has shown a sharp increase in the frequency and intensity of extreme weather events (World Bank, 2022). In recent years, some of the deadliest natural catastrophes have occurred, including the earthquakes in Haiti (230,000 deaths in 2010 and 2,248 deaths in 2021), the Brumadinho mudslide in Brazil (300 deaths in 2019), and hurricanes Maria (3,059 deaths in 2017) and Eta (183 deaths in 2020) (UNDP, 2022). The number of people in the region affected by natural disasters has also increased substantially over the last decades. Between 2000 and 2019, the Emergency Events Database (EM-DAT) database indicates that 41 million people have been affected by floods, while droughts have impacted the lives of approximately 53 million people. In this study, we look at natural disasters and the mechanisms of households to cope with them.

We measure vulnerability to poverty by considering natural hazards' damage, exposure, and coping mechanisms in seven countries of LAC. The definition of vulnerability, followed by international organizations such as the World Bank, the Intergovernmental Panel on Climate Change (IPCC), the European Commission, and the ISO standards, among others, encompasses a variety of concepts and elements, including sensitivity or susceptibility to harm and lack of capacity to cope and adapt. Here we consider both the likely damage that comes from a natural disaster shock and the ability of the households to manage it. The second element of the definition is crucial to understanding the household's resilience and recovery possibilities.

One of the best ways to understand the capacity to recover, considering the household's current characteristics and future shocks, is to involve the well-being dynamics perspective in the vulnerability assessments through long-term panel data (Chaudhuri, 2003). However, even though the quality and the number of panel data have increased, long-term panel databases still need to be available in the region. Therefore, here we develop vulnerability measures using cross-sectional data. Literature has built measures of vulnerability to poverty, especially in the context of cross-sectional data (Chaudhuri et al., 2002; Chaudhuri, 2003; Dercon, 2006; Bérgolo et al., 2010; Hill & Porter, 2017; Skoufias et al., 2024, among others). Nevertheless, our approach presents differences from others. Based on a micro-framework, we model the probability of being poor, including current households' coping mechanisms and observable measures of proxies of natural aggregate shocks.

Chaudhuri (2003) and other earlier works measure vulnerability to poverty, estimating the consumption process and drawing inferences about future consumption prospects (mean and variance) based on unobserved idiosyncratic shocks. To do this, the authors model the idiosyncratic shocks (household-level shocks) through the variance of the disturbance term of the linear consumption equation. Skoufias et al. (2024) account for unobserved idiosyncratic and community covariate shocks through the disturbance terms, modeling consumption through multilevel models. Hill and Porter (2017), for their vulnerability computation, work with objective measures of aggregate and idiosyncratic shocks. They seek exogenous sources of shocks to estimate causal effects. They use crop losses as a measure of rainfall shocks and control for the probability of drought in a given community using the historical distribution of droughts, considering the timing of the shock as exogenous. As idiosyncratic shocks, they consider shocks such as a household member's death or job loss. Besides, other studies have introduced climate change and natural disaster impacts taking a macro-level perspective (Hallegatte et al., 2016, 2017; Jafino et al., 2020, among others).

To estimate vulnerability to poverty, we make an effort to include aggregate shocks explicitly in our model. We use objective measures of potential shocks, but unlike Hill and Porter (2017), we do not model or draw the distribution of these shocks. We also do not include idiosyncratic shocks in the model. Although we explore them when we perform the Chaudhuri procedure as a robustness exercise. Our cross-sectional measure of potential shocks assesses potential damage from natural hazards as a proxy of aggregate shocks based on a probabilistic analysis. Finally, this study aims to provide disaggregated data to policymakers to build policies to reduce vulnerability to poverty due to natural hazards in LAC in their localities.

The chapter is structured as follows. The next section presents the conceptual framework and the methodology. Section 3 describes the data, and Section 4 presents the results. Section 5 summarizes the main findings and discusses their implications.

2. MEASURING VULNERABILITY TO POVERTY CONSIDERING NATURAL HAZARDS IN LAC

2.1. Methodology

Building on the definition of vulnerability, we propose a model to measure vulnerability to poverty, including natural disasters in the region. Although a household's vulnerability is an ex-ante condition and not directly observable until the adverse shock occurs (Chaudhuri, 2003; Ravallion, 1988), it is possible to summarize it as the probability of the household's welfare falling in the future below a minimum standard. One way of including this dynamic is by using long-panel data. However, no periodic panel datasets are available in the region, and we overcome this using cross-sectional data.

On the other hand, defining household welfare is challenging and complex, and there is no perfect welfare indicator to measure it. Nevertheless, absolute poverty lines are usually a reasonable approximation of household minimum welfare in developing countries (Foster, 1998; Ravallion et al., 2008; Kakwani, 2003; Ravallion, 2010, among others), correlating with vulnerability to poverty (Chaudhuri, 2003; Ravallion, 1988). Thus, we approximate household welfare using a monetary poverty measure, and we measure households' vulnerability to absolute poverty (poverty from now on) in a setting where it is possible that households suffer damage from natural hazards. In LAC, monetary poverty is usually computed over household incomes and not consumption since all countries in the region collect income information more widely and periodically than consumption information.

Since the concept of vulnerability considered in this study includes the susceptibility to be harmed and the capacity to cope and adapt, we measure household vulnerability as the propensity of being poor conditioned to observed natural hazards' potential damage, community exposure, and current coping and adaptation strategies. We extend Chaudhuri's (2003) and Skoufias et al. (2024) approach, where shocks are unobserved, and explicitly introduce aggregate shocks through observed potential harm in the model. We also incorporate some elements of Hill and Porter's (2017) study working at the household level. And we exploit the spatial variability of the cross-sectional data as much as the household survey design allows (i.e., for some countries, we go down at the district level, and for others, at the state/province level).

The probability of being vulnerable is estimated based on the following Multilevel Mixed-Effects Probit model:

$$P(y_{hds} = 1 \mid X_{hds}, Z_{ds}) = \Phi\left(\alpha + X_{hds}\beta + Z_{ds}\gamma + \xi_s + \xi_{ds} + \varepsilon_{hds}\right), \qquad (1)$$

where P is the probability of being poor and Φ is the standard normal cumulative distribution function. y_{hds} is an indicator of household poverty. It is a dummy that takes value 1 when the per capita household income is lower than the international poverty line of USD 6.85 per day adjusted by PPP 2017 and 0 elsewhere. h represents households, d indicates districts if available when the data does allow a more disaggregate unit, and s indicates states (Table A1.2 in Appendix 1 presents the number of districts and states for each country).

Z_{ds} is a set of harm and exposure covariates at the district or state level, $Z_{ds} = [Harm_{ds}, Exposure_{ds}]$. The $Harm_{ds} = \left[Harm_{ds}^{(past)}, Harm_{ds}^{(present)} \right]$ is a vector that includes two type of variables: the number of natural events that occurred in 2000–2021 ($Harm_{ds}^{(past)}$) and indexes of the potential damage from natural hazards at the present ($Harm_{ds}^{(present)}$). The indexes of potential damage from natural hazards come from the ThinkHazard! Platform and the number of natural events that occurred in 2000–2021 come from the International Disaster Database EM-DAT of the Université Catholique de Louvain, Belgium (Guha-Sapir et al., 2022). *Exposure* is a vector of aggregate variables, including the presence of people (natural logarithm of density), infrastructure (percentage of urbanization area), and resources (percentage of cropland area).

X_{hds} are covariates at the household level. $X_{hds} = [Coping_{hds}, Demographics_{hds}]$. $Coping_{hds}$ is a vector of household variables of coping mechanisms and adapting strategies at the household level, including income diversification and occupation, social assistance, housing conditions, access to the Internet, and household head's education level. $Demographics_{hds}$ includes the size of the household, household head's age, squared age, and gender. To select coping and demographic variables at the household level, we use LASSO and select the covariates of the model that fit the poverty data more adequately (see Table A1.1 in Appendix 1).

$\xi_s \sim N\left(0, \sigma_{\xi_s}^2\right)$ is a random intercept varying over states (level 1), $\xi_{ds} \sim N\left(0, \sigma_{\xi_{ds}}^2\right)$ is a random intercept varying over districts (level 2). The random intercepts ξ_{ds} and ξ_s are assumed to be independent of each other and independent across states, and ξ_{ds} is assumed to be independent across districts as well. Both random intercepts are assumed to be independent of the covariates X_{hds} and $Z_{ds} \cdot \varepsilon_{hds}$ has a normal distribution $N(0,1)$ and is assumed to be independent of ξ_{ds}, ξ_s, X_{hds}, and Z_{ds}. The model is estimated with the maximum likelihood estimation method using the adaptive algorithm Gauss-Hermite quadrature.

In the absence of the harm and exposure terms, we expect that the estimations lead to the probability of being effectively poor. We run this as a robustness check of our model to ensure that the predicted probability of being poor leads to similar poverty rates observed in the data (for more details, see Appendix 1). The probability of being poor is written as

$$P(y_{hds} = 1 | X_{hds}, Z_{ds}) = P(I_{hds} < \zeta)$$

with $\zeta = 6.85$ USD and $I_{hds} = \alpha + X_{hds}\beta + Z_{ds}\gamma + \xi_s + \xi_{ds} + \varepsilon_{hds}$. Replacing,

$$P(y_{hds} = 1 | X_{hds}, Z_{ds}) = P(\alpha + X_{hds}\beta + Z_{ds}\gamma + \xi_s + \xi_{ds} + \varepsilon_{hds} < \zeta)$$

$$= P\left(\xi_s + \xi_{ds} + \varepsilon_{hds} < \zeta - \left(\alpha + X_{hds}\beta + Z_{ds}\gamma\right)\right)$$

$$= \Phi\left(\frac{\zeta - (\alpha + X_{hds}\beta + Z_{ds}\gamma)}{\sigma_{\xi_s + \xi_{ds} + \varepsilon_{hds}}}\right).$$

But we can assume that $P(I_{hds} < \zeta) \equiv \mathrm{P}\left(y^*_{hds} = \zeta - I_{hds}\right)$ where

$$y_{hds} = \begin{cases} 1 & y^*_{hds} > 0 \\ 0 & elsewhere \end{cases}$$

and, therefore, estimate equation (1). Vulnerability to poverty using our approach might be higher or lower than the actual poverty. The empirical strategy of estimating vulnerability to poverty conditioned to harm, exposure, and coping factors may predict a high probability of being poor even if households do not experience considerable harm. Furthermore, it may not identify households with a high susceptibility to harm as vulnerable when the potential damage of hazards correlates negatively with districts' poverty. The latter is a critical caveat of the model, and we explore the effects of this miss-allocation with the robustness checks. At first, it is not appealing to find negative harm coefficients but impose structure on the model forcing the sign of the coefficients to be positive, it is not appropriate. The introduction of the constraint may bias the estimated coefficients. We can interpret these negative coefficients as a negative correlation, knowing that in these cases, our model is better able to capture the harm in poorer districts/states than the harm in richer districts/states.

We also performed two robust checks as an extension. Following Chaudhuri (2003), we model the household income per capita considering idiosyncratic shocks. These shocks enter directly into the vulnerability estimation through the standard deviation of the income model's error term. The incidence under this model works as an upper bound as it considers other shocks and risks that fall in the disturbance term, which are not captured through the observables. Nevertheless, identifying which type of shocks and risks are operating in the disturbance term is puzzling, making this a handicap. In addition, we explore the approach proposed by Skoufias et al. (2024) by carrying out a second exercise. We estimate the household's vulnerability by proposing a three-level income model. We obtained vulnerability rates like those of our model. The details and results of these robustness checks are in Appendix 2.

Finally, the potential damage included in the model through the ThinkHazard! scores is not a projection. Although it allows us to observe the potential damage from natural events, it is worth noting that ThinkHazard! scores do not represent hazard risks and their use for risk-related assessment is discouraged. The indexes are computed based on physical hazards in the area from probabilistic models with a historical baseline. ThinkHazard! provides a general view of the hazards for a given location to promote disaster and climate resilience. It is a simple flagging system highlighting the hazards in an area. Moreover, the scores emphasize the likelihood of different natural hazards affecting areas. However, the data can show some uncertainties in specific areas that fail to cover the full range of hazard categories and intensities (see more details in ThinkHazard! Platform, 2022).

Given these caps, we run the model excluding the ThinkHazard! indexes with only the number of occurrences from EM-DAT which can be a better proxy of frequency and potential hazards. The estimations do not show significant differences between both models leading to similar patterns of vulnerability to poverty (Table A1.3 in Appendix 1).

Measuring vulnerability index

We define households as vulnerable to poverty if they have a likelihood of being poor greater than a threshold. A household is classified as vulnerable if the household has a predicted probability of being poor greater than 0.50. The choice of the threshold of 0.50 is arbitrary; nevertheless, it has been used in several studies for its simplicity and intuitive interpretation (Chaudhuri, 2003, among others). Moreover, Skoufias et al. (2024), Suryahadi and Sumarto (2001), and Suryahadi et al. (2000) argue for using the 0.50 probability threshold because 50-50 odds is an easy "focal" point, that is intuitive to understand if it faces odds better or worse. Also, the threshold corresponds to the point where the expected mean income matches the poverty line under the standard normal cumulative distribution. Nevertheless, we also conduct the analysis using different thresholds, such as 0.25 and 0.75. Additionally, we generate vulnerability curves for predicted probability thresholds ranging from 0.01 to 0.99.

Once we classify the households as vulnerable or not, we compute the incidence of vulnerability using the headcount ratio. In the cases where household data allows district representation, we compute vulnerability ratios at district levels in maps; on the contrary, we present vulnerability ratios at state levels. It is important to note that this measure of household vulnerability does not account for the depth and severity of the vulnerability.

In addition, we provide conditional and unconditional profiles to explore the coping and adaptation mechanisms of vulnerable households. The possibility of overcoming the damage caused by natural disasters depends predominantly on households' coping and adaptation mechanisms. Evidence shows that the same natural hazard affects people far more than others when their livelihoods depend on specific physical assets such as livestock, their consumption is closer to subsistence levels, and they cannot rely on savings to smooth out the impacts or even if they are going through a critical moment in life for the development of human capital, the impacts on education and health can extend the risks (Hallegatte et al., 2017).

The conditional profiles show the percentage of vulnerable households lacking the coping mechanisms included as controls in the regressions. The unconditional profiles explore the lack of coping mechanisms of the households outside of the model. In particular, we assess the percentage of vulnerable households reporting only one sector of activity and only one income earner in the household. We look at the percentage of vulnerable households without legal title ownership of the dwelling, whereas it is crucial to have dwelling and land titles to enhance investment in housing infrastructure to protect it from disasters. We compute the percentage of vulnerable households where at least one member does not have medical insurance because health costs can potentially affect the family's future well-being. Also, we see the percentage of vulnerable households without remittances because households with remittances are more likely to smooth their consumption due to this external source of income.

Furthermore, we provide the percentage of vulnerable households with children younger than 5 years old, vulnerable households with children less than 12 years old attending school, and vulnerable households with all their members being elders (65 years old or older). These measures aim to identify groups facing greater risk from natural disasters. The first two groups correspond to children who may suffer more from reductions in their investments in human capital. The third group faces a significant risk due to their low potential capacity to generate an income flow that allows them to restock their assets and wealth better.

Next, we explore whether there are differences in coping and adaptation mechanisms among poor and non-poor vulnerable households. To do this, we calculate the above household profiles, differentiating them by poor status.

3. DATA AND DESCRIPTIVE STATISTICS

The base datasets for the analysis are the national Household Surveys from the Socio-Economic Database for Latin America and the Caribbean (SEDLAC, 2022). This database provides information of coping and adaptation mechanisms at the household level and poverty status for different countries of the region. The analysis focuses on seven countries: Brazil, the Dominican Republic, Ecuador, El Salvador, Honduras, Mexico, and Peru. The most recent wave used here is 2019, before COVID-19. The household poverty rate with 6.85 dollars a day line at 2017 PPP per person rises to 20% in Brazil, 15% in the Dominican Republic, 21% in Ecuador, 23% in El Salvador, 45% in Honduras, 26% in Mexico, and 26% in Peru (Table 1.1).

The selection and construction of variables of households' coping mechanisms, adaptation strategies, and socio-demographic characteristics are detailed in Appendix 1. Here, Table 1.2 provides basic information on all seven Latin American countries. Statistics suggest low occupational protection and a lack of income diversification to deal with natural hazards. The level of informality is high; on average, in Ecuador and Peru, half of the household heads have an informal job. Moreover, in Ecuador, Honduras, and Peru, nearly one household in four reports that the household head's principal occupation is agriculture. And, in most countries, except El Salvador and Honduras, households benefit from social protection that can be adapted as a safety net to respond to natural disasters. Moreover, the results show, on average, a significant proportion of fragile infrastructure and buildings susceptible to natural disasters and limited access to toilet facilities. In El Salvador and Mexico, the percentage of households living in fragile dwellings rises to around one-quarter, and the percentage of households with access to toilet facilities linked to the sewer increases, on average, from 23% to 68%, depending on the country.

For harm variables, we exploit two types of data, the number of occurrences of natural disasters in the region in the past and the potential present harm

Table 1.1. Household Poverty Headcount Ratio Adjusted by PPP 2017 by Country.

Country	Brazil	Dominican Rep.	Ecuador	El Salvador	Honduras	Mexico	Peru
Poor HH (6.85 US$)	20%	15%	21%	23%	45%	26%	26%
Poor HH (3.65 US$)	8%	2%	6%	5%	23%	7%	8%
Poor HH (2.15 US$)	4%	1%	1%	1%	11%	2%	2%

Notes: Poverty rates are calculated over households, not individuals. Households (HH) are poor if their total income per capita falls below the a-day (2017 PPP and CPI prices adjusted) International Poverty Line.
Source: Authors' calculations based on the SEDLAC database.

expected from them. For the first one, we use the number of natural disasters that occurred in 2000–2020 at the state level from the EM-DAT. This database offers a worldwide collection of natural disasters. Fig. 1.1 shows the distribution and the number of natural disasters in LAC during 1900–2021. The distribution indicates that some natural disasters are more common than others. Thus, the study focuses on the five most common events: floods, cyclones, earthquakes, droughts, and landslides, leaving aside epidemics led by biological processes.

Also, the data shows differences by subregions, both in the types of disasters they face and how they impact the people of each country (Fig. 1.2). For example, in the Caribbean, cyclones are more common. In Central America, cyclones and floods are similarly significant, while in South America, floods represent almost half of all shocks, followed by landslides by far. In Table 1.3, we can see differences in each country, too.

For potential present damage, we use the index of ThinkHazard! Platform. This platform provides data on the potential damage of hazards triggered by geophysical, hydrologic, and meteorologic processes. The Thinkhazard! index (TH index) classifies hazards as high (potentially severe damaging events), medium (potentially damaging events), low (potentially damaging events are less likely to occur but still possible), and very low (potentially damaging effects are unlikely to occur). ThinkHazard! levels are derived from hazard maps applying the spatial distribution of hazard intensity (e.g., flood depth, ground shaking) at a given frequency or "return period" based on a probabilistic analysis (more details in Appendix 1). This index is available from level 2 of administrative units (ADM 2) of FAO's classification. In the case of Brazil, the index is used at level 1 because the geographic variable available in the Household Survey is only at the state level; thus, it is calculated as the average of the indexes of level 2 (see Appendix 1). So, this country's index cannot be compared with the other countries' TH indexes.

We use data from local areas to control for community exposure. By definition, exposure is the presence of people, livelihoods, species or ecosystems, environmental functions, services, resources, infrastructure, or economic, social, or cultural assets in places and settings that could be adversely affected by events (IPCC, 2014). We include population density (people per sq. km of the district or state area), percentage of cropland, and urbanization of the district or state area. The data source used is the MODIS 500m Landcover Dataset NASA LP DAAC at the USGS EROS Center, retrieved from Google Earth Engine Data Catalog

Table 1.2. Average of Households with Coping and Adaptation Mechanisms.

Category	Variable	Brazil	Dominican Rep.	Ecuador	El Salvador	Honduras	Mexico	Peru
Income diversification and occupation protection	HH head is salaried in the main occupation	38.9%	38.4%	43.3%	40.6%	35.8%	56.8%	33.9%
	HH head is informal in the main occupation	27.0%	36.6%	50.6%	39.6%	42.8%	32.5%	51.5%
	The non-labor income per capita PPP 2017	194.98	116.47	115.15	88.19	39.55	89.32	100.81
	Ln. non-labor income per capita PPP 2017	2.75	2.92	2.94	2.14	1.67	2.23	3.55
	Labor income as a share of total income	67.1%	74.7%	73.3%	75.6%	78.6%	77.9%	71.8%
	Dependency rate	1.8	1.7	1.7	2.1	2.2	1.8	1.9
	HH head's principal income is from agriculture	6.4%	8.4%	23.8%	14.3%	23.9%	12.8%	26.6%
Social protection	HH receives benefits from social assistance	19.3%	26.3%	18.6%	1.9%	12.2%	28.9%	47.2%
Housing	Dwelling's materials of low quality	3.2%	5.9%	19.7%	25.6%	11.4%	25.8%	12.6%
	Toilet facilities linked to sewer	67.7%	23.2%	64.0%	35.6%	38.3%	62.1%	73.0%
	Access to electricity	99.8%	99.1%	99.0%	97.6%	94.1%	99.5%	95.6%
	Overcrowding	3.5%	3.9%	28.9%	8.7%	17.0%	10.6%	8.9%
Assets ownership	Car	49.4%	20.9%	23.3%	20.2%	23.6%	42.5%	11.8%
	Fridge	98.1%	87.9%	80.8%	75.7%	72.4%	86.3%	54.5%
	Computer	41.7%	16.7%	41.7%	16.7%	17.2%	27.4%	32.7%
	Washing machine	65.9%	78.7%	41.0%	21.1%	.	67.9%	30.5%
TICs	Access to Internet	37.7%	25.9%	36.4%	23.3%	27.4%	40.6%	35.9%
Education	Years of education of HH head	8.5	8.7	8.6	6.8	6.2	8.8	8.9
Demographics	Number of HH members	3.0	3.1	6.0	3.5	4.1	3.6	3.6
	Age HH head	48	49	51	50	50	50	53
	Male HH head	52.8%	63.1%	71.3%	62.9%	65.8%	71.3%	68.8%

Note: Income converted to constant 2017 international dollars using SEDLAC CPI and PPP 2017.
Source: Authors' calculations based on the SEDLAC database.

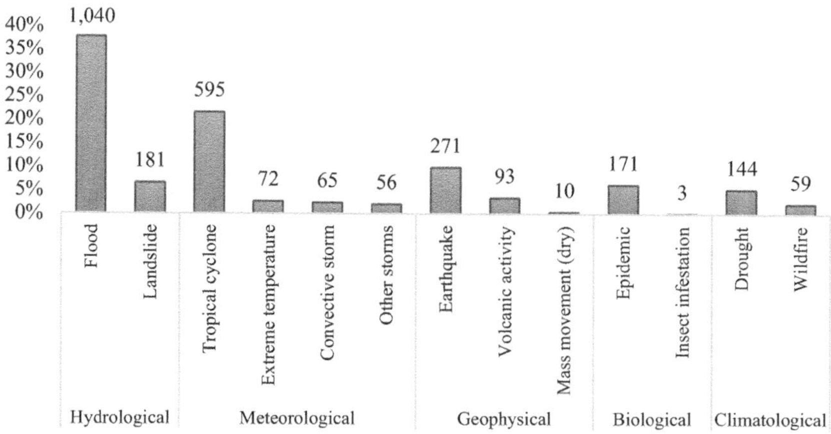

Fig. 1.1. Number of Natural Disasters Occurred in LAC During 1900–2021 by Subtype. *Source*: EM-DAT, Guha-Sapir et al. (2022).

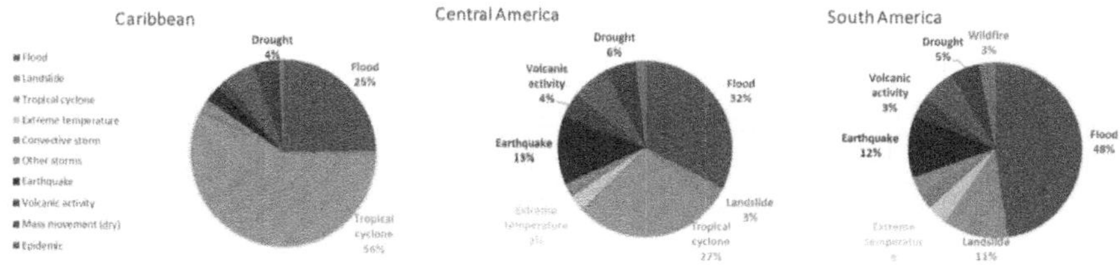

Fig. 1.2. Distribution of Natural Disasters During 1900–2021 by Subtype. *Source*: EM-DAT, Guha-Sapir et al. (2022).

based on the 2018 Images LC type 1 with 17 classes of land use. We employ class 12 for the cropland area (where at least 60% of the area is cultivated), class 13 for the urban area (at least 30% is impervious surface area, including building materials, asphalt, and vehicles), and the sum of all the classes for the total area of the administrative units at level 2.

Table 1.3 summarizes the average and standard deviation of the main variables of harm and exposure at the administrative level used in the analysis.

4. RESULTS

Table 1.4 presents the estimated coefficients from the harm term of the three-level random intercept mixed-effect probit model that includes all the natural hazards, exposure and coping controls. It also displays the estimated average marginal effects, revealing heterogeneous effects among natural hazards across countries. In the case of Brazil, both floods and droughts present a direct correlation with household poverty. Conversely, earthquakes, cyclones, and landslides

Table 1.3. Aggregate Statistics of Harm and Exposure by Country.

VARIABLES	Brazil			Dominican Rep.			Ecuador			El Salvador			Honduras			Mexico			Peru		
	Obs.	Mean	SD	Obs.	Mean	SD	Obs.	Mean	SD	Obs.	Mean	SD	Obs.	Mean	SD	Obs.	Mean	SD	Obs.	Mean	SD
Harm																					
TH index at ADM 2																					
Floods	27	2.66	0.7	134	3.10	1.1	219	2.07	1.2	211	1.74	1.1	225	1.97	1.2	878	1.98	1.2	181	1.64	1.1
Landslides	27	1.53	0.4	135	2.90	0.8	222	3.27	1.0	225	3.23	0.8	227	3.48	0.7	882	2.45	1.2	182	3.36	0.8
Earthquake	27	1.19	0.3	136	3.00	0.0	223	3.28	0.5	225	4.00	0.0	230	3.29	0.5	880	2.09	1.0	182	3.23	0.5
Cyclones	5	1.00	0.0	22	4.00	0.0	82	1.00	0.0	2	4.00	0.0	28	4.00	0.0	902	3.94	0.3	4	1.00	0.0
Droughts	27	1.59	0.7	136	3.00	0.0	223	1.00	0.0	225	3.00	0.0	230	2.11	0.3	902	2.31	0.9	182	1.41	0.7
EM-DAT: Number of events (2000–2021) at ADM 1																					
Floods	23	6.87	6.36	32	6.75	2.51	24	5.08	3.49	14	5.50	1.70	16	6.69	2.63	32	3.19	3.16	25	9.20	3.74
Landslides	23	0.39	0.94	32	0.00	0.00	24	0.29	0.55	14	0.07	0.27	16	0.00	0.00	32	0.25	0.80	25	0.56	0.87
Earthquake	23	0.04	0.21	32	0.13	0.34	24	0.67	0.82	14	1.86	0.66	16	0.50	0.73	32	0.78	1.39	25	1.60	1.53
Cyclones	23	0.09	0.29	32	11.66	1.77	24	0.00	0.00	14	5.64	1.28	16	4.00	2.22	32	6.63	5.97	25	0.00	0.00
Droughts	23	1.57	1.53	32	0.00	0.00	24	0.29	0.46	14	2.07	1.07	16	3.38	1.78	32	0.50	0.67	25	1.20	0.41
Exposure at ADM 2																					
Density	27	75.7	119.9	135	350	1173	25	84	80	225	599	1290	230	124	135	902	746	2094	182	68	296
Ln. density	27	3.4	1.5	135	4.8	1.2	25	3.9	1.3	225	5.6	1.1	230	4.4	0.9	902	4.9	1.9	182	3.0	1.4
Area	27	314,318	376,072	135	325	302	223	1,131	1,884	225	86	91	230	387	743	902	1,462	3,201	182	6,829	13,195
% cropland area	27	5%	7%	135	6%	11%	223	3%	10%	225	5%	11%	230	2%	6%	902	18%	25%	182	2%	4%
% urbanization area	27	1%	2%	135	3%	9%	223	2%	6%	225	2%	8%	230	0%	1%	902	4%	15%	182	1%	4%

Notes: Harm and exposure in Brazil are at the state level and density in Ecuador is at state level. The statistics are computed before imputations.
Source: Authors' calculations based on ThinkHazard!, EM-DAT, and SEDLAC database.

positively correlate with poor households in the Dominican Republic. Poverty in Ecuador and Peru correlates positively with the number of landslides and poverty in El Salvador with the number of droughts and earthquakes. In Honduras, the hazards that positively relate to poverty are cyclones, and droughts. Finally, cyclones and floods are positively associated with the poverty rate in Mexico. Also, the estimations indicate the relevance of coping mechanisms (they are similar to those estimated with the initial poverty model presented in Appendix 1). For instance, having an informal household head, a high dependency ratio, and a primary income from agriculture increases household's vulnerability to falling into poverty, and larger households are also more likely to be vulnerable. Receiving benefits from social assistance programs is positively correlated with the household's vulnerability. Households with salaried household heads, those with a larger share of labor income, better housing conditions, and assets are less likely to be vulnerable.

We also estimate marginal effects, Fig. 1.3 presents the average marginal effects of each natural hazard of these estimations. Positive marginal effects indicate a positive relationship between household poverty and the harm of the event. In Brazil, floods, landslides, earthquakes, and droughts show total positive effects, *ceteris paribus*. In the Dominican Republic, the number of earthquakes and landslides' potential damage positively correlate to poverty. The number of landslides and the earthquake's potential damage in Ecuador positively correlate to poverty. The droughts and the number of earthquakes matter in El Salvador. In Honduras, mainly droughts are associated with household poverty. In Mexico, cyclones are the natural hazards associated with household poverty. In Peru, the number of landslides positively associates with poverty.

The results (presented in Fig. 1.4) show that Honduras has the highest vulnerability to poverty rate (40%), and the Dominican Republic has the lowest (7%). The vulnerability incidence in Peru is 24%, indicating that almost a quarter of the households have a predicted probability over 0.50 of falling into poverty. In Mexico, the vulnerability rate is 20%, El Salvador and Brazil 16%, and Ecuador 13%.

In Fig. 1.5, the maps show the percentage of vulnerable households in each state. In the case of Brazil, the results show higher vulnerability in the north in line with the fact that poverty, exposure, and harm concentrate more in that region and that households in this area have fewer coping mechanisms than those in the south. The Dominican Republic shows that some administrative units present a vulnerability rate notably higher than the national average. The vulnerability rate of the provinces Baoruco, Independencia, and Pedernales is 29.5%, 29%, and 20%, respectively. Also, the map shows that Barahona, Dajabon, and Puerto del Plata have districts with a higher vulnerability rate than the rest.

In Ecuador, the vulnerable households are concentrated in the east, the region with more effective poverty rates. But where the TH index of landslides suggests more potential damage is in the central region, where some cantons also show a high vulnerability. El Salvador's vulnerability rate varies across its provinces. San Salvador has a vulnerability rate of around 6%, while a group of provinces have rates between 15% and 17%. Other provinces have rates between 20% and 30%, while Morazan and Ahuachapan have rates over 30%. In particular, some

Table 1.4. Multilevel Mixed Effects Probit Model Estimations Including All Hazards.

	Brazil		Dominican Republic		Ecuador		El Salvador		Honduras		Mexico		Peru	
	Mixed Probit	Mg. Effects	Mixed Probit	Mg. Effects	Mixed Probit	Mg. Effects	Mixed Probit	Mg. Effects	Mixed Probit	Mg. Effects	Mixed Probit	Mg. Effects	Mixed Probit	Mg. Effects
TH index Flood	0.333	0.041	0.035	0.005	0.006	0.001	–0.005	–0.001	–0.042	–0.009	0.006	0.001	–0.071	–0.012
	[0.111]***	[0.014]***	[0.043]	[0.006]	[0.021]	[0.004]	[0.018]	[0.004]	[0.030]	[0.007]	[0.012]	[0.003]	[0.022]***	[0.004]***
Number of	–0.036	–0.004	–0.044	–0.006	0.013	0.002	–0.003	–0.001	–0.059	–0.013	0.025	0.005	0.007	0.001
Floods	[0.017]**	[0.002]**	[0.034]	[0.005]	[0.015]	[0.003]	[0.025]	[0.005]	[0.017]***	[0.004]***	[0.014]*	[0.003]*	[0.017]	[0.003]
TH index	0.170	0.021	0.082	0.012	–0.045	–0.008	–0.023	–0.005	0.026	0.006	0.009	0.002	–0.012	–0.002
Landslides	[0.164]	[0.020]	[0.064]	[0.009]	[0.030]	[0.005]	[0.023]	[0.005]	[0.040]	[0.009]	[0.015]	[0.003]	[0.031]	[0.005]
Number of	–0.036	–0.004			0.109	0.020	–0.039	–0.008			–0.028	–0.006	0.043	0.007
Landslides	[0.066]	[0.008]			[0.080]	[0.015]	[0.133]	[0.028]			[0.056]	[0.012]	[0.072]	[0.012]
TH index	–0.143	–0.018			0.111	0.020			–0.005	–0.001	–0.035	–0.008	–0.049	–0.008
Earthquake	[0.124]	[0.015]			[0.054]**	[0.010]**			[0.084]	[0.019]	[0.022]	[0.005]	[0.041]	[0.007]
Number of	0.197	0.024	0.353	0.052	–0.089	–0.016	0.015	0.003	0.041	0.009	0.043	0.009	–0.040	–0.007
Earthquakes	[0.210]	[0.026]	[0.250]	[0.037]	[0.055]	[0.010]	[0.048]	[0.010]	[0.047]	[0.010]	[0.036]	[0.008]	[0.044]	[0.007]
TH index											0.123	0.026		
Cyclones											[0.053]**	[0.011]**		
Number of			0.008	0.001			–0.008	–0.002	0.029	0.006	0.006	0.001		
Cyclones			[0.033]	[0.005]			[0.026]	[0.005]	[0.024]	[0.005]	[0.007]	[0.001]		
TH index	0.149	0.018							0.020	0.004	–0.029	–0.006	–0.024	–0.004
Drought	[0.079]*	[0.010]*							[0.111]	[0.025]	[0.021]	[0.004]	[0.037]	[0.006]
Number of	0.159	0.019			–0.066	–0.012	0.018	0.004	0.055	0.012	0.082	0.017	–0.220	–0.036
Droughts	[0.048]***	[0.006]***			[0.084]	[0.015]	[0.030]	[0.006]	[0.026]**	[0.006]**	[0.060]	[0.013]	[0.168]	[0.028]
Ln. density	0.101	0.012	–0.077	–0.011	–0.107	–0.019	0.022	0.005	–0.082	–0.018	–0.022	–0.005	0.010	0.002
	[0.058]*	[0.007]*	[0.048]	[0.007]	[0.045]**	[0.008]**	[0.025]	[0.005]	[0.036]**	[0.008]**	[0.009]**	[0.002]**	[0.019]	[0.003]
% cropland	0.210	0.026	0.384	0.057	0.338	0.061	–0.293	–0.061	–0.158	–0.035	0.075	0.016	1.665	0.274
(Res 500)	[0.672]	[0.082]	[0.597]	[0.087]	[0.232]	[0.042]	[0.198]	[0.041]	[0.505]	[0.112]	[0.072]	[0.015]	[0.590]***	[0.097]***
% urbanization	5.908	0.724	0.563	0.083	–0.656	–0.118	0.092	0.019	1.097	0.243	–0.027	–0.006	–1.095	–0.181
and built-up (Res 500)	[8.361]	[1.026]	[0.437]	[0.065]	[0.302]**	[0.054]**	[0.235]	[0.049]	[1.332]	[0.294]	[0.108]	[0.023]	[0.386]***	[0.063]***
HH head is	–0.197	–0.024	0.166	0.025	–0.247	–0.044	–0.336	–0.068	–0.340	–0.075	-0.209	-0.045	-0.153	-0.025
salaried in main occupation	[0.013]***	[0.002]***	[0.074]**	[0.011]**	[0.012]***	[0.003]***	[0.030]***	[0.006]***	[0.056]***	[0.012]***	[0.016]***	[0.004]***	[0.028]***	[0.005]***

HH head is informal in main occupation	0.338	0.042	0.158	0.023	0.365	0.066	0.197	0.041	0.283	0.064	0.323	0.071	0.218	0.036
	[0.014]***	[0.002]***	[0.071]**	[0.011]**	[0.012]***	[0.003]***	[0.026]***	[0.006]***	[0.049]***	[0.011]***	[0.014]***	[0.003]***	[0.027]***	[0.004]***
Ln. non labor income per capita PPP 2017	−0.438	−0.054	−0.171	−0.025	−0.286	−0.052	−0.277	−0.057	−0.302	−0.067	−0.322	−0.069	−0.806	−0.133
	[0.007]***	[0.001]***	[0.023]***	[0.004]***	[0.005]***	[0.002]***	[0.012]***	[0.003]***	[0.023]***	[0.005]***	[0.007]***	[0.002]***	[0.014]***	[0.003]***
Labor income as a share of total income (monetary)	−2.124	−0.260	−2.114	−0.311	−2.087	−0.376	−1.922	−0.398	−2.261	−0.500	−2.371	−0.506	−4.246	−0.700
	[0.037]***	[0.005]***	[0.142]***	[0.025]***	[0.031]***	[0.013]***	[0.079]***	[0.016]***	[0.148]***	[0.030]***	[0.041]***	[0.011]***	[0.070]***	[0.014]***
Dependency rate (members/ number of income earners)	0.690	0.085	0.337	0.050	0.242	0.044	0.456	0.094	0.361	0.080	0.265	0.057	0.338	0.056
	[0.008]***	[0.001]***	[0.030]***	[0.005]***	[0.006]***	[0.002]***	[0.013]***	[0.003]***	[0.025]***	[0.005]***	[0.008]***	[0.002]***	[0.013]***	[0.002]***
HH head's principal income is from agriculture	0.117	0.015	0.356	0.058	0.113	0.021	0.328	0.072	0.362	0.084	0.154	0.034	0.373	0.064
	[0.019]***	[0.002]***	[0.090]***	[0.016]***	[0.015]***	[0.003]***	[0.033]***	[0.008]***	[0.067]***	[0.016]***	[0.018]***	[0.004]***	[0.028]***	[0.005]***
Receive benefits from a social assistance program	1.441	0.228	0.125	0.019	0.429	0.086	0.613	0.141	0.837	0.194	0.675	0.155	0.458	0.077
	[0.017]***	[0.004]***	[0.065]*	[0.010]*	[0.015]***	[0.004]***	[0.077]***	[0.019]***	[0.079]***	[0.018]***	[0.018]***	[0.005]***	[0.027]***	[0.005]***
Dwelling's materials of low quality	0.123	0.015	0.252	0.040	0.273	0.052	0.225	0.048	0.192	0.043	0.130	0.028	0.120	0.020
	[0.026]***	[0.003]***	[0.088]***	[0.015]***	[0.014]***	[0.003]***	[0.027]***	[0.006]***	[0.082]**	[0.019]**	[0.016]***	[0.004]***	[0.033]***	[0.006]***
Toilet facilities linked to the sewer	−0.104	−0.013	−0.048	−0.007	−0.119	−0.022	−0.193	−0.039	−0.183	−0.041	−0.164	−0.036	−0.212	−0.036
	[0.014]***	[0.002]***	[0.083]	[0.012]	[0.015]***	[0.003]***	[0.039]***	[0.008]***	[0.058]***	[0.013]***	[0.017]***	[0.004]***	[0.026]***	[0.005]***
Dwelling have access to electricity	−0.258	−0.033	−0.013	−0.002	−0.052	−0.010	−0.072	−0.015	−0.065	−0.014	−0.159	−0.035	−0.090	−0.015
	[0.084]***	[0.011]***	[0.199]	[0.030]	[0.051]	[0.009]	[0.066]	[0.014]	[0.117]	[0.026]	[0.077]**	[0.017]**	[0.041]**	[0.007]**
Number of HH members over the number of bedrooms > 3	0.207	0.026	0.222	0.035	0.290	0.055	0.115	0.024	0.199	0.045	0.216	0.048	0.134	0.022
	[0.029]***	[0.004]***	[0.102]**	[0.018]**	[0.014]***	[0.003]***	[0.038]***	[0.008]***	[0.065]***	[0.015]***	[0.020]***	[0.005]***	[0.035]***	[0.006]***

(Continued)

Table 1.4. *(Continued)*

	Brazil		Dominican Republic		Ecuador		El Salvador		Honduras		Mexico		Peru	
	Mixed Probit	Mg. Effects	Mixed Probit	Mg. Effects	Mixed Probit	Mg. Effects	Mixed Probit	Mg. Effects	Mixed Probit	Mg. Effects	Mixed Probit	Mg. Effects	Mixed Probit	Mg. Effects
Has a car	−0.584	−0.072	−0.593	−0.074	−0.024	−0.004	−0.548	−0.103	−0.334	−0.074	−0.394	−0.085	−0.420	−0.067
	[0.015]***	[0.002]***	[0.099]***	[0.011]***	[0.015]	[0.003]	[0.043]***	[0.007]***	[0.067]***	[0.015]***	[0.016]***	[0.004]***	[0.052]***	[0.008]***
Has a fridge	−0.204	−0.026	−0.186	−0.029	−0.332	−0.065	−0.345	−0.075	−0.439	−0.104	−0.241	−0.054	−0.366	−0.062
	[0.034]***	[0.004]***	[0.087]**	[0.014]**	[0.013]***	[0.003]***	[0.028]***	[0.006]***	[0.060]***	[0.015]***	[0.020]***	[0.005]***	[0.028]***	[0.005]***
Has a computer	−0.204	−0.025	−0.431	−0.056	−0.257	−0.046	−0.384	−0.074	−0.320	−0.071	−0.248	−0.052	−0.266	−0.044
	[0.031]***	[0.004]***	[0.107]***	[0.012]***	[0.017]***	[0.003]***	[0.058]***	[0.010]***	[0.084]***	[0.019]***	[0.022]***	[0.005]***	[0.036]***	[0.006]***
Has a washing	−0.314	−0.039	−0.123	−0.018	−0.026	−0.005	−0.359	−0.070			−0.203	−0.045	−0.345	−0.056
machine	[0.014]***	[0.002]***	[0.067]*	[0.010]*	[0.013]**	[0.002]**	[0.049]***	[0.009]***			[0.015]***	[0.004]***	[0.042]***	[0.007]***
Access to internet	−0.301	−0.036	−0.335	−0.046	−0.271	−0.048	−0.284	−0.056	−0.338	−0.076	−0.302	−0.064	−0.369	−0.061
in the HH	[0.033]***	[0.004]***	[0.084]***	[0.011]***	[0.018]***	[0.003]***	[0.046]***	[0.009]***	[0.066]***	[0.015]***	[0.019]***	[0.004]***	[0.037]***	[0.006]***
Years of education	−0.049	−0.006	−0.044	−0.006	−0.030	−0.005	−0.045	−0.009	−0.050	−0.011	−0.037	−0.008	−0.036	−0.006
of HH head	[0.002]***	[0.000]***	[0.007]***	[0.001]***	[0.002]***	[0.000]***	[0.004]***	[0.001]***	[0.007]***	[0.002]***	[0.002]***	[0.000]***	[0.003]***	[0.001]***
Number of HH	0.174	0.021	0.353	0.052	0.099	0.018	0.172	0.036	0.117	0.026	0.220	0.047	0.180	0.030
members	[0.005]***	[0.001]***	[0.021]***	[0.004]***	[0.002]***	[0.001]***	[0.009]***	[0.002]***	[0.015]***	[0.003]***	[0.004]***	[0.001]***	[0.008]***	[0.001]***
HH head's age	−0.000	−0.000	−0.027	−0.004	−0.019	−0.003	−0.026	−0.005	−0.037	−0.008	−0.015	−0.003	−0.008	−0.001
	[0.002]	[0.000]	[0.009]***	[0.001]***	[0.002]***	[0.000]***	[0.004]***	[0.001]***	[0.008]***	[0.002]***	[0.002]***	[0.001]***	[0.004]*	[0.001]*
HH head's age	−0.000	−0.000	0.000	0.000	−0.000	−0.000	0.000	0.000	0.000	0.000	0.000	0.000	−0.000	−0.000
squared	[0.000]***	[0.000]***	[0.000]	[0.000]	[0.000]*	[0.000]*	[0.000]***	[0.000]***	[0.000]***	[0.000]***	[0.000]	[0.000]	[0.000]	[0.000]
Male HH head	−0.203	−0.025	−0.279	−0.043	−0.085	−0.016	−0.083	−0.017	−0.191	−0.042	0.034	0.007	0.024	0.004
	[0.013]***	[0.002]***	[0.063]***	[0.010]***	[0.012]***	[0.002]***	[0.028]***	[0.006]***	[0.055]***	[0.012]***	[0.016]**	[0.003]**	[0.026]	[0.004]
Constant	−0.367		1.059		2.197		1.069		3.181		1.608		5.008	
	[0.503]		[0.615]*		[0.263]***		[0.265]***		[0.460]***		[0.257]***		[0.354]***	
Observations	137,364	137,364	5,742	5,742	135,336	135,336	20,115	20,115	4,999	4,999	66,513	66,513	33,350	33,350
Number of groups	23		32		24		14		16		32		25	

Notes: *** $p < 0.01$, ** $p < 0.05$, * $p < 0.1$. Standard errors clustered by districts in brackets (by states in Brazil and Ecuador).
Source: Authors' calculations based on ThinkHazard!, EM-DAT, and SEDLAC database.

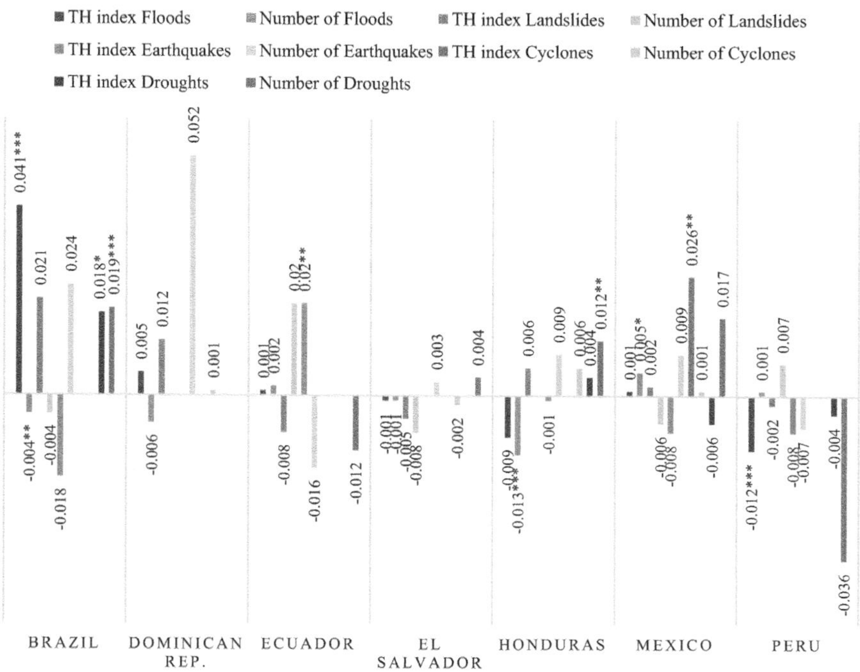

Fig. 1.3. Average Marginal Effects from the Models with Natural Hazards Separately. *Notes*: *** $p < 0.01$, ** $p < 0.05$, * $p < 0.1$. Each family color bar corresponds to a specification that includes one type of natural hazard controlled by exposure, coping mechanisms, and region. *Source*: Authors' calculations based on ThinkHazard!, EM-DAT, and SEDLAC database.

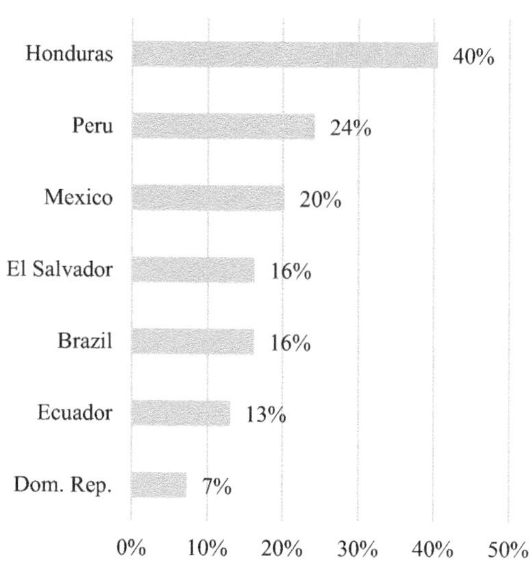

Fig. 1.4. Vulnerability Incidence (% of Vulnerable Households with a Predicted Probability Greater than 0.50). *Source*: Authors' calculations based on ThinkHazard!, EM-DAT, and SEDLAC database.

districts of Morazan and Ahuachapan show a high rate in comparison to districts of other provinces. Honduras shows that the administrative unit at level 1 with the highest percentage of vulnerable households is Lempira (84%). The map shows that many other districts present a sizeable rate. But, in Lempira's case, all their districts present a significant rate. Lempira is located in the west, corresponding to a region with significant potential earthquake damage. Mexican households show a high vulnerability rate in Chiapas (61%), Oaxaca (49%), and Guerrero (49%), then followed by Veracruz (40%) and Tabasco (37%). Furthermore, these provinces broadly suffer from a high amount of cyclone activity. From the results obtained for Peru, we derive that the pacific coastal regions have the lowest

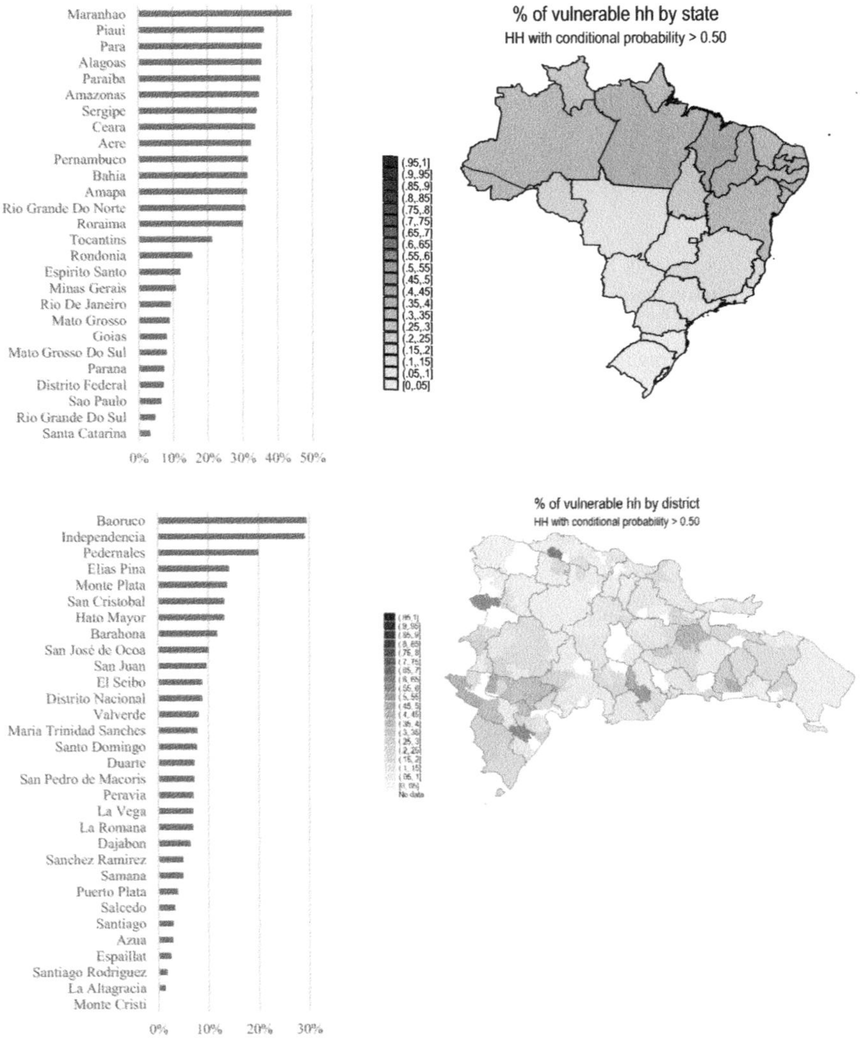

Fig. 1.5. (*Continued*)

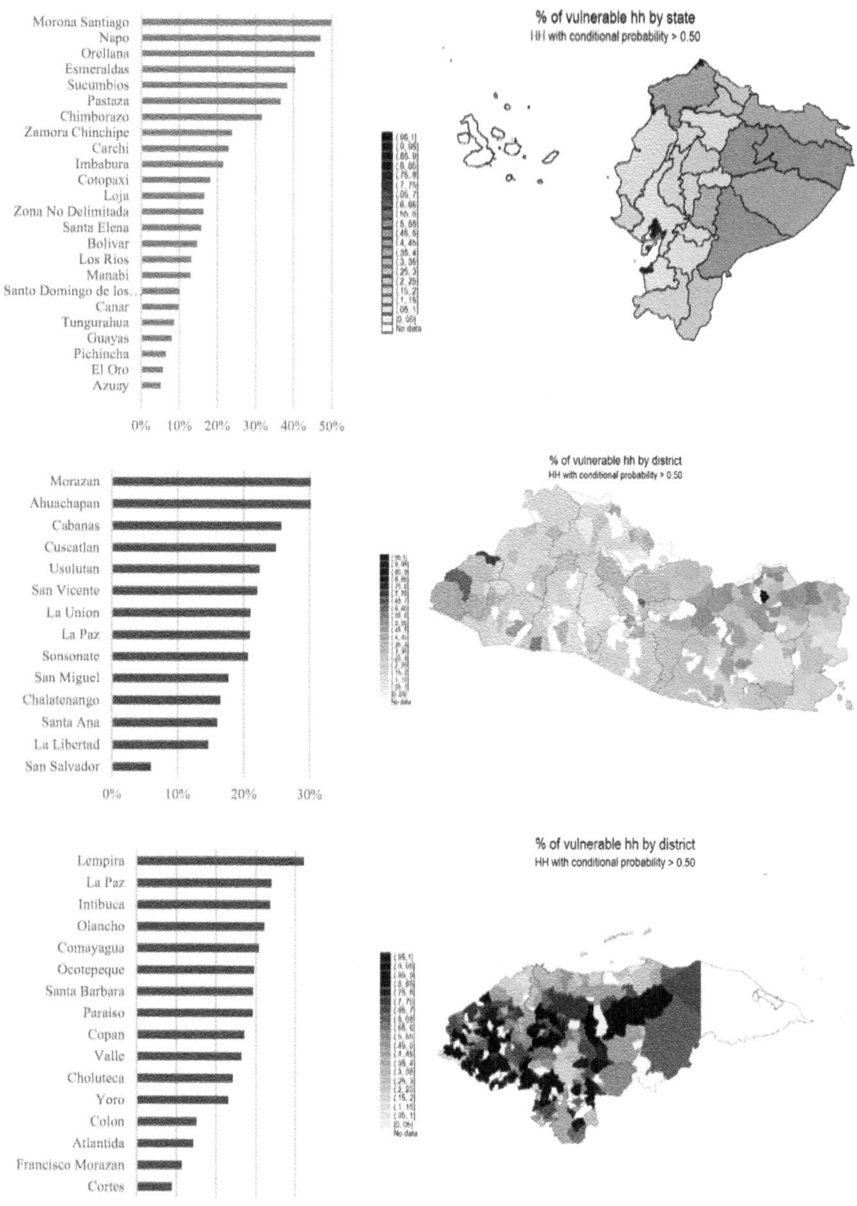

Fig. 1.5. (*Continued*)

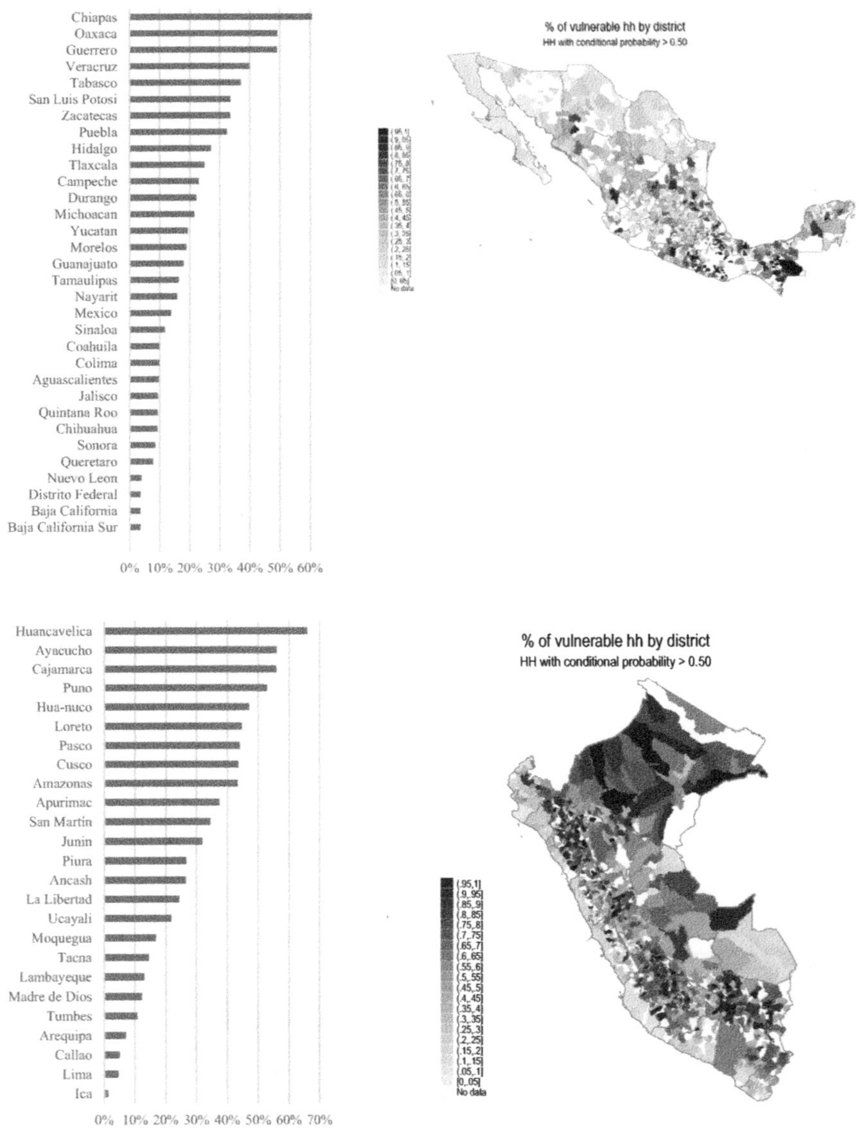

Fig. 1.5. Vulnerability Incidence Using a Threshold of 0.50 by State. *Note*: Maps display the vulnerability rates from the bar charts in intervals of 5%. *Source*: Authors' calculations based on ThinkHazard!, EM-DAT, and SEDLAC database.

vulnerability. The percentage of vulnerable households increases in the mountain regions in the center and tropical regions in the east. In the eastern is where floods are more potentially damaging. Even though Loreto province experiences more potential damage from floods, administrative units in the mountain regions with high poverty rates show the most significant vulnerability rates, such as Huancavelica, followed by Ayacucho and Cajamarca.

Following the literature, we are using a threshold of 0.50, but we also perform the analysis for other thresholds obtaining vulnerability curves (Fig. A3.1 in Appendix 3 shows results with other thresholds). Although the levels are different, the pattern and conclusions are as expected. They resemble the ones for the threshold of 0.50.

We also perform two robust checks, and most results hold regardless of the exercise. First, we estimate the model proposed by Skoufias et al. (2024), which is a multilevel model with two levels. In our analysis, we estimated a three-level model closely following the procedure outlined by Skoufias. The results that we named the Skoufias model are presented in Fig. 1.6. The comparison between our model and the Skoufias model shows that the vulnerability rates are very similar between both approaches. Second, we follow the procedure outlined in Chaudhuri (2003) and estimate the income per capita distribution based on the income generation process under Chaudhuri's model, and then we make distributional assumptions in the error variance to draw the poverty rate. Chaudhuri proposed to estimate the model equations using a three-step feasible generalized least squares. The results highly correlate with the vulnerability measures from our model (see Appendix 2 for more details).

Nonetheless, the chapter's main contribution, explored in the next section, is the analysis of these vulnerable households' coping and adaptation mechanisms.

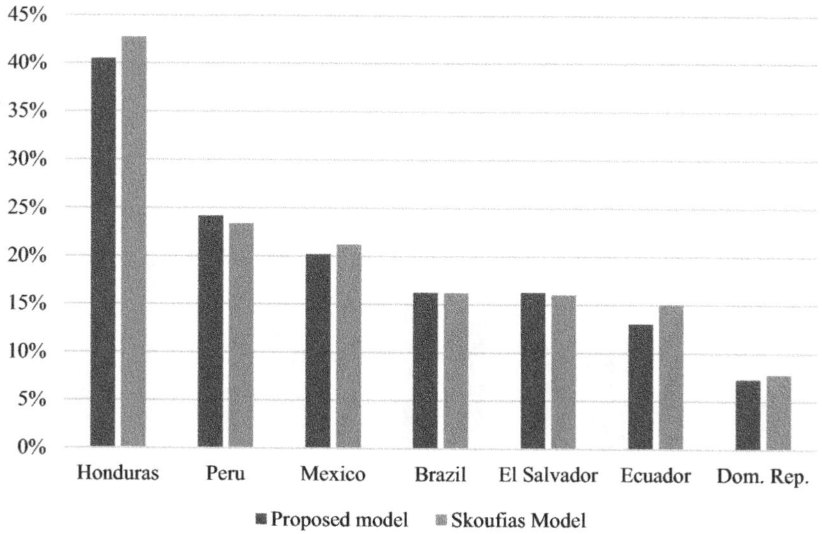

Fig. 1.6. Vulnerability Rates Comparison Between Models. *Notes*: The results correspond to the model proposed including all the natural hazard, exposure, and coping mechanisms, and the model proposed in Skoufias et al. (2024) with three levels. *Source*: Authors' calculations based on ThinkHazard!, EM-DAT, and SEDLAC database.

Vulnerability profiles

We perform a profile assessment to understand the strategies of vulnerable households for coping or adapting in the face of natural disasters. For each country, we compute the percentage of vulnerable and non-vulnerable households that have a household head non-salaried worker, only one sector of activity reported, only one income earner in the household, household head's primary income from agriculture, dwelling's materials of low quality, benefits from social assistance, and households without remittances from abroad. We also compute the percentage of households with children under 5 years old, children under 12 years old, and households with all their members' elders 65 years old or older. Table A3.1 in Appendix 3 shows these percentages at the country level for the seven countries according to vulnerability status.

In Fig. 1.7, we show Mexico's profile. The percentage of households with primary income from agriculture and salaried household heads is higher among the vulnerable than the non-vulnerable. Risk assessments show that agricultural production and income from agriculture can be depressed for years as an additional impact of natural hazards (Hallegatte et al., 2017). Households highly dependent on agriculture and ecosystems are more exposed to natural hazards. Thus, diversification of incomes, safety nets to smooth consumption, and climate-smart agriculture practices need to be on the country's agenda. In addition, physical infrastructure and housing with more climate and disaster resilience to reduce damage to dwellings are also needed. The percentage of households living in fragile dwellings is significantly higher among the vulnerable, showing that these dwellings can be particularly affected by cyclones and other natural events. The rate of households with kids is higher among the vulnerable than the non-vulnerable, but this is not the case for elders. Therefore, vulnerability reduction

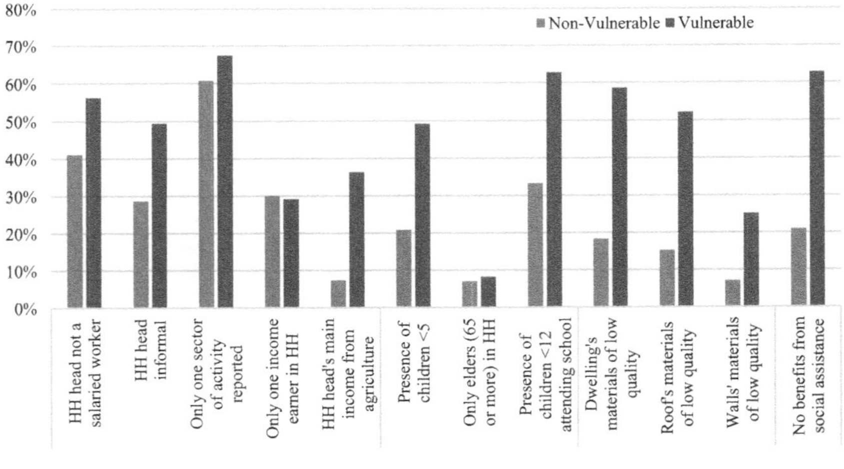

Fig. 1.7. Mexican Households' Coping Mechanisms and Adaptation Strategies. *Source*: Authors' calculations based on ThinkHazard!, EM-DAT, and SEDLAC database.

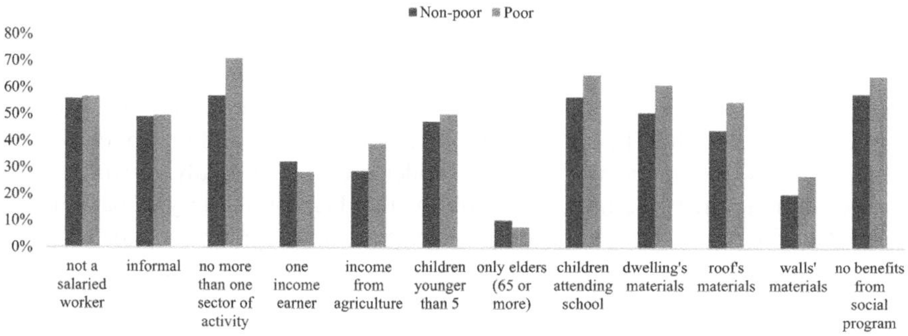

Fig. 1.8. Vulnerable Mexican Households' Coping Mechanisms and Adaptation Strategies by Poor Status. *Source*: Authors' calculations based on ThinkHazard!, EM-DAT, and SEDLAC database.

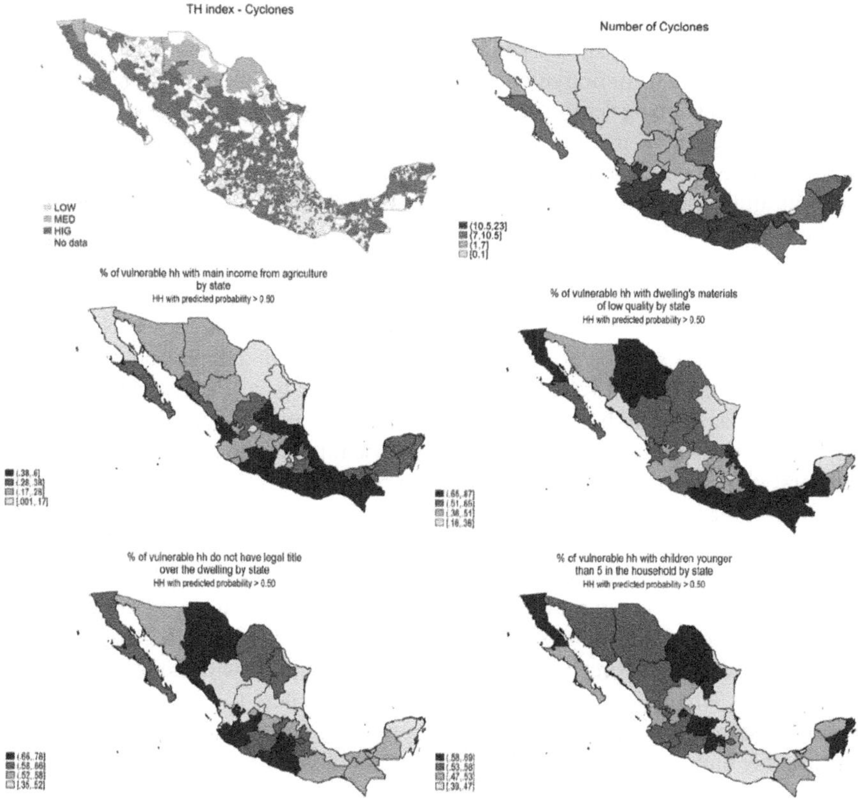

Fig. 1.9. Percentage of Mexican Households Lacking Coping Mechanisms and Adaptation Strategies by Geographic Units. *Source*: Authors' calculations based on ThinkHazard!, EM-DAT, and SEDLAC database.

measures need to include responses to avoid or diminish the permanent impacts of natural hazards, especially on children's education and health.

To check for differences between poor and non-poor households, we divided the sample of vulnerable households by household's poor status. Fig. A3.1 in Appendix 3 shows that the vulnerability rate includes poor and non-poor households. This is due to the vulnerability model used in the analysis, which may include, among the vulnerable, households with a high probability of being poor (a probability over 0.50) even when they are not actually poor. Nonetheless, the percentage of non-poor households vulnerable to poverty is lower than that of poor households. Fig. 1.8 shows that vulnerable households present a similar lack of coping mechanisms and adaptation strategies, whether poor or non-poor.

The profiles at the national level of the other countries are in Table A3.1 in Appendix 3. The results suggest that in Brazil, strengthening vulnerable households to engage in multiple economic sectors is necessary. Vulnerable households report more working only in one sector of activity and having only one income earner compared to non-vulnerable households. Also, the incidence of households with children is higher among vulnerable households. Children's incidence and lack of health insurance in the Dominican Republic are mainly distinguished among vulnerable from nonvulnerable households. In Ecuador, the prevalence of diversification from agricultural income and dwelling materials shows that fragile buildings and lack of income diversification mainly encompass vulnerable households. In El Salvador and Honduras, vulnerable households lack income diversification and occupation protection, and they also show a significant percentage of households with children whose human capital may be affected by natural hazards. In Peru, the lack of income and occupation diversification is noticeable, leaving households less able to cope and recover.

Moreover, these profiles can be analyzed at the state or district level, depending on the survey's scope. and see the degree of lack of adaptation and coping mechanisms of different regions. For example, the maps in Fig. 1.9 present at the state level the potential harm from cyclones, the percentage of households without coping mechanisms, and specific groups of households at significant risk in Mexico. The first two maps at the top of the figure correspond to all households (vulnerable and non-vulnerable), and the following maps correspond to only vulnerable households showing the incidence of a specific characteristic. The maps display that the region where more cyclones have occurred is the region with more vulnerable households obtaining their main income from agriculture and having fragile buildings. Also, some states such as Guerrero, Colima, and Jalisco with great potential damage show a high percentage of vulnerable households without legal title over the dwelling, which discourages investing in their dwelling to reduce damage from natural hazards. Further, Quintana Ro, followed by Michoacan and Jalisco show a remarkably high percentage of vulnerable households with children under 5, which can suffer more cyclone effects by reducing investments in their human capital.

Fig. 1.10 shows that in Brazil, a significant percentage of vulnerable households from Minas Gerais depend on agricultural income, an area also prone to drought. Likewise, Paraiba and Pernambuco states are prone to the effects of droughts, and access to water supply systems is not easy among vulnerable

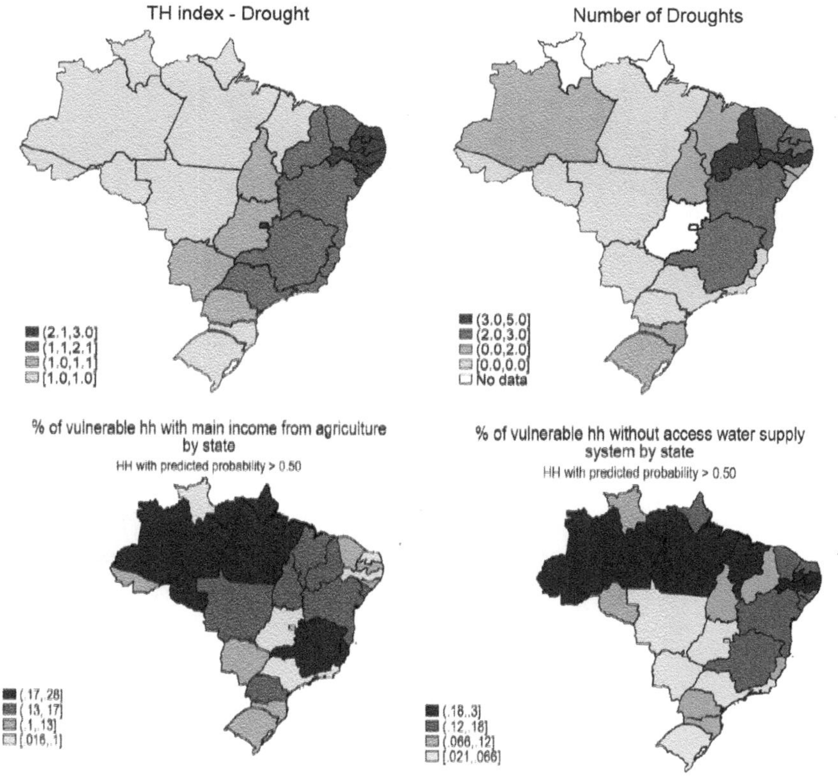

Fig. 1.10. Percentage of Brazilian Households Lacking Coping Mechanisms and Adaptation Strategies by Geographic Units. *Source*: Authors' calculations based on ThinkHazard!, EM-DAT, and SEDLAC database.

households in this area. The water scarcity likelihood of the northeast of Brazil makes water management a key factor for water security, food security, and productive activities in these states.

In Central America and the Caribbean, remittances are a source of household resilience, increasing income diversification, and typically remain relatively stable after disasters (Hallegatte et al., 2017). Fig. 1.11 shows for the Dominican Republic that although vulnerable households benefit from remittances, the regions suffering higher landslides potential damage are the regions where the percentage of vulnerable households receiving remittances is lower.

In Ecuador, some states that face potential damage from landslides show a high percentage of households that do not own their dwellings. This is challenging to improve the houses to face landslides damages and be affected as little as possible because, without home ownership, these types of investments in the dwellings are significantly less. The dwellings' improvement programs of risk mitigation may not have the expected response while the regulation and legal ownership do not change, and other adaptation and coping strategies to face potential damages to dwellings and infrastructure would be needed in these states (Fig. 1.12).

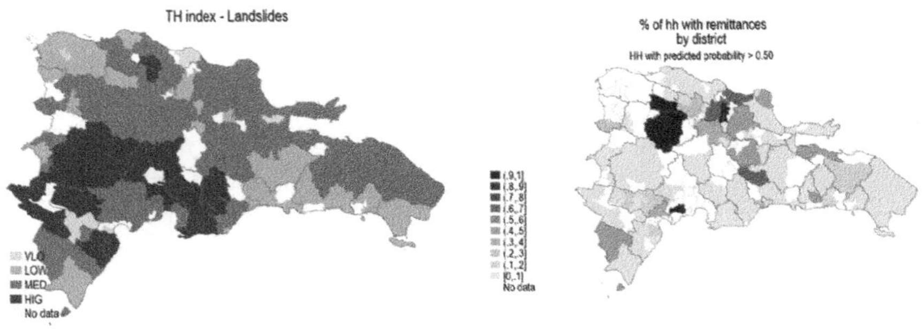

Fig. 1.11. Percentage of Dominican Republic Households with Remittances as a Coping Mechanism to Landslide's Potential Damage by Geographic Units. *Source*: Authors' calculations based on ThinkHazard!, EM-DAT, and SEDLAC database.

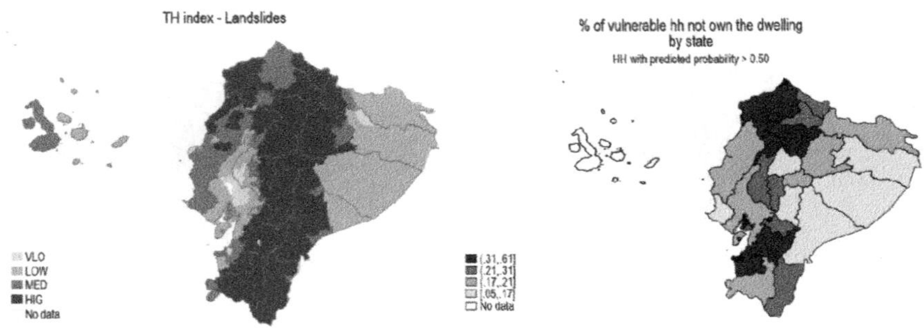

Fig. 1.12. Percentage of Ecuadorian Households That Do Not Own Their Dwellings as a Lack of Dwelling's Adaptative Strategy to Landslide's Potential Damage by Geographic Units. *Source*: Authors' calculations based on ThinkHazard!, EM-DAT, and SEDLAC database.

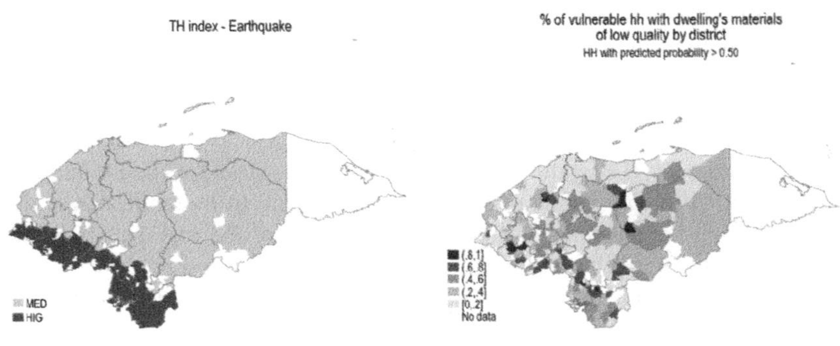

Fig. 1.13. Percentage of Honduran Households Living in Fragile Dwellings to Face Earthquake's Potential Damage by Geographic Units. *Source*: Authors' calculations based on ThinkHazard!, EM-DAT, and SEDLAC database.

Maps in Fig. 1.13 show that some districts have a large percentage of vulnerable households living in dwellings with materials of low quality, which can be particularly affected by earthquakes. These districts can be targeted for future decisions on projects or policies that upgrade the infrastructure to reduce the vulnerability of their buildings.

5. CONCLUSIONS

We use a nationally representative dataset of seven countries of the LAC region merged with natural disaster and area data to estimate the household vulnerability to poverty in the context of natural hazards. We find considerable heterogeneities in terms of the vulnerability to poverty among countries. Among others, cyclones in Mexico and earthquakes in Honduras imply a substantial increase in vulnerability to poverty. Brazilian and Salvadorean households present a higher vulnerability when drought-prone areas are considered. In Ecuador, landslides and earthquakes relate more to vulnerability. Many households in the region are unable to cope and adapt to these events, primarily through the lack of income diversification and dwelling material.

In terms of policy, the results highlight specific regions with a higher incidence of vulnerability. The methodology proposed in this chapter can be an initial tool to explore households' coping strategies and the weakened capacity to respond to natural hazards of different regions to identify priorities for action to reduce households' vulnerability. This chapter examines a few mechanisms in the profiles and maps. But the analysis can be extended depending on the action and the country in evaluation. Safety nets generally increase the household's resilience to events and risks. However, other risk management instruments such as insurance, land use, and building regulations can help households manage flood and landslide risks more. On the other hand, early warning systems can also reduce cyclones' impacts, and the awareness of being prepared can help for earthquakes.

Finally, the methodology avoids several limitations of cross-sectional data by using explicitly natural hazard potential damage data. However, caveats to the analysis concerning unobserved household characteristics, actual natural hazard impact on vulnerability (causality), and the inter-relationship between hazards and other climate change impacts remain. Including climate change measures, such as extreme temperatures and rains, as well as other types of disasters (e.g., pluvial and coastal floods), is the following apparent step. Also, in this study, the scarce availability of long-panel data limits the consistent estimates of vulnerability to poverty. Performing our approach using short synthetic panels to include dynamics in the model is a forward step that could enhance the analysis. Synthetic panels based on matching individuals with the same time-invariant characteristics in consecutive cross-sections have been recently proposed as a substitute for such data (Moreno et al., 2021). Here, we collapse the number of occurrences in a period but using short synthetic panels, we could include the time variability and explore observable households' strategies to cope with hazards across periods.

REFERENCES

Alkire, S., & Santos, M. E. (2010). *Acute multidimensional poverty: A new index for developing countries.* [OPHI Working Paper No. 38].

Amemiya, T. (1977). The maximum likelihood and the nonlinear three-stage least squares estimator in the general nonlinear simultaneous equation model. *Econometrica*, 45(4), 955–968. https://doi.org/10.2307/1912684

Bandyopadhyay, S., & Skoufias, E. (2015). Rainfall variability, occupational choice, and welfare in rural Bangladesh. *Review of Economics of the Household, 13*(3), 589–634.

Bérgolo, M., Cruces, G., Gasparini, L., & Ham, A. (2010). *Vulnerability to poverty in Latin America Empirical evidence from cross-sectional data and robustness analysis with panel data.* [Working paper, 170, Chronic Poverty Research Centre].

Chaudhuri, S. (2003). *Assessing vulnerability to poverty: Concepts, empirical methods, and illustrative examples* (p. 56). Mimeo. Department of Economics, Columbia University, New York.

Chaudhuri, S., Jalan, J., & Suryahadi, A. (2002). *Assessing household vulnerability to poverty from cross-sectional data: A methodology and estimates from Indonesia.* [Discussion Paper #:0102-52, Department of Economics, Columbia University, New York].

Chicco, D., & Jurman, G. (2020). The advantages of the Matthews correlation coefficient (MCC) over F1 score and accuracy in binary classification evaluation. *BMC Genomics, 21*, 1–13. https://doi.org/10.1186/s12864-019-6413-7

Dercon, S. (2006). Vulnerability: A micro perspective. *Securing Development in an Unstable World, 30*, 117–146.

Figal Garone, L., León, S., Olarte Rodríguez, L., & Peña, X. (2019). *Home durables and access to credit among the low-income in Latin America and the Caribbean: Trends and challenges.* [Development through the Private Sector Series TN No. 15, IDB Invest, Washington DC].

Foster, J. E. (1998). Absolute versus relative poverty. *The American Economic Review, 88*(2), 335–341. http://www.jstor.org/stable/116944

Gasparini, L., Marchionni, M., Olivieri, S., & Sosa Escudero, W. (2011). *Multidimensional poverty in Latin America and the Caribbean. New evidence from the Gallup World Poll.* Manuscript, CEDLAS.

Guha-Sapir, D., Below, R., & Ph. Hoyois. (2022). *EM-DAT: The CRED/OFDA International Disaster Database* – www.emdat.be – Université Catholique de Louvain – Brussels – Belgium.

Hallegatte, S., Bangalore, M., Bonzanigo, L., Fay, M., Kane, T., Narloch, U., Rozenberg, J., Treguer, D., & Vogt-Schilb, A. (2016). Shock waves: Managing the impacts of climate change on poverty. *Climate Change and Development.* World Bank. https://doi.org/10.1596/978-1-4648-0673-5. License:

Hallegatte, S. (2014). Trends in hazards and the role of climate change. In *Natural disasters and climate change.* Springer. https://doi.org/10.1007/978-3-319-089331_4

Hallegatte, S., Vogt-Schilb, A., Bangalore, M., & Rozenberg, J. (2017). Unbreakable: Building the Resilience of the poor in the face of natural disasters. In *Climate change and development series.* World Bank. https://doi.org/10.1596/978-1-46481003-9

Hill, R. V., & Porter, C. (2017). Vulnerability to drought and food price shocks: Evidence from Ethiopia. *World Development, 96*, 65–77.

IPCC. (2014). Summary for policymakers. In Climate *change* 2014: Impacts, *adaptation, and vulnerability.* Part A: Global *and sectoral aspects.* Contribution of Working Group II to the Fifth Assessment Report of the Intergovernmental Panel on Climate Change [Field, C.B., V.R. Barros, D.J. Dokken, K.J. Mach, M.D. Mastrandrea, T.E. Bilir, M. Chatterjee, K.L. Ebi, Y.O. Estrada, R.C. Genova, B. Girma, E.S. Kissel, A.N. Levy, S. MacCracken, P. R. Mastrandrea, and L. L. White (eds.)]. Cambridge University Press, Cambridge, United Kingdom and New York, NY, USA, pp. 1–32.

Jafino, B. A. Walsh, B. Rozenberg, J. & Hallegatte, S. (2020). *Revised estimates of the impact of climate change on extreme poverty by 2030.* [Policy Research Working Paper; No. 9417. World Bank, Washington, DC]. © World Bank. https://openknowledge.worldbank.org/handle/10986/34555 License: CC BY 3.0 IGO.

Kakwani, N. (2003). *Issues in setting absolute poverty lines*. [Poverty and social development papers No. 3. Asian Development Bank].

MODIS Landcover Collection. (2018). *MCD12Q1.006 MODIS Land Cover Type Yearly Global 500m* from Earth Engine Data Catalog https://developers.google.com/earth-engine/datasets/catalog/MODIS_006_MCD12Q1#description, maintained by the NASA EOSDIS Land Processes Distributed Active Archive Center (LP DAAC) at the USGS Earth Resources Observation and Science (EROS) Center, Sioux Falls, South Dakota. Retrieved March 2022.

Moreno, H., Bourguignon, F., & Dang, H. A. (2021). *On synthetic income panels*. [IZA Discussion Papers, No. 14236, Institute of Labor Economics (IZA), Bonn].

Ravallion, M. (1988). Expected poverty under risk-induced welfare variability. *The Economic Journal*, *98*(393), 1171–1182.

Ravallion, M. (2010). *Poverty lines across the world*. [World bank policy research working paper, (5284), The World Bank]. https://doi.org/10.1596/1813-9450-5284

Ravallion, M., Chen, S., & Sangraula, P. (2008). *Dollar a day revisited* (Vol. *4620*). World Bank Publications.

Rozenberg, J., & Hallegatte, S. (2015). *The impacts of climate change on poverty in 2030 and the potential from rapid, inclusive, and climate-informed development*. [World Bank Policy Research Working Paper, (7483), The World Bank]. https://ssrn.com/abstract=2688381

SEDLAC. (2022, March). *Socio-Economic Database for Latin America and the Caribbean: CEDLAS and The World Bank*. https://www.cedlas.econo.unlp.edu.ar/wp/en/estadisticas/sedlac/.

Skoufias, E., Vinha, K., & Beyene, B. M. (2024). Quantifying vulnerability to poverty in the drought-prone lowlands of Ethiopia. *Journal of African Economies*, *33*(2), 167–184. https://doi.org/10.1093/jae/ejad003

Sokolova, M, Japkowicz, N., & Szpakowicz, S. (2006). Beyond accuracy, F1-score and ROC: A family of discriminant measures for performance evaluation. In *Proceedings of advances in artificial intelligence (AI 2006), Lecture Notes in Computer Science* (Vol. *4304*, pp. 1015–1021). Springer. https://doi.org/10.1007/11941439_114

Stampini, M., & Tornarolli, L. (2012). *The growth of conditional cash transfers in Latin America and the Caribbean: did they go too far?* [IZA Policy Paper. No. 49].

Sulla-Menashe, D., & Friedl, M. A. (2018). *User guide to collection 6 MODIS land cover (MCD12Q1 and MCD12C1) products*. USGS: Reston, VA, USA, *1*, 18.

Suryahadi, A., & Sumarto, S. (2001). *The chronic poor, the transient poor, and the vulnerable in Indonesia before and after the crisis*. [SMERU Working paper]. https://smeru.or.id/sites/default/files/publication/vulnerability2susenas.pdf

Suryahadi, A., Sumarto, S., & Pritchett, L. (2000). *Quantifying vulnerability to poverty: A proposed measure, applied to Indonesia*. [World Bank Publications, No. 2437]. https://doi.org/10.1596/1813-9450-2437

ThinkHazard!. (2017). *Methodology report. Updated for ThinkHazard! Version 2*. Global Facility for Disaster Reduction and Recovery (GFDRR Labs). The World Bank. https://gfdrr.github.io/thinkhazardmethods/#meteo-climatological-hazards

ThinkHazard! Platform. (2022, March). *Global Facility for Disaster Reduction and Recovery (GFDRR Labs)*. The World Bank. https://thinkhazard.org/.

UNDP. (2022). *Social protection in times of uncertainty. Technical Note: Recalibrating… Getting Back on Track Towards the SDGs*. XIV Ministerial Forum for Development in Latin America and the Caribbean.

World Bank. (2022). *Hoja de ruta para la acción climática en América Latina y el Caribe 2021-2025*.

Zhang, H., Zhao, Y., & Pedersen, J. (2020). Capital assets framework for analyzing household vulnerability during disasters. *Disasters*, *44*(4), 687–707.

APPENDIX 1. DATA SOURCES, DATABASE CONSTRUCTION, AND VARIABLES SELECTED FOR THE ANALYSIS

The database for the analysis is the most recent wave of 2019 Household Surveys of the studied countries standardized under the SEDLAC's methodology before COVID-19. These datasets contain rich information on the households' coping mechanisms, adaptation strategies, and socio-demographic characteristics. We merged each household database with harm and exposure aggregate data at the most disaggregated geographic unit level, which can correspond to a canton, a district, a municipality, or a province/state, depending on the country. In the case of Mexico and Peru, the units correspond to districts; in the Dominican Republic, El Salvador, and Honduras, they are municipalities; in Ecuador, they are cantons; and in Brazil, they are provinces (states).

For harm from natural hazards, we look at the five more common hazards in Latin America and the Caribbean (LAC): river floods, landslides, earthquakes, droughts, and cyclones. We use potential damage information from ThinkHazard! indexes to measure households' susceptibility to harm. This index classifies natural hazards as High (potentially severe damage), Medium (potentially damaging effects), Low (potentially damaging events less likely to occur but still possible), and Very Low (potentially damaging effects unlikely to occur). Following ThinkHazard!'s classification, "… *Hazard levels are derived from hazard maps presenting the spatial distribution of hazard intensity (e.g., flood depth, ground shaking) at a given frequency, or 'return period.' The timeframe for each hazard depends on the timescales over which the hazard causal processes operate and historical data available to assess long-term averages*" (ThinkHazard!, 2017). The classification is made at the scale of the more disaggregated local administrative units following the ADM 2 of the FAO Global Administrative Unit Layers (GAUL) division. In the case of Brazil, the Household Survey allows us to work at the province/state level and not at the district level. Although the ThinkHazard! Platform provides an index at ADM 1 level, it is not used in Brazil because ThinkHazard! follows the maximum method where the level of potential damage at ADM 1 units is defined as the maximum hazard level by all its lower ADM 2 units. This aggregation process shows very little variability between provinces (e.g., two provinces, one with only one district with potentially severe damage and the other with potentially severe damage in all its districts, would have the same ThinkHazard! index at ADM 1). Therefore, we decided to aggregate to ADM 1 using the indexes at ADM 2. We compute the ThinkHazard!'s index at province level as the average of the municipalities indexes.

We also consider another measure of aggregate harm related to observed frequency using the data from the Emergency Events Database (EM-DAT) of the Université Catholique de Louvain (Guha-Sapir et al., 2022). This database provides a collection of natural disasters in the studied countries from 1900 to the present. The database reports the impacted administrative units by the event since 2000. Therefore, we decided to work with the number of events from 2000 to 2021 that occurred in each country at the state level.

Merging aggregate harm data and household survey data is not straightforward in all countries. Even though we have information on natural hazards in most of the ADM 2 units, in some cases, we do not have the corresponding unit in the SEDLAC database. For example, in Ecuador, the canton Eloy Alfaro from Esmeraldas province is not in the SEDLAC database, and in Honduras, Gracias a Dios and Islas de Bahía states are not in the SEDLAC database. In these cases, we do not include these units in the final database. Meanwhile, in other cases, we have units in the SEDLAC database without natural hazard data. In these cases, we impute hazard data of their nearest and similar unit neighbor. We carried out this imputation in the Dominican Republic, Mexico, and Honduras. For example, in the Dominican Republic, we imputed the hazard level of Villa Hermosa by the one of La Romana, which is 14 km of distance; Villa Montellano by Puerto Plata (14 km); Puñal by Santiago (15 km); and Guayacanes by San Pedro de Macoris (19 km).

After the corresponding imputation, we obtain that in the Dominican Republic, all ADM 2 units (hereinafter "districts" for all countries) of the SEDLAC database have aggregate natural hazard information. In Ecuador, all districts in the SEDLAC database have natural hazard information too. In Honduras, we impute hazard data with the nearest neighbor method in four districts (Jutiapa by La Ceiba; Trojes by Danlí; San Francisco Opalaca by La Iguala; Nueva Frontera by Macuelizo), obtaining only 170 observations in the SEDLAC database without hazard information (0.7% of the sample). In Mexico, we re-coded Oaxaca and six San Luis de Potosi districts and imputed 33 districts of twelve states with the nearest neighbor method, reaching 0.9% of observations of the sample without hazard information distributed among 22 districts across nine states.

For aggregate exposure, we use the population weighting the survey observations at the state or district level, depending on the country. In Brazil and Ecuador, the weighted population is at the state level, and in the other countries, at the district level. We also use the area of districts or, in Brazil's case, the area of provinces. We retrieved the area data from Google Earth Engine Data Catalog using the MODIS 500m Landcover Dataset of the NASA LP DAAC at the USGS EROS Center with a spatial resolution of 500 meters. The area data corresponds to the 2018 landcover images from LC type 1, which includes 17 classes of land use (the total area is computed as the sum of them). Based on these datasets, we use three variables of exposure, the natural logarithm of density (population/area in km^2) as a proxy of the presence of people, the percentage of urbanization area as a proxy of infrastructure developed, and the percentage of cropland as a proxy of resources of the region. In the data, urban areas are those where at least 30% of the surface area is built-up, including building materials, asphalt, and vehicles, and the cropland areas are those where at least 60% of the surface area is cultivated cropland. One limitation of using 500 m is that in areas of the tropics where cropland field sizes tend to be much smaller than a MODIS pixel, agriculture is sometimes underrepresented and can be labeled as natural vegetation instead (Sulla-Menashe & Friedl, 2018).

In addition, for the model, we select variables of coping mechanisms, adaptation, and demographics at the household level that are good enough to predict effective household poverty in the absence of harm and exposure. For this selection of households' coping mechanisms and adaptation strategies to natural disasters, we follow the Unbreakable Report (Hallegatte et al., 2017). We choose the following variables as a proxy of income diversification and occupation: the household head is a salaried worker; the household head is informal; natural logarithm of the household's non-labor income per capita, labor income as a share of total income, dependency rate, and household head's principal income is from agriculture. Also, as a proxy of assistance, we choose a dummy indicating if the household receives benefits from social assistance. For housing conditions, we select low-quality materials in the dwelling, toilet facilities linked to sewer, access to electricity, overcrowding, assets ownership (including car, fridge, computer, washing machine), and access to the Internet. And as socio-demographics, we choose the years of education of the household head, the number of household members, the household head's age and squared age, and the gender of the household head. Next, we explained the selected coping and adaptation variables.

It is well known that natural disaster events have socio-economic consequences such as job losses and falling incomes. Hallegatte et al. (2017) illustrate from a survey of 200 households in Mumbai that floods cause problems with transport and fuel availability. Affected households lose workdays, implying a loss of income, productivity, and sometimes jobs. A **salaried job** can provide minimal protection to lost workdays, and the probability of losing the job is lower than in another type of occupation, and there is the benefit of receiving a paycheck if the job is lost. Furthermore, **informality** is a primary concern, as households whose head is employed informally frequently do not have access to safety nets and protection when shocks hit.

Diversifying income sources is a coping mechanism for households in any disaster event. Higher diversification leads to lower-income losses. Therefore, we use **labor income as a share of total income** to measure the diversification of income sources. We also consider the **household's nonlabor income per capita** as a proxy of adaptation strategy. However, as Hallegatte et al. (2017) based on Bandyopadhyay and Skoufias (2015) point out, diversifying incomes helps households at all income levels to cope, but mainly with small shocks and no larger ones. Further, households with high **dependency** ratios are likelier to be vulnerable (Chaudhuri, 2003). The number of income earners (the ratio's denominator) provides a proxy of the household's risk, especially if the household has only one income earner.

The sector of activity of household members can also contribute to the risks faced by the household. For example, the **income from agriculture** can be significantly depressed by a natural disaster through agriculture productivity decline and loss of agricultural production. "*…Poor people, especially in rural areas without functioning markets, are highly dependent on agricultural income and ecosystems, and they are therefore vulnerable to the impacts of natural disasters on yields and the health and functioning of ecosystems.*" (Hallegatte et al., 2017, p. 47).

On the other hand, social protection systems can protect poor people. Following Stampini and Tornarolli (2012), Conditional Cash Transfers (CCTs) have spread in the LAC region in the last years, reaching poor households. **Social assistance programs' benefits** contribute to household income diversification and reduce risk. In any natural disaster, these benefits can work as a buffer. In addition, they can operate as a channel to reach the casualties more quickly.

Also, following Hallegatte et al. (2017) the poor and non-poor household's typical asset portfolio is very different. "... *Poor people tend to have less diversified portfolios: they hold a larger percentage of their assets in material form and save 'in kind.' Moreover, ... the quality of assets owned by poor people is lower.*" (Hallegatte et al., 2017, p. 44). Households with few productive and financial assets are more likely to be exposed to adverse shocks and have limited earnings prospects and income-generating capacity (Chaudhuri, 2003). In addition, "...*in absolute terms, wealthier people lose more assets or income from a natural disaster, which is expected because they have more assets and higher incomes. In relative terms, however, poor people always lose more than the non-poor from floods and storms*" (Hallegatte et al., 2017, p. 42).

Furthermore, Zhang et al. (2020) demonstrate that owning physical assets is vital for households' recovery after a disaster. Nonetheless, according to Chaudhuri (2003), in the absence of sufficient assets or insurance to smooth consumption, a shock may lead to irreversible losses, such as permanent damage or a distressed sale of productive assets, which does not allow for a fast postdisaster recovery. The sale of these assets is a costly coping strategy, particularly for poor households. From the above considerations, we choose a variety of home durable goods as **household assets** to reflect the well-being and coping of the households. Following Alkire and Santos (2010), we include **car** and **refrigerator** ownership in the household assets. We also include **washing machines** and **computers** because Figal Garone et al. (2019) show that LAC has high heterogeneity in owning these household assets within countries, especially **washing machines**. Though high-income segments exhibit asset ownership close to developed countries, low-income segments have considerably lower access to these assets.

Most poor people either live in fragile buildings or dwellings with low-quality materials (Hallegatte et al., 2017). These materials make areas riskier in the event of natural hazards. Also, natural disasters, especially floods, can cause problems with the **power supply**, drinking water, household drains, and **sewers** that worsen with a weak infrastructure. Moreover,

> [...]. besides losses of private income and assets, natural disasters cause significant disruption to public infrastructure. Even though all people depend to some extent on electricity, working roads, and running water, poorer people tend to be less able to protect themselves from the consequences of disruptions in infrastructure services. (Hallegatte et al., 2017, p. 46)

Finally, following Chaudhuri (2003), a household is more likely to be exposed to adverse shocks and have limited earnings prospects and income-generating capacity if it has low levels of human capital, know-how, and access to information. Also, poor households have little access to early warnings (Hallegatte et al., 2017). Hence, we consider **household head education and Internet access as coping mechanisms.**

The estimations of the model in Table A1.1 show that the variables of coping and demographics selected are good enough to predict effective poverty. The correlation between the predicted probability of being poor and the effective poverty status goes from 0.59 to 0.77, depending on the country (Brazil presents a correlation coefficient of 0.767, Peru 0.734, Honduras 0.695, Mexico 0.641, El Salvador

Table A1.1. Estimations of the Expected Poverty Model (Conditional to Household Characteristics).

Probit Model	Brazil	Dominican Republic	Ecuador	El Salvador	Honduras	Mexico	Peru
HH head is salaried in main occupation	−0.227 [0.030]***	0.159 [0.082]*	−0.217 [0.055]***	−0.311 [0.040]***	−0.315 [0.064]***	−0.211 [0.022]***	−0.163 [0.037]***
HH head is informal in main occupation	0.320 [0.019]***	0.159 [0.079]**	0.352 [0.044]***	0.165 [0.033]***	0.339 [0.053]***	0.317 [0.019]***	0.191 [0.041]***
Ln. non labor income per capita PPP 2017	−0.409 [0.022]***	−0.165 [0.028]***	−0.291 [0.023]***	−0.263 [0.017]***	−0.311 [0.026]***	−0.287 [0.011]***	−0.674 [0.032]***
Labor income as a share of total income (monetary)	−2.113 [0.064]***	−2.003 [0.160]***	−2.162 [0.085]***	−1.928 [0.100]***	−2.319 [0.147]***	−2.244 [0.057]***	−3.662 [0.174]***
Dependency rate (members/ number of income earners)	0.692 [0.011]***	0.304 [0.040]***	0.233 [0.018]***	0.495 [0.023]***	0.348 [0.023]***	0.294 [0.012]***	0.365 [0.019]***
HH head's principal income is from agriculture	0.107 [0.040]***	0.318 [0.099]***	0.188 [0.054]***	0.324 [0.042]***	0.411 [0.061]***	0.249 [0.026]***	0.308 [0.037]***
Receives benefits from a social assistance program	1.382 [0.028]***	0.208 [0.061]***	0.454 [0.028]***	0.649 [0.104]***	0.821 [0.100]***	0.679 [0.024]***	0.469 [0.036]***
Dwelling's materials of low quality	0.148 [0.050]***	0.378 [0.123]***	0.248 [0.038]***	0.205 [0.029]***	0.184 [0.086]**	0.135 [0.023]***	0.075 [0.058]
Toilet facilities linked to the sewer	−0.082 [0.024]***	−0.005 [0.077]	−0.176 [0.049]***	−0.158 [0.058]***	−0.170 [0.059]***	−0.207 [0.023]***	−0.137 [0.040]***
Dwelling has access to electricity	−0.269 [0.121]**	−0.183 [0.212]	−0.174 [0.078]**	−0.045 [0.073]	−0.066 [0.111]	−0.091 [0.104]	−0.138 [0.049]***
Number of HH members over the number of bedrooms > 3	0.247 [0.037]***	0.237 [0.101]**	0.240 [0.040]***	0.149 [0.052]***	0.226 [0.072]***	0.235 [0.028]***	0.144 [0.054]***
Has a car	−0.584 [0.020]***	−0.639 [0.125]***	−0.022 [0.043]	−0.589 [0.053]***	−0.408 [0.093]***	−0.395 [0.021]***	−0.468 [0.079]***
Has a fridge	−0.190 [0.044]***	−0.242 [0.097]**	−0.348 [0.014]***	−0.356 [0.027]***	−0.422 [0.058]***	−0.278 [0.027]***	−0.355 [0.033]***
Has a computer	−0.126 [0.044]***	−0.490 [0.074]***	−0.224 [0.029]***	−0.416 [0.094]***	−0.230 [0.085]***	−0.253 [0.030]***	−0.216 [0.058]***

Table A1.1. (*Continued*)

Probit Model	Brazil	Dominican Republic	Ecuador	El Salvador	Honduras	Mexico	Peru
Has a washing machine	−0.371 [0.024]***	−0.166 [0.089]*	0.009 [0.026]	−0.302 [0.051]***		−0.208 [0.019]***	−0.303 [0.052]***
Access to internet in the HH	−0.370 [0.037]***	−0.319 [0.079]***	−0.316 [0.027]***	−0.270 [0.076]***	−0.386 [0.075]***	−0.349 [0.024]***	−0.377 [0.051]***
Years of education of HH head	−0.054 [0.002]***	−0.042 [0.009]***	−0.033 [0.004]***	−0.044 [0.004]***	−0.058 [0.009]***	−0.041 [0.003]***	−0.035 [0.004]***
Number of HH members	0.179 [0.007]***	0.355 [0.020]***	0.090 [0.007]***	0.161 [0.013]***	0.127 [0.021]***	0.213 [0.008]***	0.157 [0.009]***
HH head's age	−0.003 [0.003]	−0.024 [0.007]***	−0.017 [0.003]***	−0.026 [0.005]***	−0.041 [0.009]***	−0.015 [0.003]***	−0.006 [0.006]
HH head's age squared	−0.000 [0.000]***	0.000 [0.000]	−0.000 [0.000]***	0.000 [0.000]***	0.000 [0.000]***	0.000 [0.000]	−0.000 [0.000]
Male HH head	−0.210 [0.009]***	−0.291 [0.061]***	−0.039 [0.046]	−0.071 [0.043]	−0.247 [0.068]***	0.037 [0.023]	−0.016 [0.037]
Region: North east	0.273 [0.043]***						
Region: South east	−0.130 [0.050]***						
Region: South	−0.268 [0.066]***						
Region: West center	−0.262 [0.096]***						
Region: Cibao north		−0.127 [0.089]					
Region: Cibao south		−0.280 [0.169]*					
Region: Cibao north east		0.014 [0.114]					
Region: Cibao north west		−0.317 [0.137]**					
Region: Valdesia		−0.054 [0.147]					
Region: El Valle		−0.102 [0.145]					
Region: Enriquillo		0.113 [0.120]					
Region: Higuamo		0.034 [0.139]					
Region: Yuma		−0.573 [0.199]***					
Region: Coast			0.003 [0.106]				

(*Continued*)

Table A1.1. (*Continued*)

Probit Model	Brazil	Dominican Republic	Ecuador	El Salvador	Honduras	Mexico	Peru
Region: Amazonia			0.296				
			[0.084]***				
Region: Insular			−1.396				
			[0.057]***				
Region: Central I				–0.016			
				[0.050]			
Region: Central II				–0.017			
				[0.048]			
Region: Oriental				–0.005			
				[0.050]			
Region: Metropolitan area San Salvador				0.036			
				[0.064]			
Region: North					–0.001		
					[0.086]		
Region: West					0.247		
					[0.104]**		
Region: South					0.014		
					[0.090]		
Region: East					0.301		
					[0.093]***		
Region: Central					0.282		
					[0.068]***		
Region: North						0.219	
						[0.073]***	
Region: North east						0.148	
						[0.094]	
Region: Center –west						0.085	
						[0.071]	
Region: Center – east						0.018	
						[0.068]	
Region: South						0.365	
						[0.067]***	
Region: East						0.351	
						[0.072]***	
Region: Yucatan peninsula						0.046	
						[0.084]	
Region: Urban sierra							0.253
							[0.055]***
Region: Urban jungle							0.074
							[0.064]

Table A1.1. *(Continued)*

Probit Model	Brazil	Dominican Republic	Ecuador	El Salvador	Honduras	Mexico	Peru
Region: Rural coast							0.139 [0.070]**
Region: Rural sierra							0.518 [0.053]***
Region: Rural jungle							0.313 [0.067]***
Region: Metropolitan Lima							−0.089 [0.054]*
Constant	1.346 [0.124]***	1.096 [0.322]***	2.178 [0.147]***	0.991 [0.168]***	2.774 [0.277]***	1.726 [0.154]***	3.431 [0.264]***
Observations	69,362,803	3,144,980	4,527,881	1,937,964	1,966,380	33,425,611	8,801,118

Note: HH is household. *** $p<0.01$, ** $p<0.05$, * $p<0.1$. Standard errors clustered by districts in brackets (by states in Brazil and Ecuador).
Source: Authors' calculations based on SEDLAC database.

Table A1.2. Country States, Districts, and Households Covered by the Survey.

Country	Number of …		
	states	districts	households (weighted)
Brazil	27	n.a.	70,585,086
Dominican Republic	32	135	3,378,912
Ecuador	25	223	4,536,941
El Salvador	14	225	1,938,504
Honduras	16	230	2,092,981
Mexico	32	894	34,027,646
Peru	25	182	9,178,213

Source: Authors' calculations based on SEDLAC database.

0.621, the Dominican Republic 0.583, and Ecuador 0.590). These correlation coefficients are relatively significant compared with other studies, such as Alkire and Santos (2010), which find a correlation of 0.870 for 104 developing countries, and Gasparini et al. (2011), which estimate a correlation of 0.428 for LAC countries. Moreover, when we explore the headcount of households with a predicted probability of being poor larger than 0.50 and the headcount of poverty by using a poverty line of 6.85 USD PPP 2017, we find a ratio for most countries close to 1. The ratio in Brazil is 0.871, the Dominican Republic 0.916, Ecuador 0.652, El Salvador 0.717, Honduras 1.002, Mexico 0.836, and Peru 1.031.

Table A1.2 shows country by country the number of states (s), the number of districts (d), and the total number of households covered by the survey.

Table A1.3 presents the models' estimations used to estimate vulnerability, including all natural hazards variables simultaneously (those from ThinkHazard!

Table A1.3. Multilevel Mixed Effects Probit Model Estimations Including and Excluding ThinkHazard! Indexes.

	Brazil		Dominican Republic		Ecuador		El Salvador		Honduras		Mexico		Peru	
	Including TH Indexes	Excluding TH Indexes	Including TH Indexes	Excluding TH Indexes	Including TH Indexes	Excluding TH Indexes	Including TH Indexes	Excluding TH Indexes	Including TH Indexes	Excluding TH Indexes	Including TH Indexes	Excluding TH Indexes	Including TH Indexes	Excluding TH Indexes
TH index Flood	0.333		0.035		0.006		−0.005		−0.042		0.006		−0.071	
	[0.111]***		[0.043]		[0.021]		[0.018]		[0.030]		[0.012]		[0.022]***	
Number of Floods	−0.036	−0.021	−0.044	−0.047	0.013	0.015	−0.003	0.000	−0.059	−0.062	0.025	0.026	0.007	0.007
	[0.017]**	[0.011]**	[0.034]	[0.033]	[0.015]	[0.016]	[0.025]	[0.022]	[0.017]***	[0.016]***	[0.014]*	[0.016]*	[0.017]	[0.017]
TH index Landslides	0.170		0.082		−0.045		−0.023		0.026		0.009		−0.012	
	[0.164]		[0.064]		[0.030]		[0.023]		[0.040]		[0.015]		[0.031]	
Number of Landslides	−0.036	0.088			0.109	0.103	−0.039	−0.064			−0.028	−0.018	0.043	0.062
	[0.066]	[0.055]			[0.080]	[0.084]	[0.133]	[0.124]			[0.056]	[0.061]	[0.072]	[0.073]
TH index Earthquake	−0.143				0.111				−0.005		−0.035		−0.049	
	[0.124]				[0.054]**				[0.084]		[0.022]		[0.041]	
Number of Earthquakes	0.197	−0.208	0.353	0.370	−0.089	−0.057	0.015	0.012	0.041	0.038	0.043	0.021	−0.040	−0.037
	[0.210]	[0.194]	[0.250]	[0.239]	[0.055]	[0.058]	[0.048]	[0.045]	[0.047]	[0.045]	[0.036]	[0.037]	[0.044]	[0.045]
TH index Cyclones											0.123			
											[0.053]**			
Number of Cyclones			0.008	0.004			−0.008	−0.009	0.029	0.021	0.006	0.007		
			[0.033]	[0.032]			[0.026]	[0.024]	[0.024]	[0.023]	[0.007]	[0.007]		
TH index Drought	0.149								0.020		−0.029		−0.024	
	[0.079]*								[0.111]		[0.021]		[0.037]	
Number of Droughts	0.159	0.096			−0.066	−0.058	0.018	0.019	0.055	0.066	0.082	0.061	−0.220	−0.211
	[0.048]***	[0.031]***			[0.084]	[0.090]	[0.030]	[0.028]	[0.026]**	[0.024]***	[0.060]	[0.064]	[0.168]	[0.170]
Ln. density	0.101	0.107	−0.077	−0.069	−0.107	−0.111	0.022	0.034	−0.082	−0.068	−0.022	−0.022	0.010	0.016
	[0.058]*	[0.042]**	[0.048]	[0.048]	[0.045]**	[0.048]**	[0.025]	[0.022]	[0.036]**	[0.033]**	[0.009]**	[0.009]**	[0.019]	[0.019]
% cropland (Res 500)	0.210	-0.666	0.384	0.115	0.338	0.364	−0.293	−0.240	−0.158	−0.606	0.075	0.040	1.665	1.525
	[0.672]	[0.515]	[0.597]	[0.523]	[0.232]	[0.192]*	[0.198]	[0.154]	[0.505]	[0.383]	[0.072]	[0.062]	[0.590]***	[0.568]***
% urbanization and built–up (Res 500)	5.908	-3.252	0.563	0.463	−0.656	-0.437	0.092	0.064	1.097	1.012	−0.027	−0.081	−1.095	−1.210
	[8.361]	[6.781]	[0.437]	[0.431]	[0.302]**	[0.286]	[0.235]	[0.226]	[1.332]	[1.243]	[0.108]	[0.099]	[0.386]***	[0.386]***
HH head is salaried in main occupation	−0.197	−0.197	0.166	0.181	−0.247	−0.243	−0.336	−0.326	−0.340	−0.336	−0.209	−0.206	−0.153	−0.155
	[0.013]***	[0.013]***	[0.074]**	[0.074]**	[0.012]***	[0.012]***	[0.030]***	[0.029]***	[0.056]***	[0.055]***	[0.016]***	[0.016]***	[0.028]***	[0.028]***

HH head is informal in main occupation	0.338	0.338	0.158	0.156	0.365	0.363	0.197	0.192	0.283	0.292	0.323	0.322	0.218	0.218
	[0.014]***	[0.014]***	[0.071]**	[0.071]**	[0.012]***	[0.012]***	[0.026]***	[0.026]***	[0.049]***	[0.049]***	[0.014]***	[0.014]***	[0.027]***	[0.026]***
Ln. non labor income per capita PPP 2017	−0.438	−0.438	−0.171	−0.171	−0.286	−0.285	−0.277	−0.276	−0.302	−0.304	−0.322	−0.321	−0.806	−0.807
	[0.007]***	[0.007]***	[0.023]***	[0.023]***	[0.005]***	[0.005]***	[0.012]***	[0.012]***	[0.023]***	[0.023]***	[0.007]***	[0.007]***	[0.014]***	[0.014]***
Labor income as a share of total income (monetary)	−2.124	−2.124	−2.114	−2.133	−2.087	−2.085	−1.922	−1.915	−2.261	−2.280	−2.371	−2.367	−4.246	−4.248
	[0.037]***	[0.037]***	[0.142]***	[0.141]***	[0.031]***	[0.031]***	[0.079]***	[0.077]***	[0.148]***	[0.147]***	[0.041]***	[0.040]***	[0.070]***	[0.070]***
Dependency rate (members/ number of income earners)	0.690	0.690	0.337	0.337	0.242	0.242	0.456	0.465	0.361	0.360	0.265	0.267	0.338	0.339
	[0.008]***	[0.008]***	[0.030]***	[0.030]***	[0.006]***	[0.006]***	[0.013]***	[0.012]***	[0.025]***	[0.025]***	[0.008]***	[0.007]***	[0.013]***	[0.013]***
HH head's principal income is from agriculture	0.117	0.117	0.356	0.355	0.113	0.114	0.328	0.339	0.362	0.372	0.154	0.158	0.373	0.375
	[0.019]***	[0.019]***	[0.090]***	[0.089]***	[0.015]***	[0.015]***	[0.033]***	[0.032]***	[0.067]***	[0.066]***	[0.018]***	[0.018]***	[0.028]***	[0.028]***
Receive benefits from a social assistance program	1.441	1.441	0.125	0.132	0.429	0.429	0.613	0.616	0.837	0.829	0.675	0.677	0.458	0.461
	[0.017]***	[0.017]***	[0.065]*	[0.064]**	[0.015]***	[0.015]***	[0.077]***	[0.074]***	[0.079]***	[0.079]***	[0.018]***	[0.018]***	[0.027]***	[0.027]***
Dwelling's materials of low quality	0.123	0.125	0.252	0.266	0.273	0.272	0.225	0.210	0.192	0.190	0.130	0.130	0.120	0.107
	[0.026]***	[0.026]***	[0.088]***	[0.087]***	[0.014]***	[0.014]***	[0.027]***	[0.026]***	[0.082]**	[0.082]**	[0.016]***	[0.016]***	[0.033]***	[0.033]***
Toilet facilities linked to the sewer	−0.104	−0.103	−0.048	−0.045	−0.119	−0.121	−0.193	−0.186	−0.183	−0.180	−0.164	−0.163	−0.212	−0.210
	[0.014]***	[0.014]***	[0.083]	[0.083]	[0.015]***	[0.015]***	[0.039]***	[0.038]***	[0.058]***	[0.058]***	[0.017]***	[0.017]***	[0.026]***	[0.026]***
Dwelling have access to electricity	−0.258	−0.257	−0.013	0.037	−0.052	−0.054	−0.072	−0.085	−0.065	−0.080	−0.159	−0.156	−0.090	−0.086
	[0.084]***	[0.084]***	[0.199]	[0.198]	[0.051]	[0.050]	[0.066]	[0.064]	[0.117]	[0.116]	[0.077]**	[0.076]**	[0.041]**	[0.040]**
Number of HH members over the number of bedrooms > 3	0.207	0.208	0.222	0.215	0.290	0.291	0.115	0.107	0.199	0.207	0.216	0.222	0.134	0.137
	[0.029]***	[0.029]***	[0.102]**	[0.102]**	[0.014]***	[0.013]***	[0.038]***	[0.037]***	[0.065]***	[0.065]***	[0.020]***	[0.020]***	[0.035]***	[0.035]***
Has a car	−0.584	−0.585	−0.593	−0.586	−0.024	−0.024	−0.548	−0.548	−0.334	−0.343	−0.394	−0.392	−0.420	−0.421
	[0.015]***	[0.015]***	[0.099]***	[0.098]***	[0.015]	[0.015]	[0.043]***	[0.042]***	[0.067]***	[0.066]***	[0.016]***	[0.015]***	[0.052]***	[0.052]***
Has a fridge	−0.204	−0.205	−0.186	−0.206	−0.332	−0.334	−0.345	−0.348	−0.439	−0.428	−0.241	−0.248	−0.366	−0.372
	[0.034]***	[0.034]***	[0.087]**	[0.086]**	[0.013]***	[0.013]***	[0.028]***	[0.027]***	[0.060]***	[0.059]***	[0.020]***	[0.019]***	[0.028]***	[0.027]***

(Continued)

Table A1.3. *(Continued)*

	Brazil		Dominican Republic		Ecuador		El Salvador		Honduras		Mexico		Peru	
	Including TH Indexes	Excluding TH Indexes	Including TH Indexes	Excluding TH Indexes	Including TH Indexes	Excluding TH Indexes	Including TH Indexes	Excluding TH Indexes	Including TH Indexes	Excluding TH Indexes	Including TH Indexes	Excluding TH Indexes	Including TH Indexes	Excluding TH Indexes
Has a computer	−0.204	−0.204	−0.431	−0.417	−0.257	−0.256	−0.384	−0.391	−0.320	−0.321	−0.248	−0.243	−0.266	−0.266
	[0.031]***	[0.031]***	[0.107]***	[0.106]***	[0.017]***	[0.017]***	[0.058]***	[0.056]***	[0.084]***	[0.084]***	[0.022]***	[0.022]***	[0.036]***	[0.036]***
Has a washing machine	−0.314	−0.314	−0.123	−0.132	−0.026	−0.025	−0.359	−0.365			−0.203	−0.201	−0.345	−0.347
	[0.014]***	[0.014]***	[0.067]*	[0.067]**	[0.013]**	[0.013]**	[0.049]***	[0.047]***			[0.015]***	[0.015]***	[0.042]***	[0.042]***
Access to internet in the HH	−0.301	−0.302	−0.335	−0.339	−0.271	−0.272	−0.284	−0.285	−0.338	−0.337	−0.302	−0.306	−0.369	−0.368
	[0.033]***	[0.033]***	[0.084]***	[0.084]***	[0.018]***	[0.017]***	[0.046]***	[0.044]***	[0.066]***	[0.065]***	[0.019]***	[0.018]***	[0.037]***	[0.037]***
Years of education of HH head	−0.049	−0.049	−0.044	−0.045	−0.030	−0.030	−0.045	−0.045	−0.050	−0.052	−0.037	−0.037	−0.036	−0.036
	[0.002]***	[0.002]***	[0.007]***	[0.007]***	[0.002]***	[0.002]***	[0.004]***	[0.003]***	[0.007]***	[0.007]***	[0.002]***	[0.002]***	[0.003]***	[0.003]***
Number of HH members	0.174	0.174	0.353	0.355	0.099	0.099	0.172	0.167	0.117	0.118	0.220	0.219	0.180	0.179
	[0.005]***	[0.005]***	[0.021]***	[0.021]***	[0.002]***	[0.002]***	[0.009]***	[0.008]***	[0.015]***	[0.015]***	[0.004]***	[0.004]***	[0.008]***	[0.008]***
HH head's age	−0.000	−0.000	−0.027	−0.026	−0.019	−0.019	−0.026	−0.025	−0.037	−0.039	−0.015	−0.016	−0.008	−0.008
	[0.002]	[0.002]	[0.009]***	[0.009]***	[0.002]***	[0.002]***	[0.004]***	[0.004]***	[0.008]***	[0.008]***	[0.002]***	[0.002]***	[0.004]*	[0.004]*
HH head's age squared	−0.000	−0.000	0.000	0.000	−0.000	−0.000	0.000	0.000	0.000	0.000	0.000	0.000	−0.000	−0.000
	[0.000]***	[0.000]***	[0.000]	[0.000]	[0.000]*	[0.000]**	[0.000]***	[0.000]***	[0.000]***	[0.000]***	[0.000]	[0.000]	[0.000]	[0.000]
Male HH head	−0.203	−0.203	−0.279	−0.280	−0.085	−0.086	−0.083	−0.078	−0.191	−0.198	0.034	0.033	0.024	0.023
	[0.013]***	[0.013]***	[0.063]***	[0.062]***	[0.012]***	[0.012]***	[0.028]***	[0.027]***	[0.055]***	[0.054]***	[0.016]**	[0.016]**	[0.026]	[0.026]
Constant	−0.367	0.930	1.059	1.424	2.197	2.392	1.069	0.862	3.181	3.231	1.608	1.992	5.008	4.601
	[0.503]	[0.142]***	[0.615]*	[0.539]***	[0.263]***	[0.177]***	[0.265]***	[0.231]***	[0.460]***	[0.327]***	[0.257]***	[0.134]***	[0.354]***	[0.295]***
Observations	137,364	137,364	5,742	5,796	135,336	136,329	20,115	21,326	4,999	5,087	66,513	69,378	33,350	33,407
Number of groups	23	23	32	32	24	24	14	14	16	16	32	32	25	25
Variance constant level states	0.011	0.017	0.044	0.041	0.025	0.030	0.005	0.004	0.000	0.000	0.031	0.038	0.073	0.078
	[0.004]***	[0.005]***	[0.034]	[0.032]	[0.010]***	[0.011]***	[0.003]	[0.003]	[0.000]	[0.000]	[0.010]***	[0.011]***	[0.023]***	[0.024]***
Variance constant level districts			0.029	0.033	0.038	0.038	0.009	0.008	0.000	0.000	0.051	0.050	0.051	0.052
			[0.028]	[0.031]	[0.006]***	[0.006]***	[0.004]**	[0.004]**	[0.000]	[0.000]	[0.005]***	[0.005]***	[0.008]***	[0.008]***

Notes: HH is household. The columns denote different specifications for each country. Column 1of each country presents the estimations to specifications, including both type of natural hazard, TH indexes and EM–DAT occurrences, while column 2 includes only EM–DAT occurrences. *** $p < 0.01$, ** $p < 0.05$, * $p < 0.1$. Standard errors clustered by districts in brackets (by states in Brazil and Ecuador).

Source: Authors' calculations based on ThinkHazard!, EM-DAT, and SEDLAC database.

and EM-DAT database) and also presents the estimations excluding ThinkHazard! indexes, leaving only the EM-DAT occurrences.

Table A1.4 displays measures of the area under the ROC curve (AUC) to assess how close the predicted probability of being poor is to the observed frequencies. It also includes performance measures such as accuracy, F1 score, and Matthew's correlation coefficient (Chicco & Jurman, 2020; Sokolova et al., 2006), considering a probability threshold of 0.50.

In addition, some variables not included in the model are relevant to explore households' coping mechanisms and adaptation. Therefore, we examine them in the profiles of vulnerability. In the profiles, we explore the incidence of households among vulnerable households that report only **one sector of activity**, only **one income earner**, and that receive benefits from **remittances** from abroad and assistance mechanisms as income diversification. We also explore the percentage of vulnerable households living in **dwellings with legal ownership**. This latter is particularly important because legal ownership allows a more feasible improvement of the infrastructure of the dwelling (Hallegatte et al., 2017). Also, insurance markets play a fundamental role in the event of a natural disaster. Unfortunately, the databases do not provide much information on different types of insurance. But there is information on household **health insurance** that is relevant as natural events' health impacts can be pervasive, especially when the public health system is deficient, pushing households to poor health and catastrophic health expenditures.

Likewise, specific demographic groups can face more risks from a natural disaster. **Children** are often the main ones affected, with permanent impacts on health and education. Hence, we compute the percentage of vulnerable households with children under five years old and children under 12 years old attending school. We also identify vulnerable households where all their members are older than 65. Older adults' coping and adaptation mechanisms can be insufficient if their losses are significant. The **elderly** usually retire from the labor market and have already made investments during their active lifetime. Thus, a negative shock can make them permanently disabled from generating new incomes and coping with losses.

Table A1.4. Performance Measures.

Indicator	Brazil	Dominican Rep.	Ecuador	El Salvador	Honduras	Mexico	Peru
Estimated area under the ROC curve (AUC)	0.95	0.89	0.88	0.89	0.90	0.90	0.94
Performance measures							
Accuracy	0.87	0.80	0.84	0.82	0.80	0.79	0.85
F1 score	0.70	0.45	0.56	0.59	0.78	0.61	0.72
Matthew's correlation coefficient	0.62	0.34	0.49	0.48	0.60	0.47	0.62

Source: Authors' calculations based on model estimations.

APPENDIX 2. ROBUSTNESS EXERCISES

A first robustness check comes from performing Chaudhuri's procedure. Following the procedure outlined in Chaudhuri (2003), we estimate vulnerability considering unexplained idiosyncratic shocks. The procedure uses the expected mean of income and the variance of the unexplained part of the income process. We assume the following simple, functional form for the household income per capita:

$$\ln y_h = X_h \beta + u_h$$

where y_h is the income per capita of the household h (to simplify, we drop the geographic subindexes), $X_h = (Harm, Exposure, Coping_h, D_h)$ is a vector of variables of harm, exposure, coping, and demographics used in the primary model and u_h is the disturbance term that we assume its variance depends on the observable variables as follows

Table A2.1. Vulnerability Rates Comparison to Chaudhuri Procedure Considering the Specification with All Hazards Together.

	Multilevel Mixed Probit		Chaudhuri	
% HH with	Mean	SD	Mean	SD
Brazil				
predicted prob. > 0.25	25%	0.435	95%	22%
predicted prob. > 0.50	17%	0.372	72%	45%
predicted prob. > 0.75	10%	0.302	30%	46%
Dominican Rep.				
predicted prob. > 0.25	18%	0.384	n.a.	n.a.
predicted prob. > 0.50	7%	0.260	n.a.	n.a.
predicted prob. > 0.75	3%	0.172	n.a.	n.a.
Ecuador				
predicted prob. > 0.25	28%	0.451	58%	0.494
predicted prob. > 0.50	13%	0.337	28%	0.448
predicted prob. > 0.75	5%	0.225	10%	0.305
El Salvador				
predicted prob. > 0.25	34%	0.473	n.a.	n.a.
predicted prob. > 0.50	16%	0.369	n.a.	n.a.
predicted prob. > 0.75	7%	0.248	n.a.	n.a.
Honduras				
predicted prob. > 0.25	60%	0.490	77%	0.420
predicted prob. > 0.50	40%	0.491	45%	0.498
predicted prob. > 0.75	25%	0.432	17%	0.376
Mexico				
predicted prob. > 0.25	37%	0.483	51%	0.500
predicted prob. > 0.50	20%	0.402	21%	0.406
predicted prob. > 0.75	9%	0.287	5%	0.208
Peru				
predicted prob. > 0.25	36%	0.480	53%	0.499
predicted prob. > 0.50	24%	0.428	27%	0.443
predicted prob. > 0.75	15%	0.353	7%	0.253

Source: Authors' calculations based on ThinkHazard!, EM-DAT, and SEDLAC database.

Table A2.2. Vulnerability Rates Comparison Between Model Proposed and Skoufias Model.

	Vulnerability Incidence	
Country	Model	Skoufias Model
predicted prob. > 0.50		
Brazil	16.22%	16.18%
Dom. Rep.	7.27%	7.75%
Ecuador	13.02%	15.00%
El Salvador	16.25%	16.03%
Honduras	40.47%	42.72%
Mexico	20.21%	21.19%
Peru	24.16%	23.35%

Source: Authors' calculations based on ThinkHazard!, EM-DAT, and SEDLAC database.

$$\sigma_{u,h}^2 = X_h\theta.$$

We estimate β and θ by the three-step feasible generalized least squares (FGLS) method (Amemiya, 1977). See the estimation's details in Chaudhuri (2003). Then we estimate the expected natural logarithm of household income per capita and its variance:

$$\hat{E}(\ln \hat{Y}_h \mid X_h) = X_h\hat{\beta}_{FGLS},$$
$$\hat{V}(\ln \hat{Y}_h \mid X_h) = \hat{\sigma}_{u,h}^2 = X_h\hat{\theta}_{FGLS}.$$

Then, the estimated conditional probability of being vulnerable is given by:

$$\widehat{Pr}(\ln \hat{Y}_h < z \mid X_h) = \Phi\left(\frac{\ln z - X_h\hat{\beta}_{FGLS}}{\sqrt{X_h\hat{\theta}_{FGLS}}}\right),$$

where z is the poverty line of 6.85 USD (adjusted by PPP 2017), and Φ denotes the cumulative density function of the standard normal.

Chaudhuri vulnerability estimates offer an upper bound rate because it includes unobservable idiosyncratic shocks that contribute to different per capita household incomes. Nevertheless, in practice, the term $X_h\hat{\theta}_{FGLS}$ can take negative values, which is inconsistent with the fact that $\hat{\sigma}_{u,h}^2$ is positive. Chaudhuri (2003) finds that few observations fall into this issue and drop them. Here, for the Dominican Republic and El Salvador, this is a sizeable problem, with a large number of households having $X_h\hat{\theta}_{FGLS}$ under zero. Thus, we do not provide Chaudhuri estimation in these countries in Table A2.1. Estimations indicate that the Chaudhuri procedure would increase vulnerability considering the threshold of 0.50 by 1 p.p. in Mexico, 3 p.p. in Peru, 5 p.p. in Honduras, and 15 p.p. in Ecuador. In Brazil, the Chaudhuri estimation is more prominent than in other countries. Brazil's estimations are computed at the province level; thus, the measurement errors and unobserved income components can be more extensive and lead to a greater inaccuracy than at the district level.

Another robustness check is to follow the approach proposed in Skoufias et al. (2024) based on Chaudhuri (2003) model except that they use a multilevel linear model of two levels. Here, we estimate a three-level multilevel linear model. We estimate the expected income mean and the expected variance assuming the following income equation:

$$\ln I_{hds} = \alpha + X_{hds}\beta + Z_{ds}\gamma + X_{hds}Z_{ds}\theta + \xi_s + \xi_d + \varepsilon_{hds}$$

with $Z_{ds} = [Harm_{ds}, Exposure_{ds}]$ and $X_{hds} = [Coping_{hds}, Demographics_{hds}]$. The squared sum of the estimated residuals and the specific effects $(\xi_s + \xi_d + \varepsilon_{hds})^2$ is regressed on X_{hds}, Z_{ds}, and $X_{hds}Z_{ds}$ to estimate the expected variance $\hat{\sigma}^2_{\xi_s+\xi_d+\varepsilon_{hds}}$..

The estimated conditional probability of being vulnerable is given by:

$$\hat{v}_{hds} = \widehat{\Pr}(\ln I_{hds} < \ln z \mid X_{hds}, Z_{ds}) = \Phi\left(\frac{\ln z - \widehat{\ln I_{hds}}}{\sqrt{\hat{\sigma}^2_{\xi_s+\xi_d+\varepsilon_{hds}}}}\right).$$

Then we re-estimated the probability of being poor and re-computed the vulnerability to poverty rates for each country. Table A2.2 presents the results under this approach and the results that we already have. Both approaches show similar vulnerability rates, according to the results.

APPENDIX 3. VULNERABILITY PROFILES

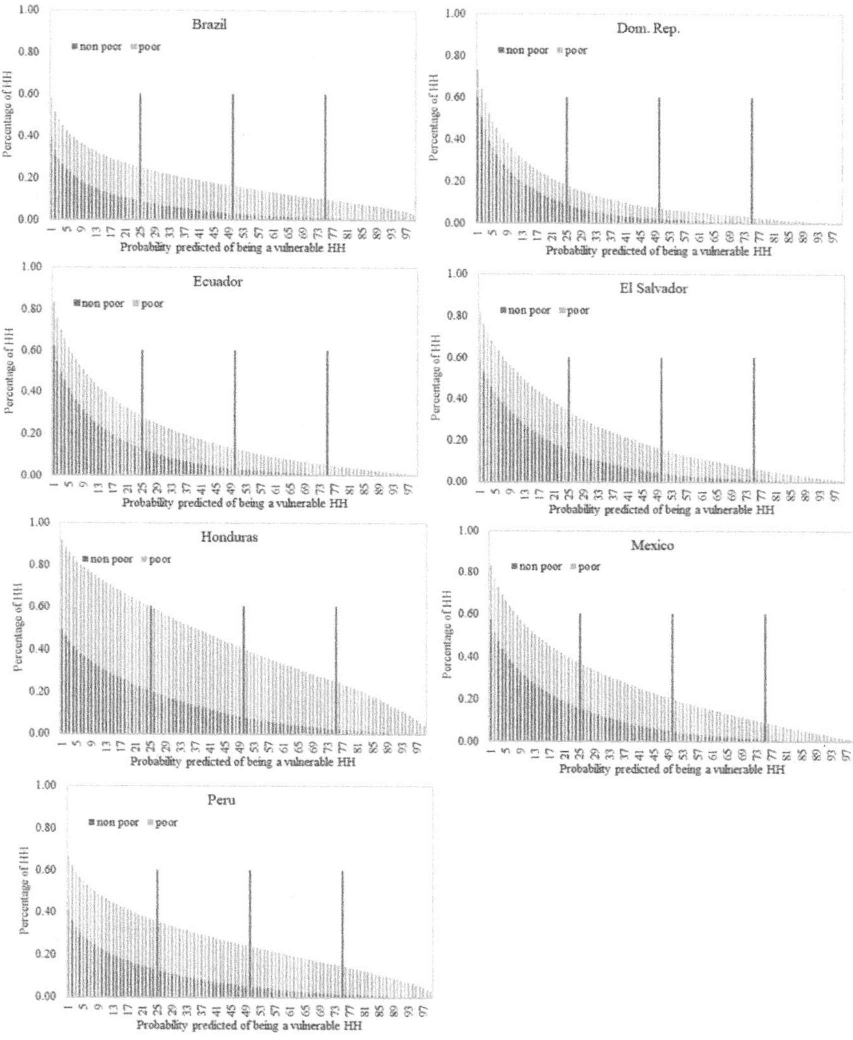

Fig. A3.1. Vulnerability Curves Considering Different Predicted Probability Thresholds by Poor Status. *Note*: The thresholds are displayed on the *x*-axis and range from 1 to 99. *Source*: Authors' calculations based on ThinkHazard!, EM-DAT, and SEDLAC database.

Table A3.1. Percentage of Households Lacking Coping Mechanisms and Adaptation Strategies.

Countries	All Households		Non-vulnerable HH with prob. < = 0.50		Vulnerable HH with prob. > 0.50		Vulnerable HH with prob. > 0.50			
							Non-poor		Poor	
	Mean	SD	Mean	SD	Mean	SD	Mean	SD	Mean	SD
Brazil										
HH head not a salaried worker	61%	0.488	58%	0.494	73%	0.442	71%	0.454	74%	0.439
Only one sector of activity reported	69%	0.464	65%	0.478	86%	0.351	77%	0.423	88%	0.330
Only one income earner in HH	36%	0.481	34%	0.474	52%	0.499	50%	0.500	53%	0.499
HH head's main income from agriculture	6%	0.245	5%	0.220	14%	0.344	14%	0.347	14%	0.343
Presence of children < 5	21%	0.406	16%	0.363	49%	0.500	42%	0.494	50%	0.500
Only elders (65 or more) in HH	8%	0.273	10%	0.297	0%	0.027	0%	0.046	0%	0.020
Presence of children < 12 attending school	26%	0.437	20%	0.400	57%	0.496	51%	0.500	58%	0.494
Dwelling's materials of low quality	3%	0.177	2%	0.154	7%	0.257	5%	0.222	8%	0.264
Roof's materials of low quality	3%	0.160	2%	0.149	4%	0.205	4%	0.195	4%	0.207
Walls' materials of low quality	5%	0.225	4%	0.205	10%	0.297	8%	0.264	10%	0.304
Benefits from social assistance	19%	0.394	10%	0.306	67%	0.471	55%	0.498	70%	0.460
No remittances from abroad	n.a.	n.a.	n.a.	n.a.	n.a.	n.a.	n.a.	n.a.	n.a.	n.a.
At least one member without health insurance	n.a.	n.a.	n.a.	n.a.	n.a.	n.a.	n.a.	n.a.	n.a.	n.a.
Dominican Republic										
HH head not a salaried worker	62%	0.486	63%	0.484	78%	0.417	72%	0.453	80%	0.403
Only one sector of activity reported	68%	0.468	67%	0.471	85%	0.354	77%	0.422	88%	0.323
Only one income earner in HH	38%	0.484	37%	0.482	52%	0.500	54%	0.501	51%	0.501
HH head's main income from agriculture	8%	0.278	8%	0.275	12%	0.330	10%	0.297	13%	0.341
Presence of children < 5	24%	0.428	20%	0.403	65%	0.477	67%	0.473	65%	0.479

Table A3.1. (*Continued*)

Countries	All Households		Non-vulnerable HH with prob. < = 0.50		Vulnerable HH with prob. > 0.50		Vulnerable HH with prob. > 0.50			
							Non-poor		Poor	
	Mean	SD	Mean	SD	Mean	SD	Mean	SD	Mean	SD
Only elders (65 or more) in HH	8%	0.273	9%	0.284	0%	0.000	0%	0.000	0%	0.000
Presence of children < 12 attending school	30%	0.459	27%	0.442	67%	0.469	68%	0.468	67%	0.470
Dwelling's materials of low quality	6%	0.236	5%	0.225	13%	0.338	10%	0.297	14%	0.350
Roof's materials of low quality	52%	0.499	49%	0.500	66%	0.474	55%	0.499	70%	0.460
Walls' materials of low quality	22%	0.413	19%	0.390	32%	0.468	25%	0.436	35%	0.477
Benefits from social assistance	26%	0.440	25%	0.431	31%	0.463	36%	0.481	29%	0.457
No remittances from abroad	89%	0.309	89%	0.311	89%	0.315	84%	0.369	91%	0.293
At least one member without health insurance	42%	0.494	39%	0.487	70%	0.460	64%	0.482	72%	0.452
Ecuador										
HH head not a salaried worker	57%	0.495	55%	0.498	69%	0.464	65%	0.478	70%	0.458
Only one sector of activity reported	58%	0.494	56%	0.497	71%	0.456	56%	0.496	75%	0.431
Only one income earner in HH	13%	0.333	13%	0.332	13%	0.332	14%	0.345	12%	0.327
HH head's main income from agriculture	24%	0.426	19%	0.392	55%	0.497	49%	0.500	57%	0.494
Presence of children < 5	30%	0.457	26%	0.437	57%	0.495	51%	0.500	60%	0.491
Only elders (65 or more) in HH	9%	0.283	10%	0.295	3%	0.170	7%	0.253	2%	0.127
Presence of children < 12 attending school	43%	0.495	39%	0.487	69%	0.463	54%	0.498	74%	0.438
Dwelling's materials of low quality	20%	0.398	15%	0.360	49%	0.500	41%	0.493	51%	0.500
Roof's materials of low quality	62%	0.485	59%	0.491	79%	0.406	74%	0.437	81%	0.393
Walls' materials of low quality	16%	0.365	12%	0.327	40%	0.490	32%	0.466	43%	0.494
Benefits from social assistance	19%	0.389	13%	0.340	53%	0.499	42%	0.493	56%	0.496
No remittances from abroad	97%	0.170	97%	0.175	98%	0.135	97%	0.165	98%	0.123
At least one member without health insurance	82%	0.388	80%	0.401	93%	0.259	92%	0.274	93%	0.253

(*Continued*)

Table A3.1. (*Continued*)

Countries	All Households		Non-vulnerable HH with prob. < = 0.50		Vulnerable HH with prob. > 0.50		Vulnerable HH with prob. > 0.50			
							Non-poor		Poor	
	Mean	SD	Mean	SD	Mean	SD	Mean	SD	Mean	SD
El Salvador										
HH head not a salaried worker	59%	0.491	58%	0.494	68%	0.468	71%	0.455	66%	0.472
Only one sector of activity reported	67%	0.470	65%	0.478	79%	0.408	68%	0.465	83%	0.379
Only one income earner in HH	43%	0.495	39%	0.489	64%	0.481	62%	0.487	64%	0.479
HH head's main income from agriculture	14%	0.351	10%	0.298	38%	0.485	36%	0.481	38%	0.486
Presence of children < 5	26%	0.440	21%	0.405	54%	0.498	48%	0.500	57%	0.495
Only elders (65 or more) in HH	8%	0.268	9%	0.287	2%	0.123	2%	0.143	1%	0.115
Presence of children < 12 attending school	34%	0.472	28%	0.450	61%	0.488	56%	0.497	63%	0.483
Dwelling's materials of low quality	26%	0.436	20%	0.397	57%	0.495	51%	0.500	59%	0.492
Roof's materials of low quality	76%	0.425	77%	0.418	70%	0.459	72%	0.448	69%	0.462
Walls' materials of low quality	23%	0.420	18%	0.381	51%	0.500	47%	0.499	53%	0.499
Benefits from social assistance	2%	0.136	1%	0.102	6%	0.232	4%	0.192	6%	0.244
No remittances from abroad	78%	0.412	77%	0.420	84%	0.365	82%	0.383	85%	0.359
At least one member without health insurance	87%	0.333	85%	0.356	98%	0.135	96%	0.188	99%	0.110
Honduras										
HH head not a salaried worker	64%	0.479	58%	0.493	74%	0.439	76%	0.431	74%	0.441
Only one sector of activity reported	65%	0.478	56%	0.496	74%	0.439	66%	0.476	76%	0.428
Only one income earner in HH	32%	0.467	28%	0.448	40%	0.490	44%	0.497	39%	0.488
HH head's main income from agriculture	24%	0.426	9%	0.282	47%	0.499	33%	0.470	51%	0.500
Presence of children < 5	36%	0.479	27%	0.443	51%	0.500	47%	0.500	52%	0.500
Only elders (65 or more) in HH	5%	0.209	3%	0.181	3%	0.161	5%	0.221	2%	0.143
Presence of children < 12 attending school	43%	0.496	34%	0.474	59%	0.492	51%	0.500	61%	0.488

Table A3.1. *(Continued)*

Countries	All Households		Non-vulnerable HH with prob. < = 0.50		Vulnerable HH with prob. > 0.50		Vulnerable HH with prob. > 0.50			
							Non-poor		Poor	
	Mean	SD	Mean	SD	Mean	SD	Mean	SD	Mean	SD
Dwelling's materials of low quality	11%	0.318	3%	0.163	24%	0.427	15%	0.358	26%	0.440
Roof's materials of low quality	78%	0.414	83%	0.380	71%	0.454	73%	0.447	71%	0.456
Walls' materials of low quality	38%	0.486	19%	0.392	64%	0.479	50%	0.501	68%	0.467
Benefits from social assistance	12%	0.327	5%	0.219	24%	0.427	17%	0.375	26%	0.437
No remittances from abroad	83%	0.373	80%	0.401	87%	0.340	81%	0.390	88%	0.325
At least one member without health insurance	n.a.	n.a.	n.a.	n.a.	n.a.	n.a.	n.a.	n.a.	n.a.	n.a.
Mexico										
HH head not a salaried worker	43%	0.495	41%	0.492	56%	0.496	56%	0.497	56%	0.496
Only one sector of activity reported	62%	0.486	61%	0.488	67%	0.469	57%	0.495	71%	0.455
Only one income earner in HH	30%	0.457	30%	0.458	29%	0.454	32%	0.467	28%	0.450
HH head's main income from agriculture	13%	0.334	7%	0.260	36%	0.481	29%	0.451	39%	0.487
Presence of children < 5	27%	0.442	21%	0.406	49%	0.500	47%	0.499	50%	0.500
Only elders (65 or more) in HH	7%	0.256	7%	0.254	8%	0.273	10%	0.300	8%	0.264
Presence of children < 12 attending school	39%	0.489	33%	0.471	63%	0.484	57%	0.496	65%	0.478
Dwelling's materials of low quality	26%	0.437	18%	0.386	59%	0.493	51%	0.500	61%	0.488
Roof's materials of low quality	22%	0.415	15%	0.359	52%	0.500	44%	0.497	55%	0.498
Walls' materials of low quality	10%	0.305	7%	0.254	25%	0.434	20%	0.399	27%	0.443
Benefits from social assistance	29%	0.453	21%	0.406	63%	0.484	58%	0.494	64%	0.479
No remittances from abroad	95%	0.210	96%	0.201	93%	0.251	90%	0.298	94%	0.234
At least one member without health insurance	34%	0.473	34%	0.473	35%	0.476	38%	0.486	34%	0.472
Peru										
HH head not a salaried worker	66%	0.473	61%	0.488	86%	0.350	80%	0.401	87%	0.335

(Continued)

Table A3.1. (*Continued*)

Countries	All Households		Non-vulnerable HH with prob. < = 0.50		Vulnerable HH with prob. > 0.50		Vulnerable HH with prob. > 0.50			
							Non-poor		Poor	
	Mean	SD	Mean	SD	Mean	SD	Mean	SD	Mean	SD
Only one sector of activity reported	57%	0.495	52%	0.500	74%	0.436	62%	0.485	77%	0.418
Only one income earner in HH	32%	0.468	29%	0.455	42%	0.494	45%	0.498	42%	0.493
HH head's main income from agriculture	27%	0.442	15%	0.356	67%	0.471	54%	0.499	70%	0.458
Presence of children < 5	25%	0.435	21%	0.410	35%	0.477	32%	0.467	36%	0.480
Only elders (65 or more) in HH	11%	0.312	10%	0.302	14%	0.351	14%	0.343	15%	0.354
Presence of children < 12 attending school	30%	0.458	26%	0.441	40%	0.490	36%	0.480	41%	0.492
Dwelling's materials of low quality	13%	0.332	11%	0.310	20%	0.397	17%	0.373	20%	0.402
Roof's materials of low quality	9%	0.290	8%	0.268	8%	0.278	8%	0.264	9%	0.281
Walls' materials of low quality	45%	0.497	33%	0.471	82%	0.388	67%	0.469	85%	0.356
Benefits from social assistance	47%	0.499	36%	0.479	86%	0.342	77%	0.419	89%	0.315
No remittances from abroad	98%	0.136	98%	0.150	99%	0.076	99%	0.117	100%	0.061
At least one member without health insurance	42%	0.493	45%	0.498	28%	0.450	40%	0.491	25%	0.435

Source: Authors' calculations based on ThinkHazard!, EM-DAT, and SEDLAC database.

CHAPTER 2

THE EFFECT OF US CLIMATE POLICY ON FINANCIAL MARKETS: AN EVENT STUDY OF THE INFLATION REDUCTION ACT

Michael D. Bauer[a], Eric A. Offner[b], and Glenn D. Rudebusch[c]

[a]*Federal Reserve Bank of San Francisco and CEPR, USA*
[b]*Frankfurt School of Finance and Management, Germany*
[c]*Brookings Institution and New York University, USA*

ABSTRACT

The Inflation Reduction Act of 2022 (IRA) represents the largest climate policy action ever undertaken in the United States. Its legislative path was marked by two abrupt shifts as the likelihood of climate policy action fell to near zero and then rose to near certainty. The authors investigate equity price reactions to these two events, which represent major realizations of climate policy transition risk. Our results highlight the heterogeneous nature of climate policy risk exposure. The authors find sizable reactions that differ by industry as well as across firm-level measures of greenness such as environmental scores and emission intensities. While the financial market response to the IRA was economically significant, it did not lead to instability or financial stress, suggesting that transition risks posed by climate policies even as ambitious as the IRA may be manageable.

Econometrics of Climate, Energy, and Green Transition
Advances in Econometrics, Volume 47A, 57–90

Published under exclusive licence by Emerald Publishing Limited
ISSN: 0731-9053/doi:10.1108/S0731-90532026000047A003

Keywords: Transition risk; stranded assets; event study; carbon emissions; ESG scores; green stocks; brown stocks

JEL Classifications: *G14; G38; Q54; Q58*

1. INTRODUCTION

The IRA is widely considered to be the most ambitious climate policy action in US history. Over the next decade and beyond, a broad array of new tax credits and direct government expenditures will provide substantial financial support for clean technologies and industries. Additionally, the IRA will offer strong direct incentives for US households and firms to invest in the equipment and capital needed to reduce their carbon emissions. Bistline et al. (2023b) estimate that the cumulative budgetary effect of the climate-related parts of the IRA could be on the order of $1 trillion over the next 10 years.[1] The economic changes induced by the IRA incentives are also expected to result in significant reductions to US greenhouse gas emissions (Bistline et al., 2023a). However, such projections of the economic and climate consequences of the IRA are generally silent about any financial implications. This is true even though the financial sector is integral to supplying the requisite capital for decarbonization and determining climate policy outcomes. The forward-looking responses of financial markets will also be evident much sooner than the economic and emissions effects and can thus provide a useful early reading on policy transmission and success. In this chapter, we document the financial market responses to the IRA and provide a new climate finance perspective on this major climate policy action.

One particularly important issue for climate finance is transition risk. The substantial investment required for the transformation to a low-carbon economy will rely heavily on financial markets and institutions (e.g., Battiston et al., 2021).[2] However, the uncertain pace and consequences of decarbonization have become a major policy concern in recent years (Van der Ploeg & Rezai, 2020). If investor expectations were to adjust precipitously to new climate policies, the resulting adverse revaluations of carbon-dependent assets – potentially resulting in stranded assets – could have severe implications for financial solvency and stability along the lines of what former Bank of England governor Mark Carney termed a "climate Minsky moment" (Carney, 2016). To better quantify the potential risks to banks and other financial institutions from such abrupt shifts in business prospects and asset prices, central banks and financial supervisory authorities are developing climate scenario analyses (Acharya et al., 2023). Clearly, the pricing of transition risks in financial markets has become a first-order policy issue. The passage of the IRA – the culmination of decades of attempts to obtain significant US legislation addressing climate change – represents a major realization of climate policy transition risk.

By investigating the stock market responses to this climate policy realization across firms and industries, we can illuminate the consequences of transition risk. Our study addresses several key questions: Did this legislation materially affect stock prices in a way consistent with the specific climate policy measures? Did stocks of "green" firms – characterized by comparably low CO_2 emissions or low environmental/emissions scores – benefit from the IRA, despite the fact that the legislation did not include any carbon taxation? If there is a differential firm-level stock market response, which measures of greenness can capture this heterogeneity?

To answer these questions, we use event-study methods to examine equity price movements following key news events around the introduction of the IRA. Event studies are particularly revealing when relevant new information becomes public via discrete, definitive announcements.[3] The legislative genesis of the IRA in 2022 included two such unambiguous shifts that whipsawed the prospects for climate-related legislation. The first, which we term a "brown event," occurred when news reports surfaced late on July 14 of the withdrawal of any support for new climate spending by Senator Joe Manchin of West Virginia – the pivotal vote required for getting legislation through the Senate. The likelihood of Senate passage of climate legislation plummeted and the probability of any near-term sizable policy action fell to almost zero. The second event, a "green event," took place in the early evening of July 27, when news broke that Senator Manchin had reached a surprise agreement with Democratic leaders on new legislation that unveiled the IRA and made it nearly certain that significant climate policy would ultimately become law. Section 2 explains in more detail the provisions of the IRA and the timeline of events preceding its passage.

We carry out several complementary event-study exercises to investigate equity market responses to this climate legislation. In Section 3, we examine the returns of green and brown industries around the IRA announcements. We first employ several commonly used energy equity indices such as the S&P Global Clean Energy and S&P 500 Integrated Oil & Gas funds. Clean energy indices had sizable negative abnormal returns after the brown event on July 14 but then rebounded strongly after the July 27 IRA debut, but fossil fuel industry indices showed a reverse pattern. We also use Fama-French industry portfolios to provide insight into what sectoral shifts investors expected. Industries that stand to benefit from the provisions in the IRA for greater green product demand or subsidized production costs exhibited a strong positive response to the green announcement on July 27 while, in contrast, the oil and coal industry lost significant market value after that event.

In Section 4, we conduct a more granular analysis at the level of individual firms. The publicly listed firms in our sample are differentiated using measures of greenness based on their actual carbon emissions data as well as emissions scores and broader Environmental scores (or E scores) calculated by a provider of firm-level environmental characteristics. The heterogeneous stock market responses across these measures of greenness are statistically and economically significant and support their use in identifying climate policy exposure. Specifically, the brown event lowered the stock market values of green firms – those with relatively low emission intensities and superior E and emissions scores – and boosted the values of brown firms. By contrast, with the announcement that made this climate legislation a near-certainty, green firms benefited and brown firms did not.

Taken together, these event-study results document substantial and rapid financial asset price reactions to climate policy news. In response to these realizations of climate policy transition risk, green and brown stocks displayed sizable movements in opposite directions. From a theoretical perspective, positive news about the passage of the IRA lifted expected profitability for green firms and disadvantaged brown firms through both demand and cost channels.[4] The IRA subsidies for purchases of low-carbon products should lead to a policy-induced strengthening of customer demand for green goods and services, boosting green firm stocks as their business prospects were improved (a demand channel as in Pástor et al., 2021). Other financial incentives in the IRA include clean energy production and investment tax credits and subsidies, lowering production costs and raising profits (a cost channel). Through these channels, news about the IRA appear to have impacted expected future dividends and, ultimately, stock prices.[5]

Section 5 shows implications for calibrating climate policy transition risk using industry-level measures of risk exposure. To better understand the risks of climate change and the transition to a low-carbon economy, financial supervisors are developing climate scenario analyses and stress tests to identify potential vulnerabilities in the financial system and assess bank solvency (e.g., Financial Stability Board, 2022; NGFS, 2022a). For many climate-related risk assessments, potential losses have been calculated based on sectoral or industry classifications, in part due to limited firm-level data availability. In Section 5, we investigate whether measures of industry-level greenness can account for the cross-industry variation in the equity price responses to the climate policy news. Such metrics have been used, for example, for assessing the exposure of commercial banks to different climate policy scenarios (e.g., Jung et al., 2023). Industry-level greenness appears to be a poor predictor of an industry's responses to the climate policy announcements we study in this chapter. This finding suggests that there is a need for a more granular firm- and asset-level accounting of transition risks – much like earlier work has called for with regard to physical risk (Bressan et al., 2022).

A central contribution of our chapter is to characterize the asset price responses to a given change in climate policies. We find that declines in brown firm stock prices to the IRA policy action do not appear outsized or disorderly even though this climate policy transition realization was very large by historical comparison. Therefore, the transition risks of financial sector bankruptcies, dislocations, and crises to future climate policies may be manageable. Of course, it may be that other climate policy actions could have more dramatic financial consequences, given that the prevalence of stranded assets may depend on the specific type of climate policy implemented; e.g., taxes versus subsidies (Rozenberg et al., 2020). However, the IRA events that we consider are extraordinary not only in terms of their large fiscal magnitude but also because the policy announcements were made during narrowly circumscribed event windows. It is difficult to envisage other climate policy realizations that could serve as a more definitive event study for assessing climate transition risk. Given that the IRA climate policy action caused manageable financial market responses of brown firms and disadvantaged industries, our evidence suggests limited risk for a climate Minsky moment.

Our chapter contributes to a quickly growing literature on the pricing of climate risks in financial markets, and specifically on the pricing of transition risks in green and brown stocks; see Bolton and Kacperczyk (2021), Pástor et al. (2022), and Bauer et al. (2022), among many others. Most prior work on the effects of climate policy on financial markets has studied events with news about *possible future* climate action and shifts in perceived transition risks, often with mixed results. Ramelli et al. (2021) investigate the stock market reaction to the 2016 and 2020 US Presidential elections, finding better stock market performance of carbon-intensive firms in response to the Trump election but also higher stock returns for firms with higher climate responsibility around *both* the Trump and Biden election wins. Monasterolo and De Angelis (2020) document shifts in the risk characteristics of green and brown stock indices before and after the announcement of the 2015 Paris Agreement, but they find no appreciable penalty on the returns or valuations of high-carbon assets and firms. Other related empirical work considers larger and more heterogeneous sets of climate policy news. Barnett (2023) identifies a number of climate policy events and shows that industries with a larger exposure to changes in oil prices exhibit a more negative stock market response to events that increase the likelihood of future climate policy action. Ardia et al. (2022) show that unexpected increases in a news-based index of climate change concerns benefit green stocks over brown stocks. Cassidy (2023) constructs a dataset of climate policy announcements and documents that brown stocks perform better than green stocks around events with a large amount of climate policy news. Other studies of the effects of climate policies on financial performance more broadly include Kumar and Purnanandam (2022), Bartram et al. (2022), and Jung et al. (2021).

Only few other studies examine clearly identified events with major news about immediate climate policy action, i.e., realizations of transition risk. Ochoa et al. (2022) study the effects of an unexpected carbon tax increase in Germany and find a heterogeneous stock market response based on emission intensity but not based on *E* scores, in contrast to our findings. Carattini and Sen (2019) document which stocks benefited from news that two carbon tax initiatives in Washington State were rejected by voters. Ivanov et al. (2023) study the passage of California's cap-and-trade legislation and the failed version at the federal level (the Waxman-Markey bill) and document more constrained bank lending to high-emission firms. Hengge et al. (2023) study carbon policy news related to the European Union Emission Trading System (EU-ETS). They examine events with exogenous changes in the price of emission permits following Känzig (2023) and show that a surprise increase in the carbon price leads to negative abnormal returns of brown stocks compared with green stocks, measured using emission intensities. Our chapter provides novel evidence on the financial market response to realizations of transition risk, using the stock market response to news about the IRA – the most important climate policy in US history.

2. THE INFLATION REDUCTION ACT

To set the stage for the empirical analysis, we provide a description of the timeline of events leading up to passage of the IRA and then summarize the key climate policy ingredients of this legislation.

Table 2.1 highlights some of the key events in the legislative history of the IRA. The IRA resulted from negotiations in the Senate to rework the Build Back Better Act, which was an expansive package of climate change, health care, tax reform, and social safety net proposals. While the Build Back Better Act passed the House despite unanimous Republican congressional opposition, it faced an evenly divided Senate and would need every Democratic vote for passage. Senator Joe Manchin became the key holdout, which resulted in months of challenging negotiations and swings of sentiment regarding passage. On the evening of July 14 – after US equity markets[6] had closed – press reports surfaced that Senator Manchin had decided to oppose any further attempts to pass the Build Back Better Act and, in particular, had rejected any further climate legislation. One such report, Romm and Stein (2022), noted

> Sen. Joe Manchin III (D-W.Va.) told Democratic leaders Thursday he would not support an economic package this month that contains new spending on climate change or new tax increases targeting wealthy individuals and corporations, marking a massive setback for party lawmakers who had hoped to advance a central element of their agenda before the midterm elections this fall.

However, two weeks later on July 27, Senator Manchin and Senate Majority Leader Charles Schumer announced that they had reached a new agreement to pass climate legislation, and they unveiled the complete text of the "Inflation Reduction Act of 2022."[7] This announcement was also made after equity markets closed and was generally viewed as essentially guaranteeing passage of climate legislation. Indeed, the IRA sped through the Senate and House within two weeks and was signed into law a few days later.

Table 2.1. Timeline of Key Legislative Events for Inflation Reduction Act (IRA).

Date	Time	Event
Nov 19, 2021, Fri.	9:49 am	House passes Build Back Better climate legislation
Dec 19, 2021, Sun.	9:12 am	Manchin announces decision to vote against Build Back Better
Jul 14, 2022, Thu.	9:29 pm	Press reports Manchin will not support new climate spending
Jul 27, 2022, Wed.	5:03 pm	Manchin and Schumer announce new climate legislation: IRA
Aug 03, 2022, Wed.	3:31 pm	CBO/JCT publishes cost estimates of IRA
Aug 07, 2022, Sun.	2:45 pm	Senate passes IRA
Aug 12, 2022, Fri.	5:42 pm	House passes IRA
Aug 16, 2022, Tue.		President Biden signs the IRA into law

Notes: A timeline for major legislative events during passage of the IRA, which was a smaller, climate-focused version of the earlier Build Back Better Act. Event times (in ET) reflect initial news accounts according to Dow Jones Newswires, which is a financial news source used by investors worldwide.

The dramatic demise and rebirth of climate legislation represented by these July events – with the probability of climate policy action first falling to near zero and then jumping to close to one – are ideal for assessing the impact of the IRA on financial markets.[8] The other events in Table 2.1 are arguably of much less interest for our purposes. The two events that preceded July 2022 pertained to the more expansive Build Back Better legislation and were part of yearlong intermittent negotiations with shifting legislative priorities that included health care, education, immigration, and tax reform. Accordingly, the extent and timing of any climate news content of these earlier events is much less clear. There were also three notable IRA events after July 2022 that included the release of cost estimates and actual IRA passage by the Senate and House. However, once Senators Manchin and Schumer had reached agreement, the August 2022 events were widely anticipated, and, according to contemporaneous press accounts, any residual uncertainty was effectively resolved before the actual votes were recorded in Congress. With climate concerns front and center for the July 2022 events and with the information arrival so clearly delineated, our analysis focuses on these dates to give the cleanest read on climate policy news.

In terms of legislative initiatives to limit climate change, the IRA provides funding for clean energy through a mix of tax incentives, grants, and loan guarantees.[9] It supports investments in clean electricity and transmission, carbon capture and storage, green hydrogen, and electric transportation and energy infrastructure. There are home energy rebates to help make homes more energy efficient and new tax credits to induce consumers to buy new and used electric vehicles. The IRA also introduces a fee on methane emissions from some companies in the oil and gas industry. Relative to past initiatives, the cost of the climate actions in the IRA is enormous – accrued both by expanding existing programs and introducing new ones. The Congressional Budget Office (CBO) and Joint Committee on Taxation (JCT) estimated that US federal budgetary costs through 2031 would be $271 billion in climate-related tax credits and $121 billion for direct expenditures (Bistline et al., 2023b). However, as stressed by Bistline et al. (2023b), many of the tax credits are uncapped, so their take-up and cost depend on corporate investment decisions and household consumption decisions. Based on a detailed energy systems modeling of the US economy, Bistline et al. (2023b) project the budgetary cost of the climate-related provisions to be several times larger than the CBO/JCT estimate – perhaps as high as $1 trillion.

In terms of climate policy effectiveness, the IRA is estimated to significantly reduce carbon emissions, with projected reductions by 2030 of around 37% below 2005 levels (Bistline et al., 2023a).[10] This would seem to put the United States within reach of its 50% reduction target by 2030 under the Paris Agreement. To calibrate the magnitude of the IRA policy action, it is possible in theory to provide a rough estimate of the equivalent carbon price that would be needed to achieve the same emissions reduction. That is, a non-carbon price climate policy can be translated into an emissions-equivalent shadow carbon price, as described in Hänsel et al. (2022). Bistline et al. (2023b) estimate that the power sector policies, which account for about 70% of the IRA emissions reductions, may have similar emissions reductions to a US carbon tax of around $12 to $15 per ton of carbon dioxide (CO_2). Scaled up, this suggests that the total IRA would represent an approximate equivalent shadow carbon price of roughly on the order of $20 per ton of CO_2. By this measure, the IRA clearly represents a sizable climate policy initiative with significant effects comparable to those contemplated in the usual climate scenario analyses associated with central bank climate stress tests (NGFS, 2022a).

By using an emissions-equivalent shadow carbon price that summarizes various climate policy actions such as subsidies, taxes, and regulation (e.g., Hänsel et al., 2022; NGFS, 2022a), it is possible to provide a broad-brush account of the two key climate policy events. With the election of President Biden and Democratic majorities in both houses of Congress in 2020, there were three broad plausible paths for US climate policy: (1) further minimal incremental action, which would continue a more than decade-long trend of little progress on national climate policy; (2) a break from the past in the form of a moderately significant climate policy initiative; or (3) a very ambitious, wide-ranging policy action along the lines of a "Green New Deal" or the Build Back Better climate legislation. These three potential paths could be roughly approximated in terms of the future shadow carbon price path as (1) no change to the path, (2) a level shift upward in the path of about $20, and (3) a level shift upward of $50 or more. Before July 2022, there was a sizable transition risk associated with the uncertainty around which path would be taken. The July 14 event appeared to adopt the first option with no policy action. However, the IRA announced on July 27 locked in the middle path and represented a substantial climate policy transition realization.

Before turning to the empirical analysis, it is helpful to outline how these climate policy events might be expected to affect the stock market from a conceptual asset pricing perspective. A company's equity price depends on its expected stream of future profits and dividends and on the discount rate used to calculate their (risk-adjusted) present value. The legislative events in July 2022 likely affected stock prices predominantly by changing expected dividends (as in Ochoa et al., 2022). The shifts in the expected path for the shadow carbon price directly impacted the expected profitability of green and brown firms. Higher carbon price paths translate into higher profits for green firms, which will face less competition from carbon-dependent competitors, and lower profits for brown firms. For example, a higher carbon price will raise the production costs and lower sales and revenues of firms that are more dependent on fossil fuels in their operations. Meanwhile, lower carbon price paths benefit brown firms more than green firms. After the July 14 brown event – which established a low expected shadow carbon price path – the expected profits of brown firms would likely rise, and those of green firms would fall. Conversely, the jump in the future carbon price trajectory following the July 27 green event would push up expected profits of green firms and depress those of brown firms. Furthermore, these shifts in the expected paths for profits would have corresponding differential effects on the prices of green and brown stocks.

Considering the specifics of the IRA, there are both supply- and demand-side subsidies that favor green firms. On the supply side, the IRA includes production and investment tax credits for clean energy, which can boost green firm profits by lowering costs. The effects on stock prices might be best understood through the lens of a *cost channel*: Firms that benefit from such subsidies see their marginal cost decline and their profits, dividends, and stock prices rise. The IRA also contains demand-side subsidies to businesses and consumers to increase demand for green products. Via this *demand channel*, profits and dividends of green firms are boosted as well, again raising their stock prices.[11] Brown firms, which are relatively disadvantaged by the production and demand subsidies, would see their profits and dividends – and thus stock prices – decline. Therefore, we anticipate that the two sharp movements in the mean shadow carbon price path will have effects on profitability and equity prices that vary with the overall greenness of a firm, which, following a growing carbon finance literature, can be measured by the firm's CO_2 emissions or environmental score.

Another potential channel through which a change in climate policy could affect stock prices is via the cost of capital. An increase in transition uncertainty would raise the expected returns of firms that are exposed to this type of risk and thus lower their stock prices.[12] The signing of the 2015 Paris Agreement and, more generally, increasing concerns about climate change, raise the likelihood of future climate policy action and therefore transition risk – particularly for carbon-dependent firms. However, unlike many previous analyses of climate-related events and risks (e.g., Barnett, 2023; Jung et al., 2021; Ramelli et al., 2021), we do not interpret our event study results as operating primarily through *changes* in climate policy transition uncertainty and risk. Although some IRA implementation details are still being worked out, we view the passage of the IRA as a *realization* of transition risk, because it implements specific new climate policies.

Finally, there are, of course, complications resulting from the specific non-carbon price nature of the US climate legislation. In contrast to a broad, uniform carbon tax, the effects on cost and demand of the IRA subsidies will depend on their particular specification, the relevant market structure and segmentation, and the incidence across firms and industries. For example, subsidies in support of clean electricity may benefit utility firms and energy companies that are in industries with relatively high overall emissions footprints. As a result, the stock market effects of the IRA may depend not only on emissions/greenness of individual firms, but also on whether their industries are specifically favored and subsidized by the IRA – regardless of the greenness of that industry. This is a point that we will return to in Section 5.

3. CLIMATE POLICY RESPONSES AT AN INDUSTRY LEVEL

The first part of our analysis focuses on the response of different sectors and industries to the IRA announcements. We consider both stock market indices commonly used to represent the green and brown energy sectors, and then turn to industry portfolios using methods from empirical asset pricing. The goal of this industry-level analysis is to provide some indication of financial market participants' views about whether the IRA represents meaningful climate legislation that will be sustained going forward.

We investigate the returns of about a dozen stock market indices that are classified either as clean or green energy funds or as fossil energy funds. Our selection of indices is informed in part by Monasterolo and De Angelis (2020), who studied the reaction of various equity market indices to the 2015 announcement of the Paris Agreement.[13] Table 2.2 shows event-study results for our 11 selected indices, including six green and five brown indices. We use daily index returns based on end-of-day prices from Bloomberg, and calculate abnormal returns as the differences between raw returns and predicted returns from an estimated market model, following common practice in empirical asset pricing (MacKinlay, 1997). To estimate the market model, we regress daily returns of each index on the return of the CRSP value-weighted stock market index, a proxy for the market portfolio, from January 2016 to May 2022 to avoid overlap with the event days.[14] For each event, we report one-day and three-day returns, with the latter calculated by cumulating daily abnormal returns. As noted above, the events took place in the evenings after trading hours on July 14 and July 27, 2022. The event windows therefore start when the stock market closed on those dates and end at market close on the next day (for one-day returns) or three days later (for three-day returns).[15] In addition to the abnormal returns for each individual index, we also report returns for a green factor and a brown factor,

Table 2.2. Abnormal Returns of Green and Brown Equity Indices.

	Brown Event (July 14)		Green Event (July 27)	
	1 day	3 days	1 day	3 days
Green indices				
Nasdaq Clean Edge Green Energy	−3.4**	−0.9	6.9***	7.5***
Wilderhill Clean Energy	−2.6*	−0.8	6.3***	5.6**
S&P Global Clean Energy	−3.4***	−1.4	6.5***	7.2***
World Renewable Energy (Renixx)	−4.0**	−2.6	7.3***	7.7***
ISE Global Wind Energy	−0.5	0.6	3.3***	3.9**
MAC Global Solar Energy	−4.1**	−2.6	6.2***	6.9**
Brown indices				
S&P 500 Integrated Oil & Gas	−0.3	2.5	−0.3	2.6
FTSE Local USA Oil & Gas & Coal	−0.1	2.4	−1.6	−2.5
FTSE All World Oil & Gas & Coal	0.3	3.3	−0.4	1.0
Dow Jones Select Oil Expl. & Prod.	−0.3	3.1	−1.6	−2.6
Dynamic Energy Expl. & Prod. Intellindex	−0.3	3.7	−1.1	−1.8
Factors				
Green Factor	−2.1**	−0.5	4.3***	2.6***
Brown Factor	−0.1	1.0	−0.6	−0.2
Green−Minus-Brown	−2.1*	−1.5	4.9***	2.8**

Notes: Abnormal returns around key IRA events. Expected returns are estimated with a market model using daily value-weighted CRSP market returns from January 2016 to May 2022. Statistical significance levels are obtained from regressions of abnormal returns on event dummies; ***, **, and * denote significance at the 1%, 5%, and 10% level, respectively.

which are weighted averages of the green and brown index returns based on their first principal components. All abnormal event returns and their statistical significance levels are obtained from regressions of the abnormal index returns on dummies for the two IRA events.

Table 2.2 shows these abnormal one-day and three-day returns around the two key IRA events on July 14 and July 27. The two events had substantially different effects on green and brown indices. The direction of the differences is intuitive, and their magnitudes are sizable. After the July 14 media reports that lowered the probability that any climate policy action would pass the Senate, green indices performed worse than brown indices, both for one-day and three-day abnormal returns. For one-day returns, the green factor fell by 2.1% while the brown factor was little changed. The relative outperformance of brown indices justifies the "brown event" label. The pattern is reversed and even more stark for the July 27 "green event," when news of Senator Manchin's support for the IRA assured its passage. For the one-day window, most green indices had significantly positive abnormal returns, and the green factor was at +4.3%. The brown factor has a slightly negative abnormal return of −0.6%. The differential green-minus-brown return was significantly positive for both the one-day and three-day windows around the green event, but the green outperformance was larger and more strongly statistically significant for the one-day event.

To provide further insight on broad market moves around the policy events, Fig. 2.1 plots the cumulative returns for eight market indices from market close on July 14 to market close on August 15. These cumulative returns illustrate the persistence of the equity index reactions to climate legislation during the crucial month when climate policy was declared dead, and the IRA was announced and later signed by President Biden. The July 14 and July 27 events are indicated with vertical dashed lines.[16] The clean-energy and fossil-fuel-energy stock indices are shown as green and brown lines, respectively.[17] For the cumulative raw returns shown in Panel A, the green indices underperformed the brown ones during the two weeks following the July 14 announcement, ending about 6% lower on July 26. Similarly, the outperformance of green indices on the day after the July 27 announcement also persisted. The performance differences in green versus brown stocks are even more pronounced for the abnormal returns shown in Panel B. During the month, the gains in the green indices following the green event significantly outweighed their losses after the brown event, resulting in a cumulative outperformance ranging from 8 to 24 percentage points.

This index-level industry analysis yields a consistent picture of the financial performance of energy-related equity holdings. Indeed, the response of equity markets to major news about the likelihood of the passage of the IRA suggests that markets expected clean/renewable energy companies to benefit and oil/gas/coal firms to be disadvantaged by its policies. Differences between green and brown industry equity indices were far less apparent following the passage of the IRA in the House and Senate later in August 2022. The small impact of these two widely anticipated events is confirmed by event-study results in Appendix Table A2.1, which contains results for the other IRA-related events listed in Table 2.1. Reflecting the smaller, more diffuse releases of releases on these dates described

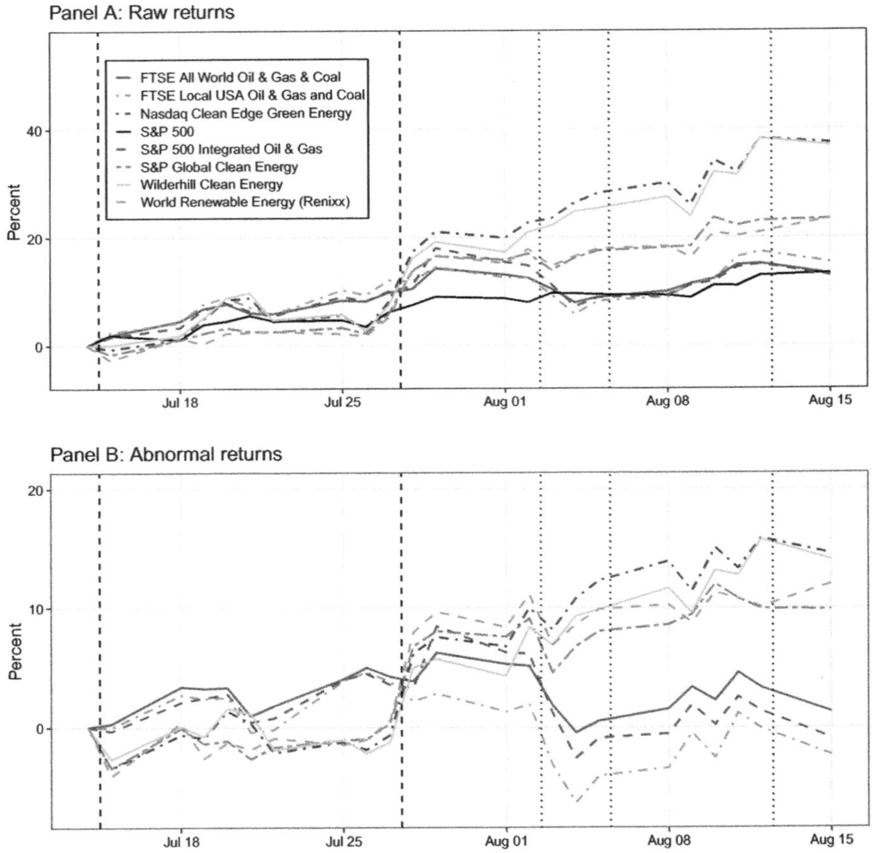

Fig. 2.1. Performance of Green and Brown Indices After Climate Policy Events. Daily cumulative returns for green and brown indices from market close on July 14 to August 15. Panel A (B) shows raw (abnormal) returns—see notes for Table 2.2. The brown and green events on July 14 and July 27, respectively, are denoted by vertical dashed lines. Three later events—described in Table 2.1—are denoted by vertical dotted lines. Each vertical line denotes the start of the event window, so the immediate observation to the right of each line shows the market response.

above, the green and brown abnormal event-returns are not dissimilar. Evidently, the two events with the largest effects on stock market indices were the news announcements on July 14 and 27 – the focus of our chapter.

We now examine the heterogeneous response of equity returns on these two dates using the 17 Fama-French industry portfolios. We use daily, equal-weighted portfolio returns, which are available on Ken French's website and are constructed using four-digit Standard Industrial Classification (SIC) codes.[18] For each of the 17 industry portfolios, we calculate abnormal returns as for the index returns and report the one-day abnormal returns across industries. The resulting abnormal portfolio returns for the 17 Fama-French industries for the brown event on July 14

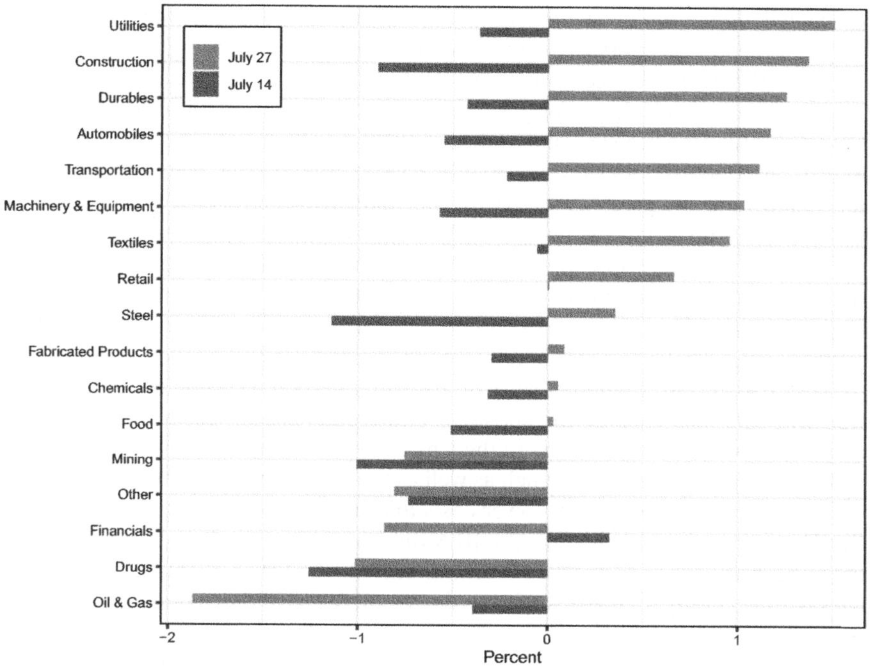

Fig. 2.2. Abnormal Industry Returns Around Green and Brown Events. Daily abnormal returns for 17 Fama-French industry portfolios (equal-weighted). Abnormal returns are calculated using the market model, estimated with daily returns and the CRSP equal-weighted market index return over the period from January 2016 to May 2022. Brown bars show returns using closing prices from July 14 to July 15 (brown event), and green bars show the returns from July 27 to July 28 (green event).

and the green event on July 27 are shown in Fig. 2.2. (Raw event returns are plotted in Appendix Fig. A2.1.) The brown event led to industry-level responses that are quite mixed and less clear-cut. But the green event produced industry winners and losers generally in line with what would be expected based on the IRA legislation.

In response to the green event, the best-performing industries were likely to benefit substantially from IRA subsidies and related measures. The utilities industry, which showed the most positive response, contains electric services and natural gas transmission/distribution/services. It stands to gain from the additional demand for electricity, which is given a significant boost by the IRA, as well from tax credits for renewable (biogas) natural gas and construction of renewable electricity plants more generally. The construction industry includes some favored clean energy companies and contractors that focus on solar installations and power generation and will be helped by the tax incentives for energy-efficient home improvements. Tax credits for electric vehicles and charging infrastructure will help the automobile and transportation industries (for an in-depth analysis, see Slowik et al., 2023). The machinery and equipment industry includes electrical equipment/machinery/distribution/components and batteries, which will play an integral part in the green transition.

At the other end, the oil & gas and mining industries stand to lose substantially from the IRA legislation and the intended decarbonization of the US economy. Consequently, stocks in these industries exhibited large negative abnormal returns around the green event. Two other industries performed poorly around this event but due to measures in the IRA unrelated to climate change. The drug industry is expected to be adversely impacted by the IRA changes to Medicare that try to lower prescription drug prices. And financial institutions are likely to be particularly affected by the 15% minimum corporate tax on large corporations, as many large banks and insurance companies pay little or no federal taxes.[19]

The cross-industry heterogeneity in the equity market response conforms quite well with the incidence of the subsidies and credits contained in the IRA. The effects can be understood through the lens of the model of Pástor et al. (2021) as working via the customer channel, as well as the cost channel defined in Section 2 whereby production subsidies lower costs and increase profits and stock returns. But it is important to note that the IRA did not necessarily benefit green industries and hurt brown industries, as commonly defined. For example, two industries with generally high levels of emissions – oil & gas and utilities – had entirely opposite responses to the green event, according to Fig. 2.2. In Section 5, we will revisit the question of whether the observed cross-industry heterogeneity in the equity response is related to emissions or other measures of industry exposure to carbon policy.

Overall, the response of both indices returns as well as portfolio returns to IRA announcements shows that market participants quickly differentiated between expected winners and losers among various industries. Differences in abnormal returns were sizable, on the order of several percentage points, after news that the IRA passage had become a near certainty.

4. CLIMATE POLICY RESPONSES OF INDIVIDUAL FIRMS

So far, we have established that the two climate policy events had substantial impacts on broad equity valuations – especially for the clean and fossil fuel energy sectors, which appeared particularly sensitive to the news about climate policy. Here, we examine the effects of these events on individual firms. The extent to which individual companies face the prospect of greater or lesser profits resulting from the policy initiatives should be reflected in changes in their equity prices. Specifically, firms will perform better if they are well-positioned to benefit – in relative terms – from clean-economy production and consumer subsidies, or more generally, from a higher (implicit) price of carbon.

Earlier research – such as Hengge et al. (2023), Bauer et al. (2022), Barnett (2023), and many others – identify green and brown firms by using firm-level measures of environmental characteristics such as firm-level CO_2 emissions.

Using such firm-level measures of greenness (G_i), including environmental scores and emissions, we investigate the equity responses to climate policy news with the following regression:

$$r_i = \alpha + \beta G_i + \delta X_i + \gamma_s + \varepsilon_i. \tag{1}$$

This specification regresses the equity returns of individual firms (r_i) on greenness (G_i), a vector of firm-level controls (X_i), and industry fixed effects (γ_s) for the green and brown event days separately. We focus our attention on estimates of the coefficient β, which captures the role of greenness for the stock market response of individual firms to climate policy news.

The requisite firm-level accounting, equity return, and environmental data are from Refinitiv.[20] We use all available US stocks after imposing some commonly used filters. Initially, our raw data set consists of the 3,601 US firms. We filter out firms without emissions scores for the year 2021, reducing the number of firms to 3,165. Following common practice in the empirical asset pricing literature, we apply a variety of standard filters to avoid unreliable returns data, which reduces our sample to 2,537 stocks.[21] Some firms released their earnings data during our event windows, which can lead to large price movements unrelated to the IRA news and thus create noise for our estimates. To mitigate this problem, we exclude firms with an earnings announcement on the event day or the following day. As a result of this additional restriction, our regression samples contain 2,520 firms for the July 14 event and 2,122 firms for the July 27 event. Given the occurrence of both IRA announcements in July 2022, we use firms' 2021 environmental and accounting data in order to best match the information set that investors likely had available when trading in response to the policy news.

For individual firms, our analysis employs several different measures of carbon dependence or greenness. Two of these are proprietary estimated measures.[22] The first is an "emissions score" that aggregates various firm-level metrics of how effective and committed a company is to reducing its emissions. This measure depends heavily on the estimated emissions data but also, for example, on assessments of the quality of a firm's "environmental management systems." The second measure is a broader environmental (E) score, which combines almost 70 metrics in three categories: emissions, innovation, and resource use. Note that the emissions score is one of the three components of the E score. Importantly, in the calculation of both of these scores, each underlying indicator is evaluated relative to peer companies in the same industry. That is, firms are categorized among 60 different industries, and green firms – those with high emissions scores or E scores – perform well within their own industry.

Finally, we also employ a very tangible, narrow measure of greenness: a firm's CO_2 emissions. This metric is widely used in economic research to measure a firm's sensitivity to climate risk and climate policy news. Similar to Ilhan et al. (2021), Ramelli et al. (2021), and many others, we use emission intensity, defined as the ratio of a firm's emissions to its market capitalization, which accounts for the effect on emission levels of firm size. In calculating emission intensity, it is also useful to differentiate between emissions as reported by firms and estimated emissions (Bauer et al., 2022). Many firms – even those in an ESG database – do not report emissions. For such firms, ESG data vendors provide estimates of emission levels that are largely based on a firm's sales or scale. These estimates have measurement error, and some have argued that using such imputed instead of reported emissions can lead to bias in some empirical analyses (Aswani et al., 2023), although event studies have not been implicated. Accordingly, our analysis using emission intensity is limited to firms with disclosed/reported emissions, which reduces our sample size by about two-thirds but arguably increases the reliability of the results.[23] However, in unreported analysis, we obtained very similar results for the much larger sample of firms available using emission intensity calculated with estimated emissions. In addition, our other two greenness metrics – *E* scores and emissions scores – incorporate the estimated emission levels, and we use the full sample of available firms for these.

The firm-level characteristics we control for include size (log total assets), market leverage (earnings before interest and taxes divided by interest expenses), revenue growth (annual growth rate in total revenues), and profitability (return on assets). Additionally, we follow Ramelli et al. (2021) and Wagner et al. (2018) and include a measure of cash effective tax rate (ETR), given that the tax burden of a firm can be an important determinant of its exposure to policy changes.[24] For the emission intensity measure of greenness, we also include the standard industry fixed effects using 17 Fama-French industries based on their SIC codes. As noted above, industry effects are already accounted for with *E* and emissions scores, which are constructed relative to peer companies in the same industry. In any case, omitting industry fixed effects completely or including them everywhere did not significantly change our results reported below.

Table 2.3 reports summary statistics for our firm-level data. The emissions and *E* scores range from 0 to 1 (as we divide the raw scores by 100). High scores indicate good environmental and emissions performance – i.e., low-carbon firms – but the median firm gets a relatively low score of around 0.2. These scores also display substantial dispersion across firms but little skewness. Emission intensity, which is available for fewer firms, ranges from 0 to 3.7 (kilotons of CO_2 per million USD market cap), with higher values indicating higher-carbon firms. As others have noted (Bauer et al., 2022; Bolton & Kacperczyk, 2021), there is a large degree of skewness in emission intensity. A small number of firms have very high emission intensities, so the mean firm has an intensity about 20 times as large as the median firm (0.2 vs 0.01). This effect is mitigated for *E* and emissions scores by their within-industry construction. The bottom panel characterizes daily returns around the two IRA events. These returns display little skewness but substantial dispersion across firms.

Table 2.4 provides estimation results for equation (1) for raw event returns, and Appendix Table A2.2 reports results for abnormal returns, which differ minimally from those for raw returns. The results in the first three columns of Table 2.4 pertain to the brown event returns on July 14–15. They show that firms with high *E* and emissions scores or low emission intensities had a significantly worse daily stock market performance around this event. This is consistent with a deterioration in the outlook for future profits of green firms by the diminished prospects

Table 2.3. Summary Statistics of Firm-Level Data.

	Mean	SD	Min	q25	Median	q75	Max	Obs.
Environmental performance								
E score	0.28	0.28	0.00	0.01	0.19	0.50	0.98	2,537
Emissions score	0.31	0.32	0.00	0.00	0.21	0.58	1.00	2,537
Emission intensity	0.20	0.58	0.00	0.00	0.01	0.08	3.70	900
Firm-level controls								
Size	21.70	1.84	17.40	20.44	21.61	22.87	26.37	2,528
Leverage	0.15	0.56	−2.20	0.01	0.09	0.24	3.51	2,133
Rev. growth	0.34	1.13	−1.00	0.04	0.14	0.30	10.39	2,428
Profitability	−0.01	0.18	−1.02	−0.02	0.02	0.07	0.37	2,503
ETR	0.11	0.31	−1.73	0.00	0.15	0.23	1.23	2,537
Daily returns								
Brown event (July 14), raw	1.92	2.60	−44.74	0.86	1.94	3.05	24.35	2,520
Brown event (July 14), abn.	−0.18	2.60	−47.54	−1.06	−0.11	0.91	22.39	2,520
Green event (July 27), raw	1.04	2.99	−26.61	−0.31	0.96	2.33	29.97	2,122
Green event (July 27), abn.	−0.25	2.97	−27.87	−1.60	−0.31	1.07	27.87	2,122

Notes: Summary statistics for firm-level environmental measures, controls, and accounting variables, and event returns. Environmental measures are described in the text. Size is the log of total assets in millions USD, market leverage is EBIT divided by interest expenses, revenue growth is annual growth in total sales, profitability is return on assets, ETR is the cash effective tax rate (total income taxes paid divided by pretax income). Returns are from market close of July 14 (27) to market close of July 15 (28), and abnormal (abn.) returns are the residuals from an estimated market model.

for comprehensive climate policy. By contrast, the differential stock market responses of green and brown firms to the green event on July 27–28 have the opposite sign. The estimated β's for the E and emissions scores are positive, while the coefficient on emission intensity is negative. These responses are also stronger and statistically more significant than for the earlier event. With the astonishing news of near-certain passage of comprehensive climate policy in the form of the IRA, green firms exhibited a substantially better stock market performance than brown ones. Specifically, in terms of E scores, a greener firm at the upper 75 percentile (with an E score of 0.58) had almost a full percentage point higher daily equity return after July 27 than a browner firm at the lower 25 percentile (with an E score of 0.01).

Overall, our results using E and emissions scores are completely consistent with those using emission intensity. All three metrics show that high-carbon firms were expected to have better prospects in the absence of climate policy and that low-carbon firms performed better when the IRA climate policy was announced. This consistency is notable because the environmental scores calculated by ESG data providers are based on relatively subjective collections of indicators using proprietary methodologies. As such, at the firm level, the information in these metrics can differ substantially across providers (Berg et al., 2022; Ehlers et al., 2022).

Table 2.4. Event Return Regressions.

	Brown Event (July 14)			Green Event (July 27)		
	(1)	(2)	(3)	(4)	(5)	(6)
E score	−0.77***			1.98***		
	(0.19)			(0.27)		
Emissions score		−0.44**			1.47***	
		(0.17)			(0.24)	
Emission intensity			0.31**			−0.43**
			(0.15)			(0.21)
Size	0.16***	0.13***	0.05	−0.15***	−0.13***	−0.21***
	(0.03)	(0.04)	(0.06)	(0.05)	(0.05)	(0.07)
Market leverage	0.30***	0.30***	0.37	0.02	0.03	−0.02
	(0.10)	(0.10)	(0.25)	(0.11)	(0.11)	(0.33)
Revenue growth	0.15*	0.15**	−0.20	−0.04	−0.05	0.28*
	(0.08)	(0.08)	(0.21)	(0.07)	(0.07)	(0.16)
Profitability	0.01	−0.04	0.89	0.45	0.50	−3.94
	(0.58)	(0.58)	(2.24)	(0.87)	(0.87)	(4.20)
ETR	0.12	0.13	−0.01	−0.04	−0.04	−0.38
	(0.19)	(0.18)	(0.16)	(0.17)	(0.17)	(0.31)
ETR missing dummy	−1.21***	−1.20***	−0.32	−0.73	−0.77*	−1.32**
	(0.43)	(0.43)	(0.72)	(0.46)	(0.46)	(0.52)
Constant	−1.23	−0.85		3.94***	3.60***	
	(0.75)	(0.77)		(1.04)	(1.06)	
Observations	2,043	2,043	824	1,693	1,693	669
R^2	0.04	0.03	0.10	0.04	0.03	0.12
Industry fixed effects	No	No	Yes	No	No	Yes

Notes: Regression results for event returns. The dependent variable is the one-day raw return from market close on July 14 to July 15 (the brown event) in the first three columns, and the return from July 27 to 28 (the green event) in the last three columns. The key regressors are the environmental pillar score (E score), the emission category score, and emission intensity, calculated as the reported level of scope 1 + 2 emissions divided by market cap (at the end of 2021). Controls include size, market leverage, revenue growth, profitability, and ETR, which are described in the text and the notes to Table 2.3. The third and sixth columns include industry fixed effects using the 17 Fama-French industries. Clustered standard errors (by industry) are reported in parentheses. ***, **, and * denote significance at the 1%, 5%, and 10% level, respectively.

Similarly, we find a modest connection between E and emissions scores and the direct measure of emission intensity: E and emissions scores have a correlation of only −0.11 and −0.08, respectively, with emission intensity. In light of the apparent noise in distinguishing green and brown firms, the consistency of our results points to the strength of the underlying effect of the climate policy news that we identify.[25]

To more finely judge the economic significance of the firm-level results, Fig. 2.3 displays the cross-section of firm-level returns using portfolio sorts. We first orthogonalize event returns and greenness measures with respect to our regression control variables (size, market leverage, revenue growth, profitability, and ETR – as well as industry fixed effects for emission intensity). Then, a univariate regression of the orthogonalized event return on the orthogonalized greenness measure would recover exactly the coefficient of interest reported in Table 2.4 (according to the Frisch-Waugh-Lovell theorem). We form decile portfolios and plot mean portfolio returns against greenness (similar to a bin scatter plot of returns on greenness). The resulting Fig. 2.3 shows the cross-sectional relationship between event returns and our three measures of greenness. The left-hand column illustrates brown event returns and shows clear negative relationships between returns and *E*/emissions scores and a positive relationship between returns and emission intensity. These correlations are completely consistent with

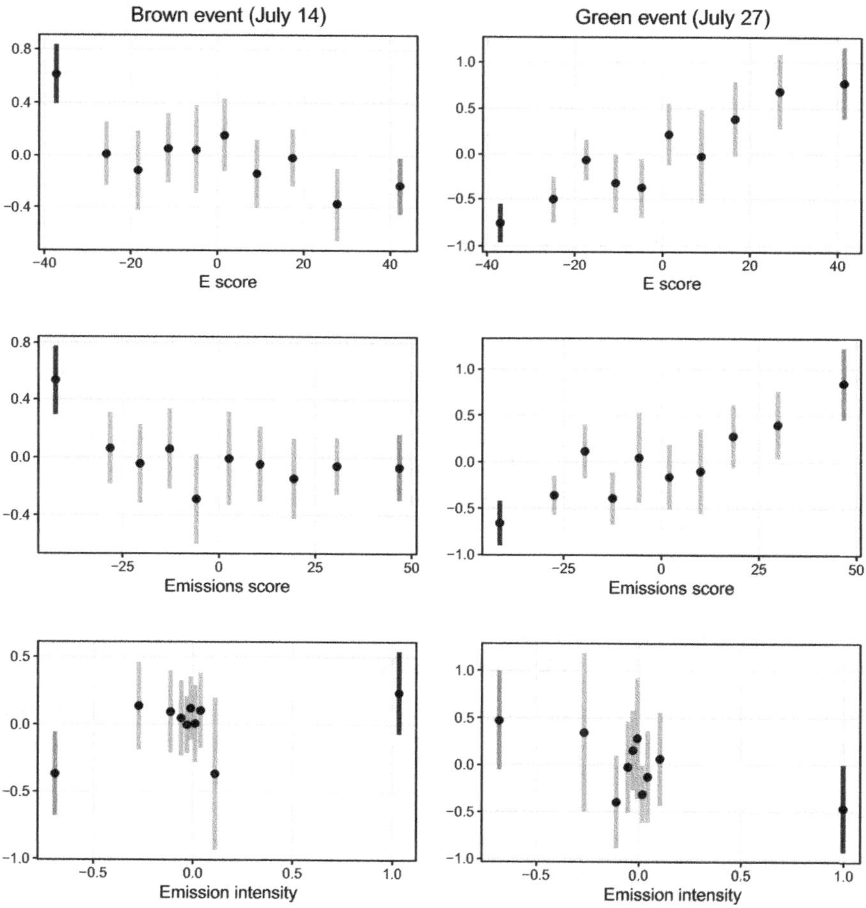

Fig. 2.3. Event Returns of Decile Portfolio. The dots measure event returns of decile portfolios formed using *E* scores (top row), emissions scores (middle row) or emission intensities (bottom row), for either the brown event on July 14 (left column) or the green event on July 27 (right column). Returns and greenness measures are orthogonalized with respect to the control variables in Table 2.4 (size, market leverage, revenue growth, profitability, and ETR). Vertical bars indicate 90% confidence intervals with greenest (brownest) deciles denoted by green (brown).

the associated coefficient estimates in Table 2.4 but allow a finely sliced reading of the firm-level results. For example, much of the response is driven by the greenest and brownest deciles of firms. These extremes are denoted by green and brown colored confidence intervals. For the brown event, the greenest firms had returns that were around 3/4 percentage point lower than brownest firms for *all* of the carbon metrics. For the green event shown in the right-hand panels, the reverse correlations between returns and greenness metrics are evident, with the high-carbon firms performing much worse across all three metrics. The announcement of the new IRA climate policy clearly led to a quantitatively significant green outperformance. Specifically, after the IRA announcement, the returns of green firms were 1.5 percentage points higher than those of brown ones using E and emissions scores and almost 1 percentage point higher using emission intensity. Furthermore, given the considerable lack of overlap of the green and brown confidence intervals in all of the panels of Fig. 2.3, the statistical significance of our results across both events is confirmed.

Our analysis provides clear and consistent evidence of the stock market impact of the two climate policy events. When negotiations for further US climate policy action publicly collapsed on July 14, investors bid up shares of brown, carbon-dependent firms while green, low-emissions firms lost value. Conversely, unveiling the IRA climate policy package benefited green stocks and hurt brown stocks. These results hold up whether environmental performance is measured using scores from ESG providers or actual emissions disclosed by the stock market companies. Again, these results are consistent with, for example, the asset pricing model of Pástor et al. (2021) in which green stocks can benefit from a policy-induced greater demand for goods and services of greener providers. In addition, clean-energy investment subsidies and similar policies appeared likely to reduce costs for green firms.

5. INDUSTRY GREENNESS AS A MEASURE OF TRANSITION RISK

So far, we have shown that surprising realizations of US climate policy had substantial effects on equity prices and that these effects differed significantly across firms. Such estimates of policy sensitivities are critical to a rapidly growing literature on the potential adverse implications of climate policy changes for the financial system. Specifically, central banks and financial supervisors are investigating the exposure and resilience of financial institutions to the transition risks posed by imperfectly anticipated efforts to facilitate and force a shift to a low-carbon economy (Acharya et al., 2023; NGFS, 2022a).

Central banks and supervisors are particularly interested in financial transition risk assessments of commercial banks, including how loans and other bank assets are revalued under a range of climate policy scenarios (Jung et al., 2023). The various climate scenarios differ in terms of the scope and pace of the policy-induced economic transformations taken to lower carbon emissions. The associated decarbonization risks include possible declines in asset prices, income, and profitability, and these risks are most material for companies with business models that rely on high carbon emissions, but firm-level emission metrics and data are only available for a subset of firms. Given the inadequate coverage of the available firm-level data, it is difficult to estimate such potential transition-related losses at a granular level. Thus, for many climate-related risk assessments, potential losses have been calculated based on sectoral or industry classifications, which are available for all of a financial institution's loans and assets. For example, Jung et al. (2023) examine the exposure of commercial banks to different climate policy scenarios by employing estimates of the effects of different carbon taxes on the output and profits of various industries as estimated from the general equilibrium models of Jorgenson et al. (2018), Goulder and Hafstead (2017), and NGFS (2022b). In effect, banks' exposures to climate policy shifts depend on the industry composition of their loan portfolio and the estimated industry-level effects of the climate policies that drive decarbonization. Similarly, Choi et al. (2020) identify high-emission firms based on their industry classification.

The climate policy events that we identified can provide a useful case study to assess the appropriateness of using industry classifications to account for climate transition risk. Specifically, we consider whether industry-level greenness metrics can account for the cross-industry variation of the equity price response to climate policy news. This analysis employs three different measures of industry-level greenness. The first two are constructed directly from our firm-level data, which we aggregate up to the 17 Fama-French industries. Industry-level emissions are the sum of all disclosed scope 1 and scope 2 emissions (in tons of CO_2 equivalents) of the firms in each industry. For these industry-level greenness metrics, we use total industry emissions and emission intensity, which divides total emissions by industry market cap (in million USD at the end of 2021).

Our final measure of industry-level greenness is based on the transition risk exposure for each industry as proxied by estimates of the differing loss in output in each sector that would be caused by a carbon tax. Jung et al. (2023) use such carbon tax sensitivities in their study of the transition risk exposures of US banks. Like them, we use the Jorgenson et al. (2018) estimates of carbon tax sensitivities, which are based on an intertemporal general equilibrium model calibrated to US industries.[26] Jorgenson et al. (2018) use the Intertemporal General Equilibrium Model industry classification. We assign the firms in each of the 60 Refinitiv industries to one of the IGEM industries, which results in 29 IGEM industries for our sample.

To calculate industry-level event returns, we aggregate firm-level abnormal returns – constructed as explained in Section 3 – into equal-weighted industry portfolios. Table 2.5 relates the industry-level event returns to the three measures of industry greenness. Note that, for all three measures, high values indicate brown industries with high transition risk. Thus, if these measures accurately captured the transition risk of the IRA policies, then we would expect to see positive coefficients in the regressions for the brown event (first three columns), and negative coefficients for the green event (last three columns). Instead, the coefficients on the emissions level variable have the wrong sign in both regressions, although they are not statistically significant. For emission intensity, the coefficients have the expected sign only for the brown event, but that is marginally statistically

Table 2.5. Event Returns and Industry-Level Green Metrics.

	Brown Event (July 14)			Green Event (July 27)		
	(1)	(2)	(3)	(4)	(5)	(6)
Emissions	−0.17			1.05		
	(0.31)			(2.56)		
Emission intensity		8.96*			−5.26	
		(4.64)			(19.38)	
Carbon tax sensitivity			−1.31			−7.06
			(3.29)			(8.83)
Constant	−0.38***	−0.49***	−0.05	−0.02	0.13	0.22
	(0.12)	(0.14)	(0.14)	(0.23)	(0.22)	(0.21)
Observations	17	17	29	17	17	29
R^2	0.004	0.067	0.004	0.024	0.003	0.047

Notes: Regressions of abnormal returns on emissions, emissions intensity, and a measure of industry sensitivity to carbon taxes. Emissions and emission intensity are aggregated to 17 Fama-French industries from firm-level data. Carbon tax sensitivity is from Jorgenson et al. (2018), the industry output sensitivity to the introduction of a $25 tax per ton of CO_2 with a 1% growth rate. ***, **, and * denote significance at the 1%, 5%, and 10% level, respectively.

significant (at the 10-percent level). Finally, the coefficients on the carbon tax sensitivity variable only have the expected sign for the green event, but again, neither is statistically significant.

To illustrate the weak relationships between greenness measures and returns, Fig. 2.4 provides the underlying scatter plot corresponding to column 5 in Table 2.5. The emission intensities of the 17 industries are measured on the horizontal axis, and the equity responses of firms in those industries are measured on the vertical axis.[27] The regression line is effectively flat indicating a very poor fit and weak predictive ability. Two industries illustrate the difficulty of using measures of greenness at an industry level: oil & gas and utilities have similar emission intensities, but they had diametrically opposed IRA equity price responses because clean power subsidies supported the utility sector.

Overall, the measured greenness of industries appears to be essentially unrelated to the equity response to the climate policy announcements. By contrast, the within-industry heterogeneity documented in Section 4 was significantly correlated with firm-level greenness. One important implication of the poor performance of the industry-level greenness measures is that, based on the climate policy transition realizations that we examined, they are likely a weak foundation for capturing and assessing transition risk. We believe that our event study considers some of the cleanest, most clearly demarcated US climate policy announcements in terms of timing. Of course, the announced policy shifts were much more complicated than the simple carbon tax changes envisioned in many climate stress tests and model simulations. However, policy complexity seems unavoidable and practical, real-world stress testing should take this into account.[28]

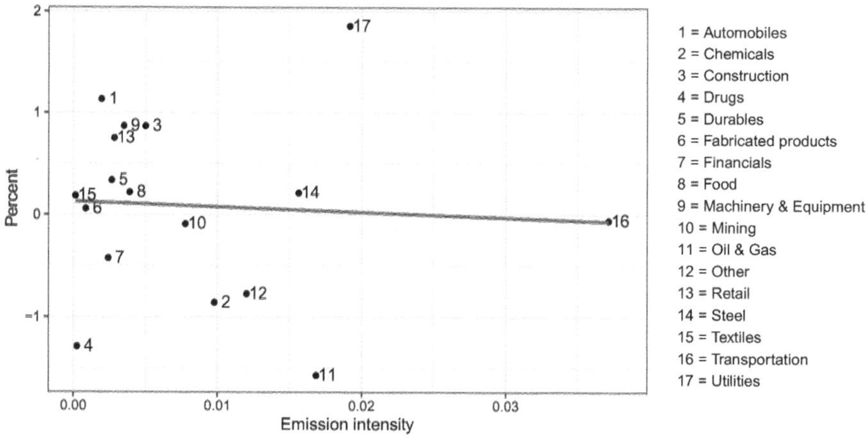

Fig. 2.4. IRA Announcement: Industry Abnormal Returns and Emission Intensity. Emission intensity and abnormal returns from July 27 to July 28 (green event) for the 17 Fama-French industries. Firm-level data are aggregated to the industry level. Abnormal returns are calculated from raw returns using a market model estimated with daily value-weighted CRSP market returns from January 2016 to May 2022. Emission intensity is constructed as the total emissions (scopes 1 and 2) divided by market cap. The best-fitting regression is shown as the blue line.

6. CONCLUSION

Our event study used the econometric identification of clearly delineated policy news to investigate how financial markets value firms' climate-related prospects. We show that the equity market responses to announcements of climate policy actions were quick, substantial, and distinctly heterogeneous with wide variation across firms and industries. Green stocks – equities of firms with lower carbon emission intensities and better environmental and emissions scores – benefited from news that the IRA would become law, while brown stocks – those of more carbon-intensive and more polluting firms – lost value. This heterogeneity of stock price responses is both statistically and quantitatively significant. We find equity movements in the opposite direction – with brown stocks outperforming green stocks – for the earlier event when the prospects for climate action shifted to negligible. These heterogeneities – particularly the increased investor demand for the stocks of low-carbon firms – are in line with the IRA's goal of fostering a transition away from fossil fuels. These results also appear consistent with several mechanisms that lead to different expected profits for green and brown firms. In particular, the heterogeneities likely reflect the varying effects of IRA tax credits and subsidies on green and brown product demand, revenues, and investment and production costs.

We also provide a cautionary note regarding the use of industry or sectoral measures of greenness for financial risk assessments and climate scenario analyses. Industries likely to benefit from the new policies – in particular, the utilities, construction, and automobile/transportation sectors – saw their stocks appreciate. However, across all industries, there was little correlation between industry-level greenness and stock market response. This finding suggests that a more granular, firm-level level approach may often be necessary to reliably capture exposure to transition risk.

Our examination of the reactions of equity prices to two major climate policy transition realizations can help policymakers, regulators, and investors better understand such transition risks and the likely financial effects of new climate policies. The results of our event study have some reassuring implications for financial transition risk assessments. The highly ambitious IRA climate policy legislation was a significant climate policy transition realization that could have increased the likelihood of stranded assets. Nevertheless, it did not result in any dramatic or disorderly repricing akin to a "climate Minsky moment." That is, the most consequential climate policy action ever in US history did not lead to firm-level equity price responses that were overwhelming or destabilizing. Of course, there are caveats to this conclusion. The impact effects on equity prices may not persist. Financial investors may have naively or sensibly underreacted to the IRA, perhaps downplaying the open-ended tax cuts, or even putting sizable odds on a future policy rollback. Alternatively, other types of climate policies – such as a precipitous and largely unexpected carbon pricing scheme – could have different implications and potentially lead to financial stress and instabilities. But given the significant scope and clear-cut timing of the climate policy news during the passage of the IRA, it is difficult to envisage another set of events that would serve as a more definitive realization for assessing climate transition risk.

NOTES

1. Many of the IRA tax credits are open-ended without fixed budgets, so the fiscal impact depends on usage and the amount claimed. The official IRA budget score by the Joint Committee on Taxation was under $400 billion, but that likely underestimates likely participation and tax credit take-up.

2. There are three broad roles that financial markets will play in the green transition (Giglio et al., 2021): allocating funds to sustainable investment, informing climate-related economic and policy decisions, and managing climate risks. As an example, information from financial markets can help pin down the long-run social discount rate used in determining the social cost of carbon (Bauer & Rudebusch, 2023).

3. See MacKinlay (1997) for a review of event-study methods. In macroeconomics, a large literature has employed event studies to examine the financial market effects of monetary policy announcements (e.g., Bauer & Rudebusch, 2014; Bauer & Swanson, 2023; Gürkaynak et al., 2005; Kuttner, 2001).

4. As noted by Bistline et al. (2023b), the economic incidence of IRA tax credits and other provisions – that is, whether they will be captured by producers or consumers – is relevant for assessing the effects of the IRA.

5. The passage of the IRA could also have shifted the cost of capital and risk premia, by changing perceptions of future climate risks, but such shifts are much less clear.

6. The New York Stock Exchange is usually open from Monday through Friday from 9:30 a.m. to 4:00 p.m.

7. As described in Romm et al. (2022): "Sen. Joe Manchin III (D-W.Va.) on Wednesday reached a deal with Democratic leaders on a spending package that aims to lower

health-care costs, combat climate change and reduce the federal deficit, [...] Under the deal, Schumer secured Manchin's support for roughly $433 billion in new spending, most of which is focused on climate change and clean energy production. It is the largest such investment in US history, and a marked departure from Manchin's position only days earlier."

8. Further supporting press accounts are included in Appendix A. It is difficult to augment these narratives with prediction market probabilities. There was a tiny New Zealand prediction market that did record bets on whether the US Senate would pass a budget "reconciliation" bill by September 2, 2022 (see https://www.predictit.org). While the reconciliation process was used to pass the IRA, the crucial issue for our event study is whether climate policy would be included in this reconciliation bill, and the prediction market is silent on this key question.

9. Besides curtailing climate change, the IRA has two other goals: restraining health-care costs and reducing the federal budget deficit. The first of these is notably aided by allowing Medicare to begin negotiating the price of select prescription drugs. Federal deficit reduction is largely achieved via a new 15% minimum tax on corporations with earnings of at least $1 billion a year.

10. Baseline projections without the IRA had reductions by 2030 of about 28% below 2005.

11. This demand channel is similar to the *customer channel* of Pástor et al. (2021) where firms benefit from additional demand in accordance with their greenness.

12. Effects on the cost of capital could also result from a shift in investor preferences for green investments, perhaps from a bandwagon effect in which IRA news increases investor interest in green assets, according to the *investor channel* of Pástor et al. (2021). While it is conceivable that new climate legislation could raise public awareness in a way that drives investors toward green investments – lowering expected returns and raising prices of green stocks – evidence of such a shift is not apparent.

13. We omit one index that was labeled green in Monasterolo and De Angelis (2020), the STOXX Global ESG Environmental Leaders index. They find that this index is just as well correlated with the brown oil and gas funds. Most tellingly, this index is heavily weighted toward bank stocks, which fared poorly with the announcement of the IRA. We also omit a European oil and gas index listed as a brown index in Monasterolo and De Angelis (2020).

14. For stock market event studies with daily data, the market model captures abnormal movements in stock returns fairly well and adding additional factors is generally found to be unnecessary (e.g., Brown & Warner, 1985; MacKinlay, 1997). Consistent with this prevailing view, we also calculated abnormal returns using the Fama-French three-factor model and found very similar results.

15. We obtained similar results using just the overnight close-to-open returns but judged that a slightly longer window better captured the market pricing of news during business hours.

16. Again, the news on these days was released after markets had closed, so these news releases are shown as occurring between the market close quotes on these event days and the subsequent days.

17. The fossil-fuel stock declines on August 3 and 4 partly reflected a plunge in benchmark crude oil prices, which were down about 6% over those two days on concerns about rising oil supplies and a deteriorating economic outlook. Oil prices posted much smaller movements around the July 14 and 27 events – up 1.8% and down 1.0%, respectively.

18. See https://mba.tuck.dartmouth.edu/pages/faculty/ken.french/Data_Library/det_17_ind_port.html (accessed 04/13/2023) for data and details on the industry definitions and return calculations. The use of value-weighted portfolios leads to qualitatively similar results. Our focus for the rest of this chapter is on daily returns, which is a common solution to the tradeoff faced in the choice of window length in event studies: longer windows allow for delayed reactions or reversion of the effects, but they also include more noise as other news unrelated to the events affect stock returns.

19. For example, among the 19 Fortune 100 companies that the Center for American Progress identified in a recent report as paying an effective federal tax rate below 10%, four belong to the financial sector (Koronowski et al., 2022).

20. Refinitiv – now rebranded as LSEG Data & Analytics – provides accounting data from the Worldscope database, stock market returns from Datastream, and environmental data from the ESG database.

21. Specifically, we filter out stocks that are not common equity, primary equity quotations, or listed in NYSE, AMEX, or NASDAQ. We also remove securities with prices lower than $1 during our estimation and event windows, and securities whose name fields indicate non-common equity affiliation (see, e.g., Bauer et al., 2022; Griffin et al., 2010; Ince & Porter, 2006).

22. Refinitiv offers a large ESG database that covers about 85% of the global market cap and draws on more than 630 different ESG metrics. For details about the proprietary methodology, see https://www.refinitiv.com/content/dam/marketing/en_us/documents/methodology/refinitiv-esg-scores-methodology.pdf (accessed 03/16/2023).

23. Specifically, we use each firms reported total 2021 scopes 1 and 2 emissions (in kilotons of CO_2 equivalents) relative to its market capitalization (in million USD at the end of 2021). We do not include scope 3 emissions because they are hard to monitor and attribute.

24. ETR is missing for a fairly large number of firms, and like Ramelli et al. (2021) we replace the missing values with zero and add an indicator variable identifying missing observations.

25. As noted earlier, Ramelli et al. (2021) find conflicting results for the stock market response to the Trump election depending on whether *E* scores and emission variables were used, but for that event, the timing of any news about the prospects for climate action was less clear-cut.

26. Specifically, we employ the estimated output sensitivities to an introduction of a $25 tax per metric ton of CO_2 equivalents, with a 1% tax growth rate.

27. There are small differences in industry returns between Figs. 2.2 and 2.4. The former are estimated using all registered firms, and the latter are estimated using only our ESG firm-level dataset. However, the same conclusion is obtained with either measure: on average across all industries, returns and greenness appear uncorrelated.

28. The Unites States may be especially prone to policy complexity, given the politicization of views on climate change (see, e.g., DiLeo et al., 2023).

ACKNOWLEDGMENTS

We thank Elías Albagli, Stefano Carattini, Christian Kontz, Sanjay Patnaik, and David Wessel for helpful comments. The views expressed here are those of the authors and do not necessarily reflect the views of others in the Federal Reserve System.

REFERENCES

Acharya, V. V., Berner, R., Engle, R., Jung, H., Stroebel, J., Zeng, X., & Zhao, Y. (2023). *Climate stress testing*. [Staff Report 1059, Federal Reserve Bank of New York].

Ardia, D., Bluteau, K., Boudt, K., & Inghelbrecht, K. (2023). Climate change concerns and the performance of green vs. brown stocks. Management Science, 69(12), 7607-7632

Aswani, J., Raghunandan, A., & Rajgopal, S. (2023). Are carbon emissions associated with stock returns? *Review of Finance* (forthcoming).

Barnett, M. (2023). *A run on oil? Climate policy and stranded assets risk*. [Working Paper, February].

Bartram, S. M., Hou, K., & Kim, S. (2022). Real effects of climate policy: Financial constraints and spillovers. *Journal of Financial Economics, 143*(2), 668–696.

Battiston, S., Monasterolo, I., Riahi, K., & Van Ruijven, B. (2021). Accounting for finance is key for climate mitigation pathways. *Science, 372*(6545), 918–920.

Bauer, M. D., Huber, D., Rudebusch, G. D., & Wilms, O. (2022). Where is the carbon premium? Global performance of green and brown stocks. *Journal of Climate Finance, 1*, 100006. https://doi.org/10.1016/j.jclimf.2023.100006

Bauer, M. D., & Rudebusch, G. D. (2014). The signaling channel for federal reserve bond purchases. *International Journal of Central Banking, 10*(3), 233–289.

Bauer, M. D., & Rudebusch, G. D. (2023). The rising cost of climate change: Evidence from the Bond Market. *Review of Economics and Statistics, 105*(5), 1255–1270.

Bauer, M. D., & Swanson, E. T. (2023). A reassessment of monetary policy surprises and high-frequency identification. *NBER Macroeconomics Annual, 37*(1), 87–155.

Berg, F., Kölbel, J. F., & Rigobon, R. (2022). Aggregate confusion: The divergence of ESG ratings. *Review of Finance, 26*(6), 1315–1344.

Bistline, J., Blanford, G., Brown, M., Burtraw, D., Domeshek, M., Farbes, J., Fawcett, A., Hamilton, A., Jenkins, J., Jones, R., King, B., Kolus, H., Larsen, J., Levin, A., Mahajan, M., Marcy, C., Mayfield, E., McFarland, J., McJeon, H., … Zhao, A. (2023). Emissions and energy impacts of the Inflation Reduction Act. Science, *380*(6652), 1324–1327.

Bistline, J., Mehrotra, N., & Wolfram, C. (2023b). *Economic implications of the climate provisions of the Inflation Reduction Act*. Brookings Papers on Economic Activity.

Bolton, P. & Kacperczyk, M. (2021). Do investors care about carbon risk? *Journal of Financial Economics, 142*(2), 517–549.

Bressan, G., Duranovic, A., Monasterolo, I., & Battiston, S. (2022). *Asset-level climate physical risk assessment is key for adaptation finance*. [SSRN working paper, March].

Brown, S. J., & Warner, J. B. (1985). Using daily stock returns: The case of event studies. *Journal of Financial Economics, 14*(1), 3–31. https://doi.org/10.1016/0304-405X(85)90042-X

Carattini, S., & Sen, S. (2019). *Carbon taxes and stranded assets: Evidence from Washington State*. Working Paper 7785, CESifo.

Carney, M. (2016). *Resolving the climate paradox*. Arthur Burns Memorial Lecture, September 22, 2016, Berlin. Retrieved February 21, 2023, from https://www.fsb.org/wp-content/uploads/Resolving-the-climate-paradox.pdf

Cassidy, W. (2023). *Elections have consequences: The impact of political agency on climate policy and asset prices*. [Working paper, Booth School of Business, University of Chicago].

Choi, D., Gao, Z., & Jiang, W. (2020). Attention to global warming. *The Review of Financial Studies, 33*(3), 1112–1145.

DiLeo, M., Rudebusch, G. D., & van't Klooster, J. (2023). *Why the Fed and ECB parted ways on climate change: The politics of divergence in the global central banking community*. [Hutchins Center Working Papers].

Ehlers, T., Elsenhuber, U., Jegarasasingam, K., & Jondeau, E. (2022). Deconstructing ESG scores: how to invest with your own criteria?

Financial Stability Board. (2022). *Climate scenario analysis by jurisdictions*. Retrieved April 25, 2023, from https://www.ngfs.net/sites/default/files/medias/documents/climate_scenario_analysis_by_jurisdictions_initial_findings_and_lessons.pdf

Giglio, S., Kelly, B., & Stroebel, J. (2021). Climate finance. *Annual Review of Financial Economics, 13*, 15–36.

Goulder, L., & Hafstead, M. (2017). *Confronting the climate challenge: US policy options*. Columbia University Press.

Griffin, J. M., Kelly, P. J., & Nardari, F. (2010). Do market efficiency measures yield correct inferences? A comparison of developed and emerging markets. *Review of Financial Studies, 23*(8), 3225–3277.

Gürkaynak, R., Sack, B., & Swanson, E. T. (2005). Do actions speak louder than words? The response of asset prices to monetary policy actions and statements. *International Journal of Central Banking, 1*(1), 55–93.

Hänsel, M. C., Bauer, M. D., Drupp, M. A., Rudebusch, G. D., & Wagner, G. (2022). *Climate policy curves: Linking policy choices to climate outcomes*. [Hutchins Center Working Papers].

Hengge, M., Panizza, U., & Varghese, R. (2023). *Carbon policy surprises and stock returns: Signals from financial markets*. [Working Paper No. 2023/13, International Monetary Fund].

Ilhan, E., Sautner, Z., & Vilkov, G. (2021). Carbon tail risk. *Review of Financial Studies*, *34*(3), 1540–1571.

Ince, O. S., & Porter, R B. (2006). Individual equity return data from Thomson Datastream: Handle with Care!. *Journal of Financial Research*, *29*(4), 463–479.

Ivanov, I., Kruttli, M. S., & Watugala, S. W. (2023). Banking on carbon: Corporate lending and cap-and-trade policy. *Review of Financial Studies* (forthcoming).

Jorgenson, D. W., Goettle, R. J., Ho, M. S., & Wilcoxen, P. J. (2018). The welfare consequences of taxing carbon. *Climate Change Economics*, *9*(01), 1840013.

Jung, H., Engle, R., & Berner, R. (2021). *CRISK: Measuring the climate risk exposure of the financial system*. [Staff Report 977, Federal Reserve Bank of New York].

Jung, H., Santos, J. A. C., & Seltzer, L. (2023). *US banks' exposures to climate transition risks*. [Staff Report 1058, Federal Reserve Bank of New York].

Känzig, D. R. (2023). *The unequal economic consequences of carbon pricing*. [Working Paper 31221, NBER].

Koronowski, R., Vela, J., Rasheed, Z., & Hanlon, S. (2022). *These 19 Fortune 100 companies paid next to nothing – or nothing at all – in taxes in 2021*. Center for American Progress. Retrieved May 09, 2023, from https://www.americanprogress.org/article/these-19-fortune-100-companies-paid-next-to-nothing-or-nothing-at-all-in-taxes-in-2021/

Kumar, M., & Purnanandam, A. (2022). *Carbon emissions and shareholder value: Causal evidence from the US power utilities*. [SSRN working paper, November].

Kuttner, K. N. (2001). Monetary policy surprises and interest rates: Evidence from the Fed funds futures market. *Journal of Monetary Economics*, *47*(3), 523–544.

MacKinlay, A. C. (1997). Event studies in economics and finance. *Journal of Economic Literature*, *35*(1), 13–39.

Monasterolo, I., & De Angelis, L. (2020). Blind to carbon risk? An analysis of stock market reaction to the Paris Agreement. *Ecological Economics*, *170*, 106571.

NGFS. (2022a). *NGFS Scenarios for central banks and supervisors*. Retrieved August 30, 2023, from https://www.ngfs.net/sites/default/files/medias/documents/ngfs_climate_scenarios_for_central_banks_and_supervisors_.pdf.pdf

NGFS. (2022b). *Running the NGFS scenarios in G-Cubed: A tale of two modelling frameworks*. Retrieved August 30, 2023, from https://www.ngfs.net/sites/default/files/medias/documents/running_the_ngfs_scenarios_in_g-cubed_a_tale_of_two_modelling_frameworks.pdf

Ochoa, M., Paustian, M. O., & Wilcox, L. (2022). *Do sustainable investment strategies hedge climate change risks? Evidence from Germany's Carbon Tax*. [FEDS Working Paper 2022-073, Federal Reserve Board].

Pástor, L., Stambaugh, R. F., & Taylor, L. A. (2021). Sustainable investing in equilibrium. *Journal of Financial Economics*, *142*(2), 550–571.

Pástor, L., Stambaugh, R. F., & Taylor, L. A. (2022). Dissecting green returns. *Journal of Financial Economics*, *146*(2), 403–424.

Van der Ploeg, F., & Rezai, A. (2020). Stranded assets in the transition to a carbon-free economy. *Annual Review of Resource Economics*, *12*, 281–298.

Ramelli, S., Wagner, A. F., Zeckhauser, R. J., & Ziegler, A. (2021). Investor rewards to climate responsibility: Stock-price responses to the opposite shocks of the 2016 and 2020 US elections. *Review of Corporate Finance Studies*, *10*(4), 748–787.

Romm, T., & Stein, J. (2022). Manchin says he won't support new climate spending or tax hikes on wealthy. *The Washington Post*, published July 14, 9:09pm EDT. Retrieved April 12, 2023, from https://www.washingtonpost.com/us-policy/2022/07/14/manchin-climate-tax-bbb/

Romm, T., Stein, J., Roubein, R., & Joselow, M. (2022). Manchin says he has reached deal with Schumer on economy, climate bill. *The Washington Post*, published July 27, 4:59pm EDT. Retrieved April 12, 2023, from https://www.washingtonpost.com/us-policy/2022/07/27/manchin-says-he-has-reached-deal-with-democrats-economy-climate-bill/

Rozenberg, J., Vogt-Schilb, A., & Hallegatte, S. (2020). Instrument choice and stranded assets in the transition to clean capital. *Journal of Environmental Economics and Management*, *100*, 102183.

Slowik, P., Searle, S., Basma, H., Miller, J., Zhou, Y., Rodríguez, F., Buysse, C., Kelly, S., Minjares, R., Pierce, L., Orvis, R., & B., Sara. (2023). *Analyzing the impact of the Inflation Reduction Act on electric vehicle uptake in the United States*. Energy Innovation and International Council on Clean Transportation. Retrieved May 09, 2023, from https://theicct.org/wp-content/uploads/2023/01/ira-impact-evs-us-jan23-2.pdf

Wagner, A. F., Zeckhauser, R. J., & Ziegler, A. (2018). Company stock price reactions to the 2016 election shock: Trump, taxes, and trade. *Journal of Financial Economics*, *130*(2), 428–451.

APPENDIX 1. SUPPLEMENTAL PRESS COVERAGE OF CLIMATE POLICY EVENTS

A1.1. PRESS REPORTS FOR JULY 14, 2022 BROWN EVENT

Joe Manchin Won't Support Climate, Tax Measures in Economic Package
Wall Street Journal, July 14, 2022, 11:48 pm ET

> Sen. Joe Manchin (D., W.Va.), the pivotal vote in Democrats' efforts to pass a bill aimed at fighting climate change, told Senate Majority Leader Chuck Schumer that he wouldn't support an economic package that raises taxes or includes climate provisions, according to people familiar with the matter. Instead, Mr. Manchin told Mr. Schumer on Thursday that he would only support a bill that includes provisions aimed at lowering the price of prescription drugs and a two-year extension of Affordable Care Act subsidies, according to one of the people.

https://www.wsj.com/articles/joe-manchin-wont-support-bill-that-includes-climate-and-tax-measures-11657848978?page=2&mod=article_inline (accessed 11/09/2023)

How Joe Manchin Doomed the Democrats' Climate Plan
The New York Times, July 15, 2022

> Senator Joe Manchin III of West Virginia, who took more campaign cash from the oil and gas industry than any other senator, and who became a millionaire from his family coal business, independently blew up the Democratic Party's legislative plans to fight climate change. [...] Privately, Senate Democratic staff members seethed and sobbed on Thursday night, after more than a year of working nights and weekends to scale back, water down, trim and tailor the climate legislation to Mr. Manchin's exact specifications, only to have it *rejected inches from the finish line*. [...] Mr. Manchin's refusal to support the climate legislation, along with steadfast Republican opposition, *effectively dooms the chances* that Congress will pass any new law to tackle global warming for the foreseeable future [...].

https://www.nytimes.com/2022/07/15/climate/manchin-climate-change-democrats.html (accessed 11/09/2023)

Manchin Pulls Plug on Climate and Tax Talks, Shrinking Domestic Plan
The New York Times, July 14, 2022

> Senator Joe Manchin III, Democrat of West Virginia, pulled the plug on Thursday on negotiations to salvage key pieces of President Biden's agenda, informing his party's leaders that he would not support funding for climate or energy programs or raising taxes on wealthy Americans and corporations. [...] The decision by Mr. Manchin [...] *dealt a devastating blow* to his party's efforts to enact a broad social safety net, climate and tax package.

https://www.nytimes.com/2022/07/14/us/politics/manchin-climate-taxes.html (accessed 11/09/2023)

A1.2. PRESS REPORTS FOR JULY 27, 2022 GREEN EVENT

Joe Manchin Reaches Deal with Chuck Schumer on Energy, Healthcare, Tax Package
Wall Street Journal, July 28, 2022, 10:28 am ET

> Sen. Joe Manchin (D., W.Va.) agreed to back a package aimed at lowering carbon emissions and curbing healthcare costs while raising corporate taxes, marking a *stunning revival* of core pieces of President Biden's economic and climate agenda that the West Virginia Democrat had *seemingly killed* earlier this month. The deal, negotiated privately between Messrs. Manchin and Senate Majority Leader Chuck Schumer (D., N.Y.) since the start of last week, would raise roughly $739 billion […]

https://www.wsj.com/articles/joe-manchin-reaches-deal-with-chuck-schumer-on-energy-healthcare-package-11658957299 (accessed 11/09/2023)

Surprise Deal Would Be Most Ambitious Climate Action Undertaken by US
The New York Times, July 28, 2022

> Senate Majority Leader Charles Schumer (D-N.Y.) and centrist Sen. Joe Manchin (D-W.Va.) on Wednesday said they had struck a climate, health and tax package deal […] The new package is a fraction of the more than $3 trillion deal once envisioned by liberal Democrats, but it still could give the party a big win ahead of midterm elections […].

https://www.nytimes.com/2022/07/28/climate/climate-change-deal-manchin.html (accessed 11/09/2023)

Manchin, Schumer announce slimmed-down deal on climate, taxes, health
The Hill, July 27, 2022, 5:38 pm ET

> The $369 billion climate and tax package forged in a surprise deal by Senate Democrats would be the most ambitious action ever taken by the United States to try to stop the planet from catastrophically overheating. The agreement, which Senate Democrats announced late Wednesday and hope to pass as early as next week, shocked even some who had been involved in the sputtering negotiations over climate legislation during the past year. The announcement of a deal, after many activists had given up hope, almost instantly reset the role of the United States in the global effort to fight climate change. And it was delivered by Senator Joe Manchin III of West Virginia, the holdout Democrat who had been reviled by environmentalists and some of his own colleagues after he said this month that he could not support a climate bill due to inflation concerns.

https://thehill.com/homenews/senate/3576965-manchin-schumer-announce-slimmed-down-670-billion-deal/ (accessed 11/09/2023)

APPENDIX 2. ADDITIONAL EMPIRICAL ANALYSIS

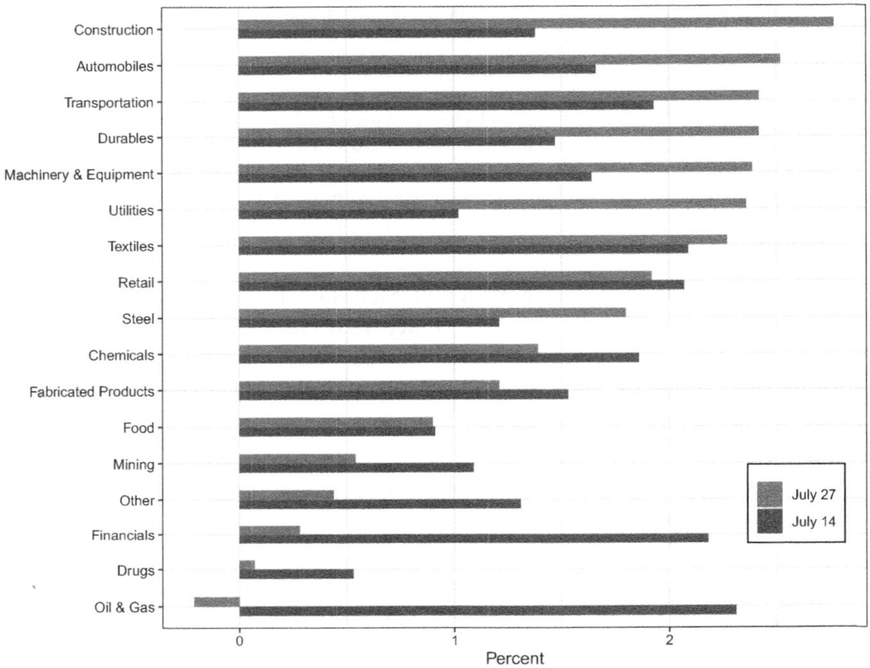

Fig. A2.1. Returns of 17 Fama-French Industry Portfolios Around Green and Brown Events. Daily returns for 17 Fama-French industry portfolios (equal-weighted). Brown bars show returns using closing prices from July 14 to July 15 (brown event), and green bars show the returns from July 27 to July 28 (green event).

Table A2.1. Abnormal Returns of Green and Brown Equity Indices with Alternative Events.

	CBO/JCT (Aug 03)		Senate (Aug 07)		House (Aug 12)	
	1 Day	3 Days	1 Day	3 Days	1 Day	3 Days
Green indices						
Nasdaq Clean Edge Green Energy	−1.7	2.1	1.5	2.5	−1.1	−5.2**
Wilderhill Clean Energy	−1.4	1.3	1.7	3.1	−1.4	−6.3**
S&P Global Clean Energy	−4.1***	−1.0	0.5	3.7	−0.1	−1.2
World Renewable Energy (Renixx)	−3.8**	−1.2	0.4	1.3	1.8	−0.7
ISE Global Wind Energy	−2.0**	−0.3	0.9	2.2	0.1	1.1
MAC Global Solar Energy	−4.6***	−0.8	0.8	3.8	−0.2	−2.2
Brown indices						
S&P 500 Integrated Oil & Gas	−4.8***	−6.7***	0.3	1.1	−2.2	−1.5
FTSE Local USA Oil & Gas & Coal	−4.9***	−5.8*	0.7	1.6	−2.2	0.0
FTSE All World Oil & Gas & Coal	−3.2**	−4.5*	1.0	1.8	−2.0	−1.0
Dow Jones Select Oil Expl. & Prod.	−5.0**	−5.8*	0.4	1.1	−2.6	−0.3
Dynamic Energy Expl. & Prod. Intellindex	−5.5***	−7.0*	−0.1	1.1	−2.9	−0.5
Factors						
Green Factor	−2.1**	0.0	0.7	1.1	−0.1	−0.9
Brown Factor	−2.7***	−2.0**	0.3	0.5	−1.4	−0.3
Green−Minus-Brown	0.6	2.1*	0.4	0.7	1.3	−0.7

Notes: Abnormal returns around other IRA-related events. Expected returns are estimated with a market model using daily value-weighted CRSP market returns from January 2016 to May 2022. Statistical significance levels are obtained from regressions of abnormal returns on event dummies; ***, **, and * denote significance at the 1%, 5%, and 10% level, respectively.

Table A2.2. Event-Study Regressions: Abnormal Returns.

	14 July 2022			27 July 2022		
	(1)	(2)	(3)	(4)	(5)	(6)
E score	−0.86***			1.93***		
	(0.19)			(0.27)		
Emissions score		−0.54***			1.41***	
		(0.17)			(0.24)	
Emission intensity			0.31**			−0.42**
			(0.14)			(0.21)
Size	0.15***	0.13***	0.07*	−0.16***	−0.13***	−0.19**
	(0.03)	(0.03)	(0.04)	(0.05)	(0.05)	(0.09)
Market leverage	0.37***	0.36***	0.43*	0.06	0.06	0.02
	(0.10)	(0.10)	(0.25)	(0.11)	(0.11)	(0.33)
Revenue growth	0.10	0.11	−0.38***	−0.07	−0.08	0.17
	(0.08)	(0.08)	(0.14)	(0.07)	(0.07)	(0.14)
Profitability	0.61	0.56	2.17	0.79	0.84	−3.22
	(0.60)	(0.60)	(2.21)	(0.88)	(0.88)	(4.22)
ETR	0.31*	0.31*	0.12	0.08	0.08	−0.27
	(0.18)	(0.18)	(0.13)	(0.16)	(0.17)	(0.32)
ETR missing dummy	−1.19***	−1.18***	−0.16	−0.72	−0.76*	−1.21**
	(0.44)	(0.44)	(0.70)	(0.45)	(0.45)	(0.52)
Constant	−3.26***	−2.93***		2.77***	2.39**	
	(0.73)	(0.75)		(1.03)	(1.06)	
Observations	2,043	2,043	824	1,693	1,693	669
R^2	0.05	0.04	0.09	0.04	0.03	0.12
Fixed Effects	NO	NO	YES	NO	NO	YES

Notes: The figure shows the industry fixed-effects regression of one-day abnormal returns on environmental pillar score (E score), emissions score, and emission intensity. Emission intensity is constructed as total emissions (scopes 1 and 2) divided by market cap. Controls include size, market leverage, revenue growth, profitability, and ETR. Fixed effects account for the Fama-French 17 industries. Clustered standard errors are reported in parentheses. ***, **, and * denote significance at the 1%, 5%, and 10% level, respectively.

CHAPTER 3

NIGHTTIME LIGHT POLLUTION AND ECONOMIC ACTIVITIES: A SPATIO-TEMPORAL MODEL WITH COMMON FACTORS IN US COUNTIES

Georges Bresson[a], Jean-Michel Etienne[b], and Guy Lacroix[c]

[a]*Department of Economics, Université Paris Panthéon-Assas, France*
[b]*Department of Economics, Université Paris-Saclay, France*
[c]*Department of Economics, Université Laval, Canada*

ABSTRACT

Excessive nighttime light is known to have detrimental effects on health and on the environment (fauna and flora). The chapter investigates the link between nighttime light pollution and economic growth, air pollution, and urban density. The authors propose an urban model of nighttime lights pollution and economic activities which accounts for spatial interactions. The model naturally leads to a dynamic general nesting spatial model with unknown common factors. The model is estimated with data for 3,071 continental US counties from 2012 to 2019 using a quasi-maximum likelihood estimator. Short run and long run county marginal effects emphasize the importance of spillover effects on radiance levels. Counties with high levels of radiance are less sensitive to

Econometrics of Climate, Energy, and Green Transition
Advances in Econometrics, Volume 47A, 91–118

ISSN: 0731-9053/doi:10.1108/S0731-90532026000047A004

additional growth than low-level counties. This has implications for policies that have been proposed to curtail nighttime light pollution.

Keywords: Nighttime light pollution; air pollution; GDP; satellite data; space-time panel data model; spatial urban model

JEL Classification: C23; Q53

1. INTRODUCTION

Nighttime lighting is intimately related to economic development and growth. Satellite recordings are now widely used by social scientists and development economists as proxies for human development and wealth in subnational regions of developing countries. In developed economies, though, night light is often perceived as a nuisance. Indeed, the presence of unwanted, inappropriate, or excessive artificial lighting has been coined "nightlight pollution". Falchi et al. (2016) and Kyba et al. (2017) have estimated that 83% of the world's population is affected by nighttime lighting and that as much as 23% of the earth's terrestrial surface is covered by night light.

Night light pollution can take many forms: light trespass, glare, over-illumination, light clutter, sky glow, etc.[1] Its impact on the health and well-being of human (Sager, 2019), animal and vegetal lifeforms has become a major concern in recent years. Humans have always evolved in an environment with a clear distinction between night and day. Ubiquitous electric lighting at home and at the workplace, and the use of light-emitting electronic devices at night have blurred this distinction (Cain et al., 2020). People now spend most waking hours surrounded by artificial lighting, reduced sunlight exposure and relatively bright nighttime lighting (Goulet et al., 2007; Martinez-Nicolas et al., 2019). Excessive nighttime light exposure can reduce circadian amplitude which has been associated with a greater incidence of depression (Burns et al., 2021; Jewett et al., 1994).

Excessive nightlight has also been shown to increase atmospheric pollution since it prevents nighttime chemical reactions that normally reduce the smog produced by the fumes emitted from cars and factories (see CIRES, 2011; Stark et al., 2011). In addition, Ścieżor and Czaplicka (2020) have shown that various types of aerosols, both of natural and anthropogenic sources, exacerbates sky glow. Particulate matter (PM) related to the combustion of solid fuels in the winter as well as mists and haze are considered important light scattering sources. Anthropogenic PM has the greatest impact on the brightness of the cloudless night sky glow in winter. In areas heavily polluted with light, fogs and mist are particularly important.

The detrimental consequences of nightlight pollution have led many to advocate eliminating or reducing it as much as possible. For example, Tucson (Arizona) has recently reduced sky glow by 7% after converting street lights. At least 18 states, the District of Columbia and Puerto Rico now have laws in place to reduce light pollution. The majority of states that have enacted so-called "dark skies" legislation have done so to promote energy conservation, public safety, esthetic interests, and astronomical research capabilities. Municipalities in a number of states have also been active on this issue, adopting light pollution regulations as part of their zoning. More and more cities are adopting policies to drastically reduce or even switch off public lighting during certain hours of the night (Dizon & Pranggono, 2022). Since the beginning of the war in Ukraine, faced with soaring energy prices, European cities are turning off their lights. Spain has made these measures compulsory, ordering stores to turn off their lights at night. Berlin has turned off the floodlights that illuminate 200 of its historic buildings and monuments, and a number of cities in Austria, Germany, and Italy have reduced street lighting or switched off commercial signs. In France, many municipalities have taken steps to switch off street lighting completely between midnight and 5 am each night (quoted by Politico, August 3, 2022). These commitments are in line with the Green New Deal for Europe proposed by the European Commission to make the EU's climate, energy, transport, and taxation policies fit for reducing net greenhouse gas emissions by at least 55% by 2030, compared to 1990 levels (European Commission, 2021).

Research suggests that light pollution is an issue primarily in industrialized countries. Gallaway et al. (2010) found that those with high rates of resource extraction typically have high levels of light pollution. Likewise, countries with high GDP and dense urban and suburban areas also had the highest rates of light pollution. Over the past decade, and since the seminal papers of Chen and Nordhaus (2011) and Henderson et al. (2011, 2012), the links between light pollution and economic activities have been extensively investigated (see Addison & Stewart, 2015, for a survey; Zhao et al., 2019). Two main approaches can be distinguished: The first uses satellite nighttime lights data as a proxy to poorly measured GDPs computed from national accounts in some developing countries and autocraties (see, e.g., Addison & Stewart, 2015; Chen & Nordhaus, 2011; Goldblatt et al., 2020; Gonzalez-Navarro & Turner, 2018; Henderson et al., 2012; Keola et al., 2015; Martinez, 2022). The second, less frequent in economics, uses economic data (GDP, population, ...) to model nightlight pollution. Hu and Yao (2022) are the only ones to our knowledge to estimate nighttime light pollution as a function of GDP. They attempt to correct GDP growth based on national accounts within a measurement errors model framework using satellite-recorded nighttime lights. They provide estimates for 162 countries over the period 1993–2013 using a simple log-linear model of the impact of the GDP growth rate on the growth rate of nighttime light pollution (without any other control variables). The estimation by Sieve maximum likelihood – to reduce the measurement error of national accounts GDP – gives a coefficient of 1.3. This estimation allows to correct reported GDPs and provide "true" GDPs.

This chapter is cast within the second strand of the literature. It investigates the links between economic activities (GDP) and light pollution at the county level across the United States. As per the literature, the analysis accounts for population level, urban density, air pollution, *etc.* Physical data (night light, urban density, and $PM_{2.5}$) are drawn from the *Visible Infrared Imaging Radiometer Suite*

(VIIRS) onboard the Suomi satellite.[2] Data on county-level GDP and population estimates are drawn from the Bureau of Economic Analysis (Aysheshim et al., 2020).[3] The purpose of the chapter is to determine the short and long-run local sensitivity of light pollution to economic growth (GDP) and other conditioning variables. Policies to mitigate light pollution may indeed be more efficient in certain areas and less so elsewhere, and may also be undermined by local economic growth. In order to achieve this, we extend the spatial urban models developed by Glaeser et al. (1995) and Brueckner (2003) in Section 2.[4] The manner in which we account for spatial interaction effects between the dependent and the explanatory variables leads to the so-called dynamic general nesting spatial model with common factors (Elhorst, 2021; Shi & Lee, 2017). This is detailed in Section 3. Section 4 gives the results and Section 5 concludes.

2. A SPATIAL URBAN MODEL OF NIGHTTIME LIGHTS POLLUTION AND ECONOMIC ACTIVITIES

Following da Silva et al. (2017), we assume that the total output of county $i(=1,...,N)$ at time $t(=1,...,T)$ is given by a Cobb-Douglas production function:

$$Q_{it} = A_{it}\, L_{it}^{\beta_L} K_{it}^{\beta_K} \bar{Z}_i^{1-\beta_L-\beta_K},$$

where L_{it} represents the population size of the county which proxies the number of workers, K_{it} denotes the traded capital and $\bar{Z}_i$ is fixed non-traded capital. A_{it} is the total factor productivity (TFP) which we assume to depend on the TFP of other counties but whose intensity decreases with distance. More formally, let

$$A_{it} = a_{it} \prod_{j(\neq i)=1}^{N} a_{jt}^{\eta w_{ij}},$$

where the TFP A_{it} is a function of county and time-specific labor productivity and technology, a_{it}, as well as those of neighboring counties, $a_{jt}\; j(\neq i)$. The parameter $\eta\left(0<\eta<1\right)$ captures the degree of interdependence among them. Although η is assumed to be constant, the interactions between counties depends on the relative location of each, w_{ij}, which are elements of a $\left(N \times N\right)$ neighborhood matrix W_N such that $0 \leq w_{ij} \leq 1$ and $w_{ii} = 0$.

Normalizing the price of capital to one, the first-order conditions with respect to capital and labor yields the following labor demand equation:

$$s_{it} = A_{it}^{\frac{1}{1-\beta_K}} \beta_L \beta_K^{\frac{\beta_K}{1-\beta_K}} L_{it}^{\frac{\beta_L+\beta_K-1}{1-\beta_K}} \bar{Z}_i^{\frac{1-\beta_L-\beta_K}{1-\beta_K}}, \tag{1}$$

where s_{it} is the wage rate.[5]

Consumers in county i are assumed to have a Cobb-Douglas utility function for tradable goods, C_{it}, and housing, H_{it}. Following Brueckner (2003), it is further assumed that the utility level is weakly separable in both the local and distant county (dis)amenities. The latter include traffic congestion, nighttime light pollution, R_{it}, air pollution, P_{it}, etc. According to Glaeser et al. (1995), potential (dis)amenities can be proxied by population size since it may be argued that quality of life is inversely related to it. Formally, we generalize the Cobb-Douglas utility functions proposed by Brueckner (2003), Glaeser et al. (1995), and da Silva et al. (2017) and write:

$$U_{it} = C_{it}^{1-\alpha} H_{it}^{\alpha} \left(R_{it}^{-\psi} \prod_{j(\neq i)=1}^{N} R_{jt}^{-\zeta w_{ij}} \right) \left(P_{it}^{-\kappa} \prod_{j(\neq i)=1}^{N} P_{jt}^{-\xi w_{ij}} \right) L_{it}^{-\varphi} \prod_{j(\neq i)=1}^{N} L_{jt}^{-\nu w_{ij}},$$

where $\psi > 0$, $\zeta > 0$, $\kappa > 0$, $\xi > 0$, $\varphi > 0$, and $\nu > 0$. Consumers maximize their utility subject to the following budget constraint:

$$C_{it} + p_{H_{it}} H_{it} = s_{it} L_{it}.$$

They choose C_{it} and H_{it}, where the price of the tradable good is normalized to 1 and the housing price is given by $p_{H_{it}}$. The housing demand is then given by:

$$H_{it} = \frac{\alpha s_{it} L_{it}}{p_{H_{it}}}.$$

As underlined by da Silva et al. (2017), spatial equilibrium conditions insure that utility equalizes across space if labor is mobile: Higher wages are required to offset local negative attributes (pollution, crime, etc.).[6,7]

Let the common utility level at a particular point in time be denoted as V_t. In equilibrium, the indirect utility function is given by

$$V_t = \alpha^{\alpha} (1-\alpha)^{1-\alpha} s_{it} p_{H_{it}}^{-\alpha} \left(R_{it}^{-\psi} \prod_{j(\neq i)=1}^{N} R_{jt}^{-\zeta w_{ij}} \right) \left(P_{it}^{-\kappa} \prod_{j(\neq i)=1}^{N} P_{jt}^{-\xi w_{ij}} \right) L_{it}^{1-\varphi} \prod_{j(\neq i)=1}^{N} L_{jt}^{-\nu w_{ij}}. \quad (2)$$

Following da Silva et al. (2017) and Glaeser and Gottlieb (2009), housing floor space is produced competitively either by land (l) or by height (h). If the supply of land at a particular location is fixed, or becomes available only gradually, the prices of land (p_l) and housing (p_H) are endogenous, and thus the cost of producing hl units of structure on top of l units of land is given by $c_0 h^{\delta} l$, where $\delta > 1$. If developer maximizes profits, the housing supply is given by:

$$hl = \left(p_{H_{it}} / \delta c_0 \right)^{\frac{1}{\delta - 1}} l.$$

The housing price equation derives from the equilibrium condition on the market:

$$p_{H_{it}} = \left(\frac{\alpha s_{it} L_{it}}{l} \right)^{\frac{\delta-1}{\delta}} (\delta c_0)^{\frac{1}{\delta}}. \quad (3)$$

Solving the system formed by labor demand (1), indirect utility (2), and housing prices (3) for the (dis)amenities R_{it} yields:

$$\log R_{it} = \frac{1}{\psi}\left\{\frac{\delta(1-\alpha)+\alpha}{\delta(1-\beta_K)}\right\}\log A_{it} + \Theta \log L_{it} - \sum_{j(\neq i)=1}^{N} \nu w_{ij} \log L_{jt}$$
$$- \sum_{j(\neq i)=1}^{N} \zeta w_{ij} \log R_{jt} - \kappa \log P_{it} - \sum_{j(\neq i)=1}^{N} \xi w_{ij} \log P_{jt} + \Phi_{it}. \quad (4)$$

Φ_{it} is a rather cumbersome function of individual-specific effects through $\log \bar{Z}_i$ and time effects through $\log V_t$. It can be shown that:

$$\log A_{it} = (1-\beta_K)\log Q_{it} - \beta_L \log L_{it} + (\beta_K - 1)\eta \sum_{j(\neq i)=1}^{N} w_{ij} \log Q_{jt}$$
$$+\beta_L \eta \sum_{j(\neq i)=1}^{N} w_{ij} \log L_{jt} + D_{it}. \quad (5)$$

D_{it} is a complex function of individual-specific effects through $\log \bar{Z}_i$, $\sum_{j(\neq i)=1}^{N} \log \bar{Z}_j$ and time effects through $\sum_{j(\neq i)=1}^{N} \log a_{jt}$. By substituting equation (5) in equation (4) and by pooling N individuals (i.e., dual pooling), we get for a single time period:

$$\left(I_N + \frac{\zeta}{\psi} W_N\right)\log R_t = \left(\frac{\left\{\frac{\delta(1-\alpha)+\alpha}{\delta(1-\beta_K)}\right\}(1-\beta_K)}{\psi} I_N + \frac{\left\{\frac{\delta(1-\alpha)+\alpha}{\delta(1-\beta_K)}\right\}(\beta_K - 1)\eta}{\psi} W_N \right) \log Q_t$$
$$+ \left(\frac{\Theta - \beta_L \left\{\frac{\delta(1-\alpha)+\alpha}{\delta(1-\beta_K)}\right\}}{\psi} I_N + \frac{\beta_L \left\{\frac{\delta(1-\alpha)+\alpha}{\delta(1-\beta_K)}\right\} - \nu}{\psi} W_N \right) \log L_t$$
$$- \left(\frac{\kappa}{\psi} I_N + \frac{\xi}{\psi} W_N\right) \log P_t + \Phi_t + D_t \left\{\frac{\delta(1-\alpha)+\alpha}{\delta(1-\beta_K)}\right\}, \quad (6)$$

where $\log R_t$, $\log Q_t$, $\log L_t$ and $\log P_t$ are $(N \times 1)$ vectors, I_N is an $(N \times N)$ identity matrix and W_N is the $(N \times N)$ spatial weight matrix. Φ_t is the $(N \times 1)$ vector of Φ_{it} and D_t is the $(N \times 1)$ vector of D_{it}. Equation (6) gives the static desired level of the (log) nighttime lights pollution of own economy (i) and its neighbors (j) linked to explanatory variables. It can be simply written as

$$Y_t^* = X_t a + W_N X_t b + \mu_t,$$

where $Y_t = \left(I_N + \frac{\zeta}{\psi} W_N \right) \log R_t$, $X_t = \left[\log Q_t, \log L_t, \log P_t\right]$, and $W_N X_t = [W_N \log Q_t$, $W_N \log L_t, W_N \log P_t]$. Furthermore, $\mu_t\left(= \Phi_t + D_t\left(\delta(1-\alpha)+\alpha\right)/\left(\delta(1-\beta_K)\right)\right)$ defines individual- and time-specific effects through functions of $\log \bar{Z}_i$, $\sum_{j(\neq i)=1}^{N} \log \bar{Z}_j$ and time effects through $\log V_t$ and $\sum_{j(\neq i)=1}^{N} \log a_{jt}$.

Over time, counties face adjustment costs due to growth in population, economic activities, and related (dis)amenities. Thus, as in the literature on factor demands, one can assume a partial adjustment process. Whether expectations are adaptive or rational, a dynamic process of the following form is assumed (see, e.g., Blundell et al., 1996; Bresson et al., 1996; Hendry et al., 1984; Kennan, 1979):

$$Y_t - Y_{t-1} = (1-\phi)\left(Y_t^* - Y_{t-1}\right) + u_t,$$

where $0 < \phi < 1$ and u_t is a $(N \times 1)$ vector of idiosyncratic shocks, leading to

$$\begin{aligned} \log R_t = {} & \lambda W_N \log R_t + \phi \log R_{t-1} + \rho W_N \log R_{t-1} + \beta_1 \log Q_t + \theta_1 W_N \log Q_t + \\ & \beta_2 \log L_t + \theta_2 W_N \log L_t + \beta_3 \log P_t + \theta_3 W_N \log P_t + \phi\mu_t + u_t. \end{aligned} \tag{7}$$

The dynamics alluded to by Glaeser and Gottlieb (2009) is implicitly taken into account through the partial adjustment process of our structural model (6). This dynamics is also implicitly captured by the parameters of the reduced form (7). $\phi\mu_t$ captures both the individual and time-specific effects. To take into account the fact that they are intertwined, we incorporate the common correlated effects Γf_t, where f_t is a $(m \times 1)$ vector of m unknown common factors and Γ is a $(N \times m)$ matrix of factor loadings. We further assume that the *i.i.d.* idiosyncratic error u_t, with components $\varepsilon_t \sim (0, \sigma^2 I_N)$, possesses a spatial structure $\tilde{W}_N$, which may or may not be the same as W_N. Thus, the expression $\phi\mu_t + u_t$ in equation (7) is written as:

$$\phi\mu_t + u_t = \Gamma f_t + u_t, \text{ with } u_t = \tau \tilde{W}_N u_t + \varepsilon_t.$$

In the spatial econometrics literature, such a specification is known as a dynamic general nesting spatial model with common factors (Elhorst, 2021; Shi & Lee, 2017). The common correlated effects f_t allow to reduce any omitted variables bias and to take into account cross-sectional dependence between counties. These effects are estimated along with the other parameters of the model. In particular, the number of factors (m) is determined consistently along with their values and those associated with the $(N \times m)$ matrix of factor loadings Γ. Cross-sectional dependence is introduced through a finite number of unobservable common factors that may influence nighttime light differentially across counties. Such factors could include, for instance, aggregate technological shocks, oil price shocks, structural breaks, national policies aimed at reducing over-illumination or to promote energy conservation, state "dark skies" legislation – or even the downward trend in labor mobility – that may influence nighttime electricity consumption. The individualized factor loadings Γ reflect the impact of these unobservable common factors on the radiance of nighttime light in each county, *ceteris paribus*.

In the empirical analysis, R_{it} corresponds to the monthly average nighttime lights per square km of county i for year t, expressed in watt per square kilometer steradian, Q_{it} is be the GDP, expressed in millions of chained 2012 dollar per square km, L_{it} is the population density (population per square km) or the urban density (urban area of the county divided by the county area) and P_{it} is be the mean particulate matter ($PM_{2.5}$) concentration expressed in microgram per cubic meter ($\mu g / m^3$).

3. DATA AND EMPIRICAL STRATEGY

3.1. Data and Prima Facie Evidence

The analysis is based upon data drawn from two different sources. The physical data (nighttime light, $PM_{2.5}$ and urban density) were extracted from the from *AidData geoquery tool* (Goodman et al., 2019).[8] Data on county-level GDP, population, *etc.* were provided by the Bureau of Economic Analysis (BEA) using its *Data Retrieval Application Programming Interface (API)*.[9,10] The two datasets were merged using FIPS codes (Federal Information Processing System) and cover all $N = 3{,}071$ continental US counties for the 2012–2019 period.

Nighttime lighting corresponds to the average monthly radiance (or energy luminance) measured in watt per square kilometer steradian ($Watt/km^2/sr$. See Elvidge et al., 2017, 2021).[11] Satellite readings are provided several times a day. They are usually filtered to obtain images such as the one in Fig. 3.1, which depicts detailed point estimates of light pollution.[12] These data are then processed to obtain the average monthly radiance per county and included in the AidData geoquery tool. The observed sky glows are generally less than 100 km in diameter, but a few can be greater than 300 km or even 400 km (Duriscoe et al., 2014, 2018). Extremely large sky glows are observed in the East (from New Hampshire to Delaware), in the North (from Eastern Wisconsin to Pennsylvania), in the West (from San Francisco Bay to San Diego), in Florida, in the South (between Houston and Panama City) as well as areas around Las Vegas and Phoenix, to name but a few (see Fig. 3.2).

The top panel of Fig. 3.3 shows the county-wise distribution of average monthly nighttime lights, R, for the year 2012. Not surprisingly, most densely populated cities/counties have high levels of radiance.[13] Yet, close inspection of the data reveals that a number of small counties are also plagued by intensive nighttime lighting.[14] The bottom panel of the figure depicts the average *variation* in monthly

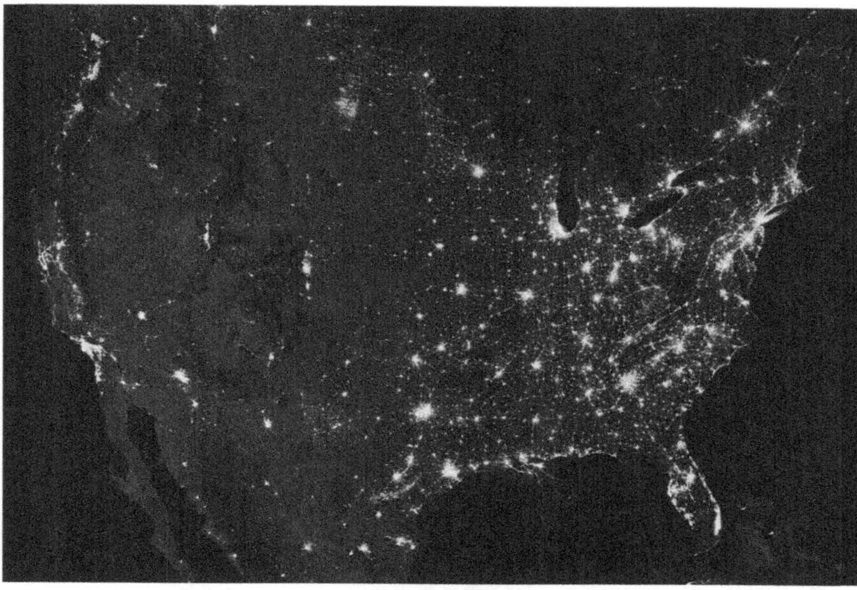

Fig. 3.1. Continental United States at Night – April–October 2012.

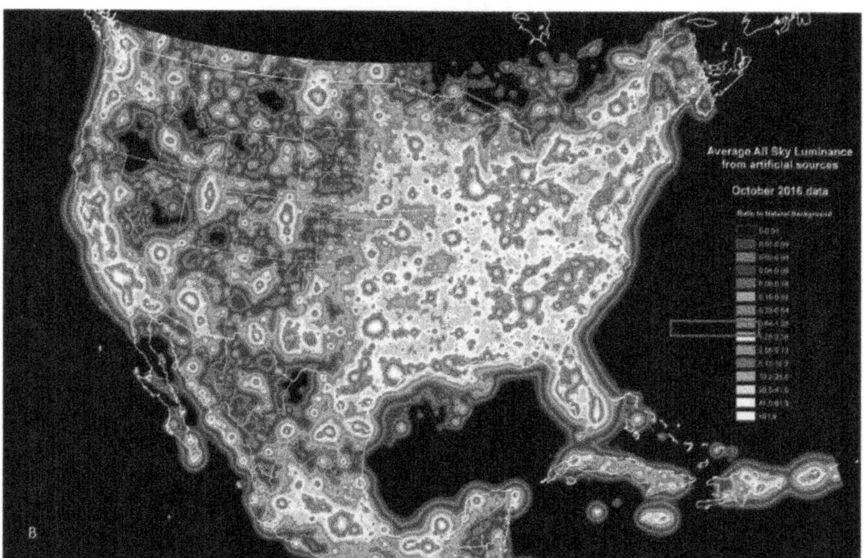

Fig. 3.2. All-Sky Luminance Ratio Over the Conterminous United States. Values of ALR of 0.3, 3.0 and >10.0, Correspond to Good, Poor Night Sky Quality, and Milky Way Invisible. (*Source*: Duriscoe et al., 2018, p. 141.)

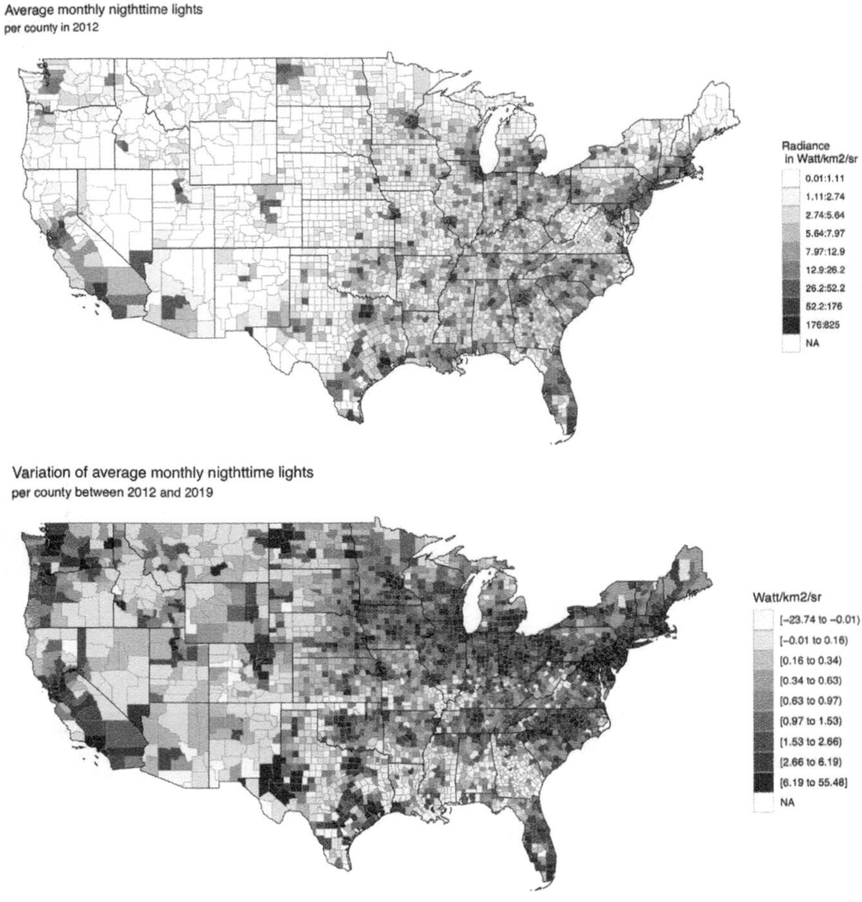

Fig. 3.3. Average Monthly Nighttime Lights Per County in 2012 and Variation Between 2012 and 2019.

radiance between 2012 and 2019. Over that period, the average US-wide annual growth rate was 2.28%. This has translated into increased radiance in most counties, but not all. Furthermore, the intensification is far from being uniform across counties. To gain some insight into the relation between nighttime lighting, R, and GDP, Fig. 3.4 plots state-level means over the entire 2012–2019 period. The relationship between the two appears to be log-linear.[15] As per Fig. 3.3, there is considerable heterogeneity across states. In particular, the District of Columbia (Washington, DC) has a radiance level (785.695 $Watt/km^2/sr$) that is 49 times higher than the national mean level and a GDP per square km that is 104 times higher than the national average. Likewise, while the states of New York, New Jersey, Massachusetts, and Maryland have both high levels of radiance and GDP per sq. km, at the other extreme, the states of Montana, Wyoming, North & South Dakota, and Idaho have low values for both.

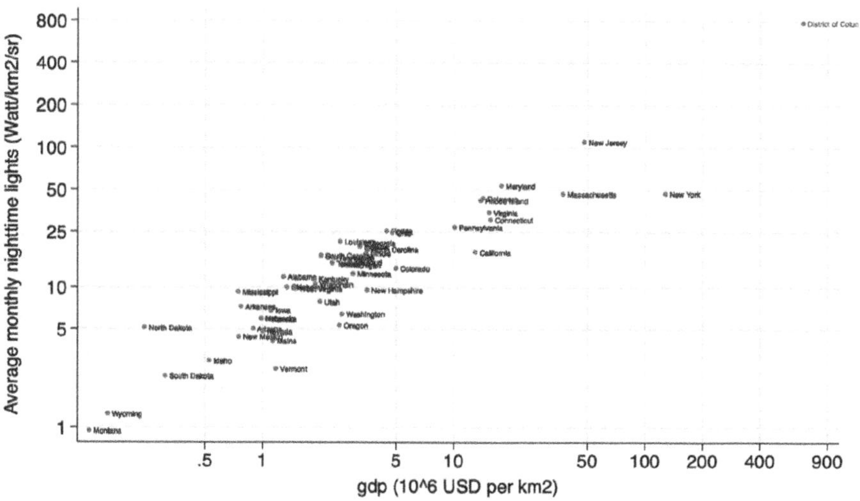

Fig. 3.4. Scatter Plot of State Means of Average Monthly Radiance and GDP/km^2.

As argued above, the heterogeneity in nighttime light exposure is very likely related to the cross-county variations in GDP as well as other factors. Table 3.1 reports the descriptive statistics of the main variables included in the econometric model. All variables exhibit wide variations, even when normalized by county surface. Thus, GDP (in 10^6 of chained 2012 \$/km^2), Q, population density/km^2, L, urban rates (urban area/county area in percent) and air pollution ($PM_{2.5}$ concentration in microgram/meter^3), P, vary considerably across counties.

As is customary with panel data, we have computed a series of CIPS unit root tests on the dependent variable as well as all exogenous variables (see Table B1 in the supplementary material).[16] The null assumption of unit roots cannot

Table 3.1. Descriptive Statistics, $N = 3{,}071$ US Counties (2012–2019).

	Mean	Min	Max	Std.dev
Radiance (R)	15.997	0.008	929.812	44.691
GDP	562.309	7.648	726943.301	24343.068
GDP/km^2 (Q)	6.384	0.026	7282.567	123.651
Population	103.615	0.008	10094.865	330.881
Population density	80.354	0.049	18769.750	486.056
Urban rate	2.748	0.000	85.912	7.901
$PM_{2.5}$ (P)	8.916	3.333	19.501	2.139

Notes: Radiance: average monthly radiance in *Watt/km^2/sr*.
GDP: in millions of chained 2012 dollar.
GDP/km^2: in millions of chained 2012 dollar/km^2.
Population: in thousands of inhabitants.
Population density: population/km^2.
Urban rate: urban area/county area (in %).
$PM_{2.5}$: particulate matter ($PM_{2.5}$) concentration in microgram per cubic meter ($\mu g/m^3$).

be rejected for log-R (radiance), log-Q (GDP/km^2) and urban rate. Conversely, trend stationary processes are not rejected at the 5% level for log-L (population density) and the log-P (air pollution). The effect of these unit roots is likely to be neutralized by the incorporation of common correlated factors in the econometric specification. Additional unit root tests will be conducted on the estimated residuals to validate this.

For estimation purposes, we computed a spatial matrix based on Haversine distances (in km) between county centroids using their latitudes and longitudes.[17] The distances range between 6.23 km and 3,686.92 km, with an average of 1,366.36 km. These are unreasonably large (quartiles $Q_1 = 766.96$ km and $Q_3 = 1230.61$ km). Thus, we have resorted to use a spatial distance matrix based on the 15 nearest neighboring counties. Doing so yields a mean distance of 73.67 km, and 10th percentile = 37.22 km, $Q_1 = 48.43$ km, $Q_3 = 86.96$ km, and 90th percentile = 117.88 km. These are more in line with sky glow radiance which are between 6.23 km and 401.02 km (see Duriscoe et al., 2014, 2018). The choice of a smaller number of neighbors is not without consequences on the estimation of the model.[18] The widest counties are mostly located in the West and Southwest (e.g., San Bernardino (CA) and Flagstaff (AZ) counties, whose approximate diameters are around 250 km). But there are also large ones in the North and the East such as St-Louis (MN), Houlton (ME), and Eagle River (MI) counties, whose approximate diameters are greater than 140 km. This heterogeneity in the spatial dimension of counties, which could be a potential source of misspecification in a simple spatial model, is taken into account at 4 levels in our model, which is the most general of the class of spatial models. Indeed, in equation (3.2) below, spatial heterogeneity is taken into account through the definition of the 15-neighbor spatial matrix (W_N), through contemporaneous spatial correlation (λ) and spatial time lag interaction (ρ), through the spatial error component structure of u_t and finally through the introduction of factor loadings Γ associated with common correlated effects f_t.

From this spatial matrix, we define the row-normalized Haversine inverse distance matrix (W_N) which has a non-sparsity rate of 0.488% and whose non-zero weights (w_{ij}) range between 0.0229 and 0.3283 with an average of 0.0666 (see Fig. B4 in the supplementary material).

The inclusion of factors into our model is meant to capture potential cross-sectional dependence. As pointed out by Elhorst (2021) and Elhorst et al. (2021), cross-sectional dependence can range from non-existent, to weak, strong, and global. Bailey et al. (2016) characterize the degree of dependence through an exponent parameter α defined over the [0, 1] interval to measure the degree of cross-sectional dependence. Weak or local (spatial) dependence ($\alpha < 1/2$) has been modeled extensively in the spatial econometrics literature with seminal contributions dating back to the 1980s. The literature on modeling strong or global cross-sectional dependence ($\alpha > 1/2$) is more recent. The initial approaches (Bai & Ng, 2002; Pesaran, 2006) suggested the use of the cross-sectional averages (i.e., time means) of the variables in the regression, or even other variables not taken into account in the regression. More recently, the principal components approach has been emphasized, hence we speak of unknown common factors.

Table 3.2. Cross-Sectional Dependence Exponent Estimation.

	α	Std. Err.	Lower Bound 95%	Upper Bound 95%
log*R*	0.9699	0.0155	0.9396	1.0001
log*Q*	0.9064	0.0192	0.8688	0.9441
Urban rate	0.8865	0.0084	0.8700	0.9030
log*P*	1.0008	0.0088	0.9837	1.0180

The latest generation of dynamic spatial model (the one we use) refers to local dependence and strong dependence (or global cross-dependence) to describe two types of dependence. The local spatial dependence is associated to the endogenous spatial lag, the exogenous spatial lags and to a spatial lag in the error term. The global cross-sectional dependence is associated with cross-sectional averages or principal components with heterogeneous coefficients. Moreover, this model accounts for dynamic effects by means of the pure dynamic effect (ϕ) and of the spatial time lag interaction (ρ).

Estimation of the exponents α on our variables is given in Table 3.2. These estimates confirm the need to specify the model with both a local cross-sectional dependence and a global cross-sectional dependence.

3.2. The Econometric Methodology

The model we specify belongs to the class of dynamic general nesting spatial models with common factors and can be estimated using the quasi maximum likelihood (QML) estimation method of Shi and Lee (2017). Indeed, the specification in equation (7) is of the form:

$$\begin{gathered} Y_t = \lambda W_N Y_t + \phi Y_{t-1} + \rho W_N Y_{t-1} + X_t \beta + \Gamma f_t + u_t \\ \text{with } u_t = \tau \tilde{W}_N u_t + \varepsilon_t, \end{gathered} \tag{8}$$

where Y_t is an N-dimensional column vector of observed dependent variables and X_t is an $(N \times (K-2))$ matrix of exogenous regressors, so that the total number of right-hand side variables is equal to K $(Y_{t-1}, W_N Y_{t-1}, X_t)$.[19] The advantage of this model is that it accommodates two types of cross sectional dependences, namely, local dependence and global (strong) dependence. Individual units are potentially impacted by time varying unknown common factors f_t, which captures global (strong) dependence. The number of unobserved factors is assumed to be a fixed constant r that is much smaller than N and T. The matrix of $(N \times r)$ factor loadings Γ and the $(T \times r)$ factors $F_T = (f_1, f_2, \ldots, f_T)'$ are not observed and are treated as parameters. The $(N \times N)$ spatial weights matrices W_N and $\tilde{W}_N$ are used to model spatial dependences. The term $\lambda W_N Y_t$ describes the contemporaneous spatial interactions, ϕY_{t-1} captures the pure dynamic effect and $\rho W_N Y_{t-1}$ is a spatial time lag of interactions that captures diffusion. λ is the spatial dependence parameter, ϕ is the autoregressive time dependence parameter and ρ is the spatio-temporal diffusion parameter. As stated above, the idiosyncratic error u_t depends on ε_t which are assumed $i.i.d.(0, \sigma^2 I_N)$, where I_N is an $(N \times N)$ identity matrix.

u_t also possesses a spatial error component structure $\tilde{W}_N$, which may or may not be the same as W_N. The specification of a dynamic general nesting spatial econometric model for spatial panels with unknown common factors (DGNSP-CCE) follows directly from the derivation of the structural model (6) associated with a partial adjustment process whose reduced form boils down to equations (7) and (8). The DGNSP-CCE specification corresponds to the *fourth generation of spatial econometric models* as coined by Elhorst (2021). According to Elhorst (2014), about halfway through the decade 2010–2020, three generations of spatial econometric models had been developed prior to the DGNSP-CCE model. The first generation consists of models based on cross-sectional data, the second generation includes non-dynamic models based on spatial panel data and the third generation encompasses dynamic spatial panel data models. Chronologically, we have moved from specific to general specifications. The DGNSP-CCE model accounts for local spatial dependence, dynamics, and global cross-sectional dependence. It generalizes the traditional controls for time-invariant and spatial-invariant variables by unit-specific and time-specific effects. With these properties, it is the most general spatial econometric model currently available, as Elhorst (2021) rightly points out.

The parameters of (8) are $\theta = (\delta', \lambda, \tau)'$ with $\delta = (\phi, \rho, \beta')'$, σ^2, Γ and F_T. The predetermined and the exogeneous variables are collected in a $(N \times K)$ matrix $Z_t = [Y_{t-1}, W_N Y_{t-1}, X_t]$. Denote $S(\lambda) = I_N - \lambda W_N$ and $M(\tau) = I_N - \tau \tilde{W}_N$. The sample-averaged quasi-log likelihood function is

$$\begin{aligned} \log Q_L\left(\theta, \sigma^2, \Gamma, F_T\right) &= -\frac{1}{2}\log 2\pi - \frac{1}{2}\log\sigma^2 + \frac{1}{N}\log|S(\lambda)M(\tau)| \\ &\quad - \frac{1}{2\sigma^2 NT}\sum_{t=1}^{T}\left(S(\lambda)Y_t - Z_t\delta - \Gamma f_t\right)' \\ &\quad \times M'(\tau)M(\tau)\left(S(\lambda)Y_t - Z_t\delta - \Gamma f_t\right). \end{aligned} \tag{9}$$

Concentrating out σ^2 from the objective function (9) and dropping the constant terms leads to

$$\begin{aligned} \log Q_L\left(\theta, \tilde{\Gamma}, F_T\right) &= \frac{1}{N}\log|S(\lambda)M(\tau)| \\ &\quad - \frac{1}{2}\log\left\{\begin{array}{l} \frac{1}{NT}\sum_{t=1}^{T}\left(M(\tau)\left(S(\lambda)Y_t - Z_t\delta\right) - \tilde{\Gamma} f_t\right)' \\ \times\left(M(\tau)\left(S(\lambda)Y_t - Z_t\delta\right) - \tilde{\Gamma} f_t\right) \end{array}\right\}, \end{aligned}$$

where $\tilde{\Gamma} = M(\tau)\Gamma$. Shi and Lee (2017) concentrate out the factors and their loadings using the principal component theory to get the following concentrated log-likelihood:[20]

$$\begin{aligned} \log Q_L(\theta) &= \max_{F_T, \tilde{\Gamma}} \log Q_L\left(\theta, \tilde{\Gamma}, F_T\right) \\ &= \frac{1}{N}\log|S(\lambda)M(\tau)| - \frac{1}{2}\log L_T(\theta) \end{aligned}$$

with

$$\log L_T(\theta)=\frac{1}{NT}\sum_{i=r+1}^{N}\varpi_i\left(\begin{array}{l}M(\tau)\left(S(\lambda)Y-\sum_{k=1}^{K}Z_k\delta_k\right)\\ \times\left(S(\lambda)Y-\sum_{k=1}^{K}Z_k\delta_k\right)'M'(\tau)\end{array}\right),$$

where Y (resp. Z_k) is the $(N\times T)$ matrix of the dependent variable (resp. of the kth explanatory variable). The estimate for $\tilde{\Gamma}$ can be obtained as the eigenvectors associated with the first r largest eigenvalues of $M(\tau)\left(S(\lambda)Y-\sum_{k=1}^{K}Z_k\delta_k\right)\left(S(\lambda)Y-\sum_{k=1}^{K}Z_k\delta_k\right)'M'(\tau)$. By inverting N and T, the estimate for F_T can be similarly obtained.

If we interpret the factors f_t as omitted variables, an exploratory first-stage regression can be used to determine how many are likely present in the data. Several approaches have been proposed to that end such as Cattell (1966)'s scree plot test, Bai and Ng (2002)'s PC and IC criteria, Onatski (2010)'s edge distribution estimator and Ahn and Horenstein (2013)'s eigenvalue ratio tests.[21]

4. ESTIMATION RESULTS

In order to investigate the robustness of our results, we have estimated three different specifications: (1) the dynamic spatial autoregressive model (DSAR) with fixed effects, (2) the dynamic spatial Durbin model (DSDM) with fixed effects and (3) the dynamic general nesting spatial panel model with common correlated effects (DGNSP-CCE) as in equation (8).[22] Note that the DSAR and DSDM models are nested within the DGNSP-CCE. As per the above discussion, we conducted a series of tests proposed by Cattell (1966), Onatski (2010), and Ahn and Horenstein (2013). All concluded that the data were compatible with $r=2$ common factors (see Section C in the supplementary material).

Table 3.3 reports the parameter estimates of the three specifications as well as several specification tests.[23,24] As shown in the bottom panel, all three models satisfy the stationarity condition ($\lambda+\phi+\rho<1$) based on a $\chi^2(1)$ Wald test (see Yu et al., 2008). Likewise, the data are consistent with the assumption that the spatio-temporal diffusion parameter is equal to the negative of the product of the spatial dependence parameter and the autoregressive time dependence parameter ($\rho=-\lambda\phi$). Parent and LeSage (2011) have shown that the latter greatly simplifies the estimation of such models. This is perhaps why it is customarily imposed in empirical work. Finally, the Juodis and Reese (2022) cross-dependence test, CD_W, confirms the independence of the estimated residuals.[25] The middle panel reports the R^2 statistics as well as the estimated variance parameter, σ^2. Overall, the three specifications yield similar estimates of σ^2 and fit the data relatively well.[26]

Table 3.3. Dynamic Spatial Panel Models of log-Average Monthly Radiance $N = 3{,}071$ US Counties, 2012–2019.

	DSAR		DSDM		DGNSP-CCE	
	Coef.	*T*-stat	Coef.	*T*-stat	Coef.	*T*-stat
λ: $W_N \log R$	0.905	212.274	0.901	205.918	0.958	317.477
φ: $\log R_{-1}$	0.748	120.529	0.747	119.708	0.338	47.014
ρ: $W_N \log R_{-1}$	−0.726	−97.051	−0.729	−95.530	−0.326	−42.345
Covariates:						
$\log Q$	0.033	5.304	0.033	4.657	0.026	3.320
$\log P$	0.021	1.059	−0.350	−7.812	0.236	2.311
Urban rate	0.001	0.383	−0.003	−0.911	0.008	2.029
Spatialized covariates:						
$W_N \log Q$			−0.015	−1.085	−0.024	−2.014
$W_N \log P$			0.428	8.257	−0.188	−1.763
W_N Urban rate			0.012	1.576	0.000	−0.673
Spatial error component:						
τ					−0.472	−17.256
σ	0.055		0.066		0.064	
R^2	0.978		0.974		0.974	
Adjusted R^2	0.978		0.974		0.964	
Tests:	Test	*P*-value	Test	*P*-value	Test	*P*-value
Wald: $\lambda + \varphi + \rho = 1$	210.255	0.000	229.523	0.000	60.470	0.000
Wald: $\rho = -\lambda\varphi$	0.000	0.999	0.000	0.999	0.906	0.341
CD_W	0.061	0.952	0.082	0.935	0.254	0.800

Notes: DSAR: Dynamic Spatial AutoRegressive model with fixed effects.
DSDM: Dynamic Spatial Durbin Model with fixed effects.
DGNSP-CCE: Dynamic General Nesting Spatial Panel model with Common Correlated Effects.
CD_W: Juodis and Reese (2022) cross-dependence test.

The main differences between the models occur with respect to the slope parameters. Though the DSAR and DSDM models yield similar estimates for λ, ϕ, and ρ, they differ with respect to the direct impact of pollution on radiance. Whereas the DSAR model finds no relation between the two, the DSDM model concludes the opposite. Note that the parameter is negative, which implies that additional air pollution lowers local radiance. Yet, the fact that the parameter of the spatialized air pollution ($W_N \log P$) is positive and statistically significant indicates that the spillover effects are important. Thus, the radiance level in county i increases with the $PM_{2.5}$ concentration in county j. Taken together, the two estimates suggest there is a positive link between air pollution and local radiance as found by e.g. Ścieżor and Czaplicka (2020). Finally, note that neither specifications find a relation between urban rate and radiance, but that both imply that spatial dependence (λ) is somewhat larger than persistence (ϕ).

The last two columns of Table 3.3 report the parameter estimates and the T-statistics of the DGNSP-CCE model. Contrary to the two other models, all the parameters are significantly different from zero (except for the spatialized urban rate, W_NUrban rate). While the impact of the spatial dependence ($\lambda = 0.9584$) is still sizable, the autoregressive time dependence effect has decreased significantly ($\phi = 0.3375$). As with the other specifications, the temporal dynamics is less important than the spatial dynamics, albeit both are much smaller in magnitude. The parameter estimates of GDP/km^2, $\log Q$, and of air pollution, $\log P$, are slightly larger in absolute value than their spatialized counterparts. For reasons mentioned below, these cannot be directly compared. Lastly, note that the parameter estimate of τ is significantly different from zero. Thus, the DGSNP-CCE specification must be preferred to the other two. The incorporation of a spatial error component structure in the disturbances u_t as in equation (8) modifies most slope parameters as well as their statistical significance. As mentioned above, the null assumption of unit roots could not be rejected for certain covariates. When computing IPS and CIPS unit root tests on the estimated residuals, as conjectured, the null hypothesis is fortunately rejected in all three specifications (see Table D2 in the supplementary material).

The parameter estimates of the DGNSP-CCE model do not correspond to marginal effects (see LeSage & Pace, 2009) and so may not be directly compared to those of the DSAR or DSDM models. On the other hand, short and long run direct, indirect and total effects may be computed through impact multipliers. Thus, let $\partial \log R_{ti} / \partial x_{k,ti}$ represent the contemporaneous direct effect on county *i*'s average monthly radiance arising from a change in its *k*th explanatory variable (see Debarsy et al., 2012; Elhorst, 2014). The cross-partial derivative $\partial \log R_{tj} / \partial x_{k,ti}$ measures the contemporaneous spatial spillover effect on county *j*, $j \neq i$, of an increase in *i*'s *k*th explanatory variable. Since the model is dynamic, the partial derivatives of a change $x_{k,ti}$ may be computed for each county at various time horizons $t+s$. Written in a matrix form, and following LeSage and Pace (2009), the cumulative direct effect (i.e., cumulative own-county impacts) is measured as the average of the diagonal elements, while the cumulative indirect effect (i.e., diffusion over space and time) is measured by the average of the row sums of the non-diagonal elements of that matrix. Naturally, the cumulative total effect is the sum of the cumulative direct and indirect effects (see Elhorst, 2021, and the supplementary material).

Table 3.4 reports the short and long run direct, indirect, and total marginal effects of various covariates on the logarithm of average monthly radiance. The direct short run elasticities of average monthly radiance relative to GDP/km^2 range between [0.026;0.027] while spillover effects range between [0.001;0.095], leading to total short run elasticities comprised between 0.027 and 0.122 with a sample mean at 0.050. In the long run, the total elasticities increase to [0.041;1.54] with a mean at 0.069. Fig. 3.5 reveals the spatial and temporal differences in the total marginal effects of a 1% increase in GPD/km^2. Interestingly, the maps show that counties with the highest short and long run elasticities are not necessarily

Table 3.4. Short Run and Long Run Direct, Indirect and Total Marginal Effects on Average Monthly Radiance.

		Min	10%	25%	50%	75%	90%	Max	Mean
GDP/km^2									
Short run	Direct	0.026	0.026	0.026	0.026	0.026	0.026	0.027	0.026
	Indirect	0.001	0.012	0.018	0.024	0.029	0.036	0.095	0.024
	Total	0.027	0.038	0.045	0.050	0.055	0.062	0.122	0.050
Long run	Direct	0.039	0.040	0.040	0.040	0.040	0.040	0.041	0.040
	Indirect	0.002	0.015	0.023	0.029	0.036	0.043	0.113	0.030
	Total	0.041	0.055	0.062	0.069	0.075	0.083	0.154	0.069
Urban rate									
Short run	Direct	0.009	0.010	0.010	0.011	0.011	0.012	0.019	0.011
	Indirect	0.011	0.093	0.142	0.183	0.225	0.275	0.733	0.186
	Total	0.020	0.103	0.153	0.194	0.235	0.286	0.752	0.197
Long run	Direct	0.013	0.015	0.016	0.016	0.017	0.018	0.028	0.016
	Indirect	0.015	0.130	0.196	0.251	0.305	0.372	0.970	0.254
	Total	0.029	0.145	0.212	0.267	0.322	0.390	0.998	0.271
$PM_{2.5}$ concentration									
Short run	Direct	0.238	0.244	0.246	0.248	0.250	0.253	0.289	0.249
	Indirect	0.052	0.449	0.685	0.884	1.083	1.324	3.535	0.898
	Total	0.291	0.694	0.932	1.132	1.332	1.577	3.824	1.147
Long run	Direct	0.360	0.368	0.370	0.373	0.376	0.380	0.429	0.374
	Indirect	0.073	0.612	0.926	1.185	1.441	1.755	4.576	1.200
	Total	0.432	0.982	1.297	1.558	1.816	2.138	5.005	1.574

those with the highest radiance. Thus, locations such as Los Angeles, Las Vegas, Phoenix, Miami, Chicago, New York, ... are little impacted by a 1% increase in their respective GDP/km^2 (see Fig. 3.3). It is as if their respective counties had reached such a level of light pollution that any increase in economic activity could hardly have any additional effect. On the other hand, nighttime light pollution of large peri-urban areas around large cities such as Seattle, San Francisco, Denver, ... is very sensitive to increases in GDP/km^2. Likewise, clusters of counties located on the Utah-Idaho border or the Washington-Idaho border, for example, are also highly sensitive. It is therefore in such areas that pollution control policies may yield the greatest benefits. Interestingly, a one-percentage point increase in urban rate increases radiance but by a much larger magnitude than GDP/km^2. In addition, spillover effects are way more important than own-effects, and total effects exhibit considerable heterogeneity in the long run ([0.029;0.998]. See Fig. 3.6). Finally, air pollution is found to have the greatest impact on radiance. A 1% increase in $PM_{2.5}$ translates into increases in radiance anywhere between 0.29–3.82 (short run) and 0.43–5.0 (long run) (see Fig. 3.7). The direct effects are relatively constant and similar in the short and long run. The indirect effects, on the other hand, increase steadily as we move along the different quantiles and dominate the direct effects almost throughout.

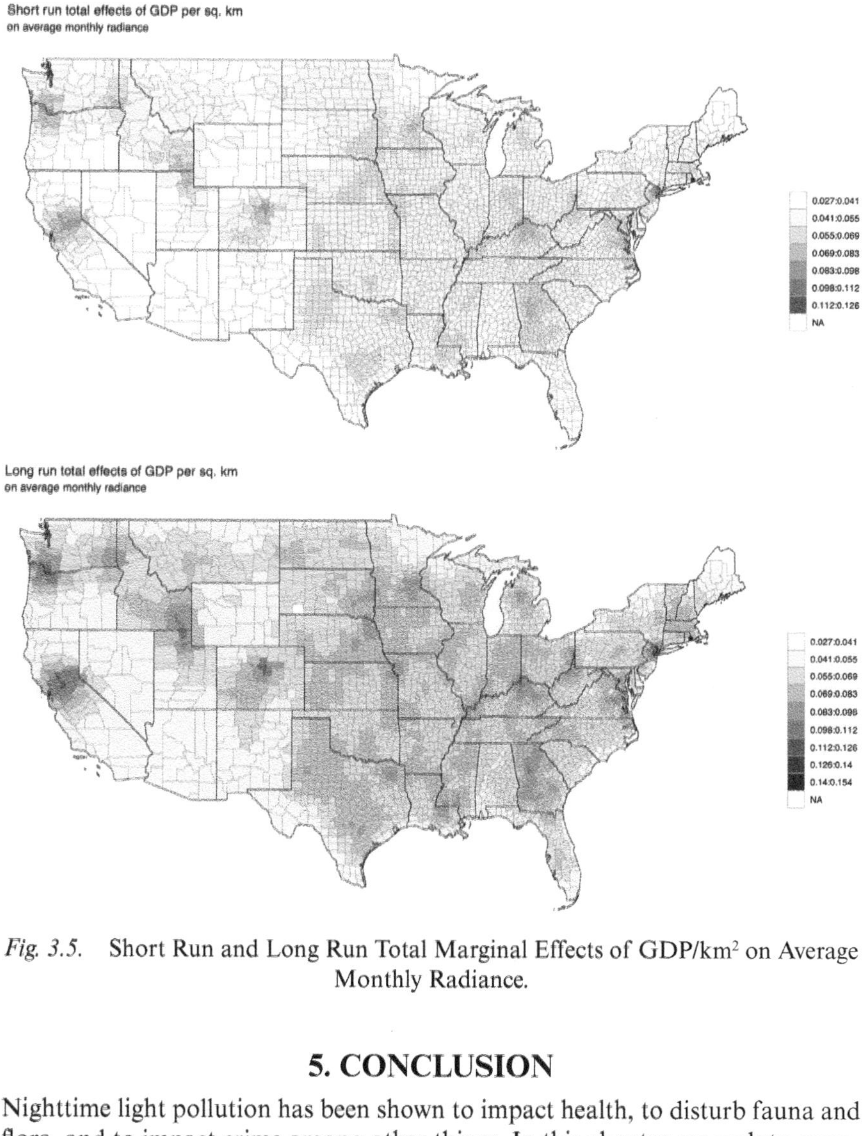

Fig. 3.5. Short Run and Long Run Total Marginal Effects of GDP/km^2 on Average Monthly Radiance.

5. CONCLUSION

Nighttime light pollution has been shown to impact health, to disturb fauna and flora, and to impact crime among other things. In this chapter, we seek to quantify the link between economic growth and nighttime light pollution. To that end, we use detailed economic and physical data for 3071 counties in the continental USA over the 2012–2019 period. We extend a standard spatial urban model à la da Silva et al. (2017) to establish a link between the two. In particular, the model shows how light pollution (radiance) depends upon wealth (GDP), urban density, and air pollution. The proposed spatial urban model additionally accounts for spatial interaction effects and leads to a dynamic general nesting spatial model with common factors. The model is estimated using a QML estimator.

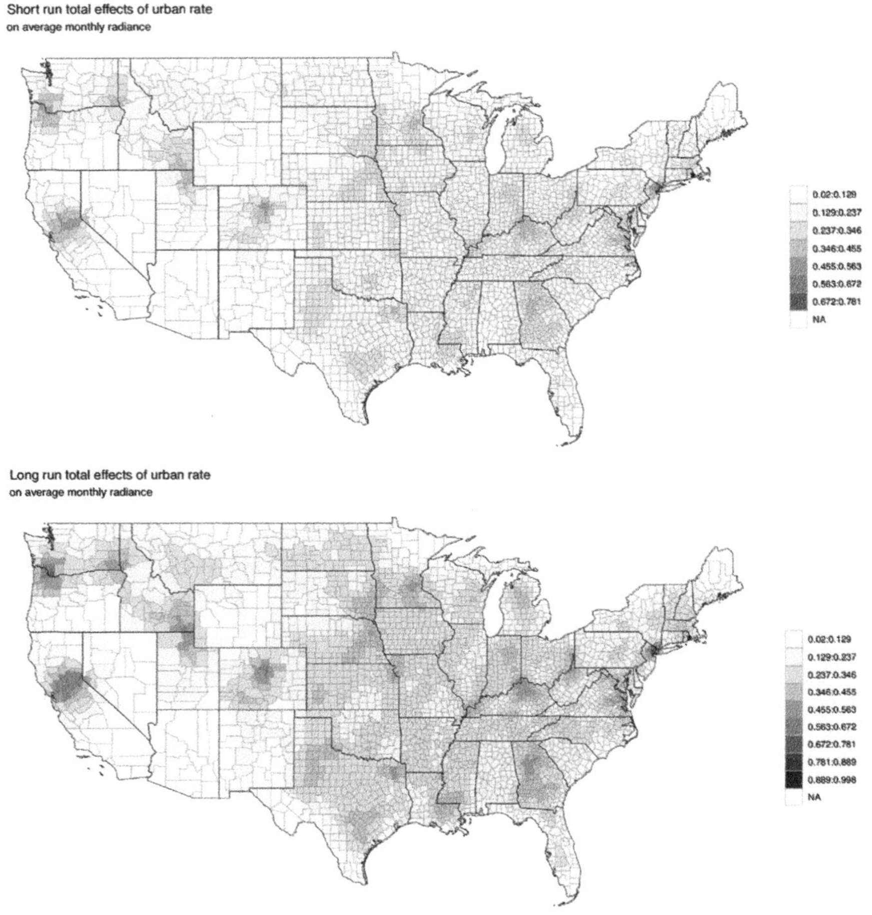

Fig. 3.6. Short Run and Long Run Total Marginal Effects of Urban Rate on Average Monthly Radiance.

According to our results, nighttime light pollution depends both upon own (direct) GDP and that of neighboring counties (spillover effects). Both the short and long run marginal effects emphasize the importance of spillover effects on radiance levels. The same applies to urban density and air pollution. Interestingly, our results unearth considerable county-wise heterogeneity in radiance response: Those with high levels of radiance are little affected by further increases in wealth. Those with lower levels are much more sensitive. It follows that policies to mitigate light pollution are likely to be more successful in the latter than in the former.

This chapter is the first to our knowledge to estimate a dynamic space-time model with unknown common factors when investigating the impact of economic activities and environmental pollution on nighttime light pollution. Previous literature has mainly focused on the interest of nighttime lights as

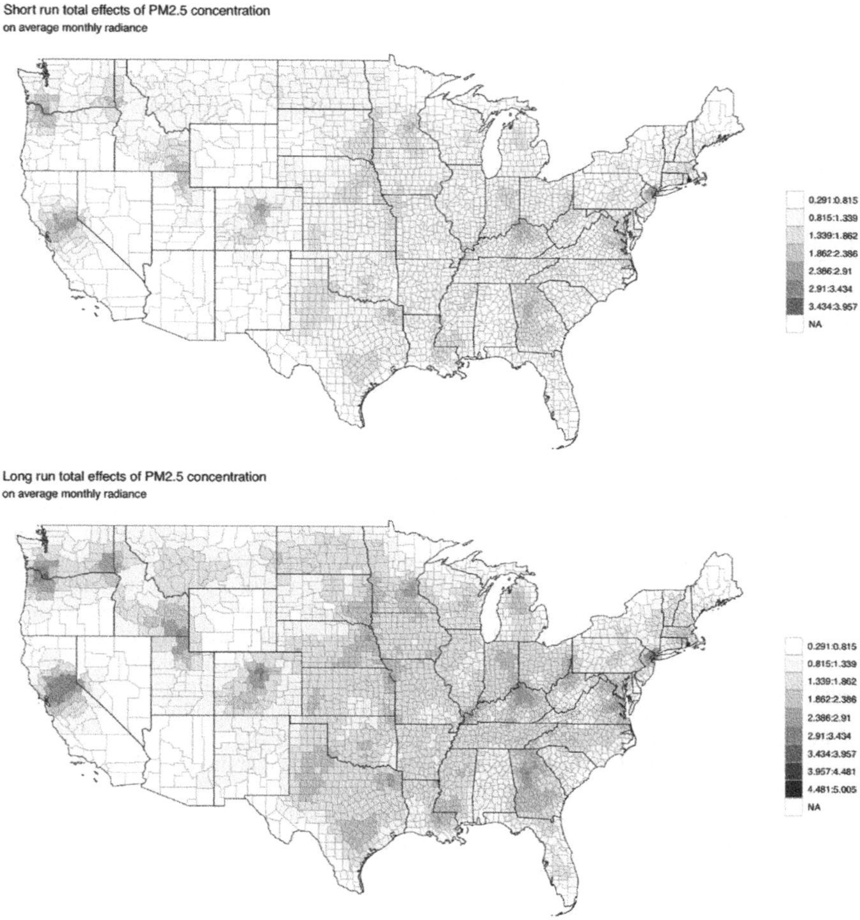

Fig. 3.7. Short Run and Long Run Total Marginal Effects of $PM_{2.5}$ Concentration on Average Monthly Radiance.

a proxy to correct the national accounts GDP, mainly from developing countries and autocracies (Martinez, 2022). Our specification and our estimates are novel in this respect. The strong statistical significance of the spatial coefficients (λ, ρ, and τ) and those associated with spatialized exogenous variables in the DGNSP-CCE model confirms the relevance of using a dynamic space-time model with unknown common factors when investigating nighttime pollution. The removal of all or any parameters in a non-spatial model would result in biased estimates due to omitted variables. This relates to the general-to-specific modeling approach and to the model selection issue. The DGNSP-CCE model, which is the most general specification, is already congruent.[27] Bailey et al. (2016)'s "α exponents" approach referred to in Section 3.1 is well suited to test the general-to-specific approach. It allows to test for the presence of weak only (local) cross-sectional dependence or for the coexistence of weak (local) and strong (global) cross-sectional dependencies. As mentioned above, the strong statistical significance of the ancillary parameters implies that our model cannot be made more parsimonious. We would conclude similarly were we to adopt a specific-to-general approach.

The dynamic general nesting spatial models with common correlated factors (DGNSP-CCE) nests both the Dynamic Spatial Autoregressive Model (DSAR) and the Dynamic Spatial Durbin Model (DSDM). The DGNSP-CCE outperforms the other two despite the fact that all three fit the data rather well. This is essentially due to the introduction of the common factors. Yet, the model could eventually be enriched by introducing additional covariates such as highway networks, transport flows, business centers, land cover classification (urban area, cropland, grassland, wetland, forest, etc.). This will be the subject of future research.

NOTES

1. Light trespass occurs when spill light, which is light that falls outside the area intended to be lit, is cast where it is not wanted. A typical light trespass problem occurs when a strong light enters the window of one's home from the outside. Glare is when light strikes your eyes directly from the source. Over-illumination is the excessive use of lighting, such as leaving lights on when they are not being used or using poorly designed lighting that illuminates areas that do not need to be illuminated. Light clutter refers to excessive groupings of lights, especially bright or flashing lights, which can generate confusion or accidents. Sky glow is the illumination of the night sky, most referred to as the "glow" effect that appears over populated areas at night. Sky glow is mainly a combination of reflected light from illuminated areas and badly directed light escaping into the sky, where it is scattered by the atmosphere and redirected back at the ground. If the sky glow is generally observed at distances lower than 100 km, some of them can be seen at more than 400 km of distance. This is the case for example of the lights of Las Vegas and Phoenix in the United States (Duriscoe et al., 2014, 2018).
2. VIIRS nighttime light data have been included in the AidData geoquery tool to allow extraction at subnational levels (see Goodman et al., 2019).
3. For population estimates, see BEA Methods Statement in https://www2.census.gov/programs-surveys/popest/technical-documentation/methodology/2020-2021/methods-statement-v2021.pdf.
4. See also Debarsy et al. (2012) and da Silva et al. (2017).
5. See Section A of the supplementary material for a detailed derivation of the model. The supplementary material can be downloaded from Emerald's website, www.emerald.com. See the prelims on the copyright page of this Volume.
6. Despite a global long-term downward trend in labor mobility in the United States, mobility is found to be increasing for the highly skilled but decreasing for the low skilled over the period 1995–2000 (Ganong & Shoag, 2017). Moreover, according to data from the American Community Surveys, the five-year outmigration flows are increasing between 2012–2017 (Coate & Mangum, 2021) and according to data from the Current Population Surveys, unconditional county-to-county flows were relatively stable over our sample window (see CPS Historical Migration/Geographic Mobility Tables).
7. As emphasized by Glaeser and Gottlieb (2009, p. 985), *"running naïve income change regressions, without also considering changes in employment and housing prices, misses the fact that labor is quite mobile across places within the United States"*. In other words, focusing on raw outmigration flows alone may be misleading.
8. https://www.aiddata.org/geoquery
9. BEA Data Retrieval Application Programming Interface (API).
10. See the appendix for a detailed description of all variables.

11. The steradian (*sr*) is a unit derived from the meter (*m*). Its expression, in base units, is $sr = m^2 \cdot m^{-2}$. It is thus a dimensionless unit. The energy intensity is expressed in watt per steradian and the radiance, in watt per square meter steradian. The original data in the AidData geoquery tool was measured in $nanoWatt/cm^2/sr$ which we converted into $Watt/km^2/sr$.

12. See https://www.nasa.gov/mission_pages/NPP/news/earth-at-night.html for details.

13. This includes the Northeast region between Washington and Boston, coastal Florida, the regions of Chicago, San Francisco, Los Angeles, but also Las Vegas, Phoenix, Houston, Dallas, Denver, Seattle, Salt Lake City, etc.

14. For example, the counties of McKenzie, Mountrail, and Williams in North Dakota, the county of Bernalillo in New Mexico, the counties of Modland, Ector, Winkler in Texas and the counties of Ada, Canyon in Idaho, etc.

15. The same applies for population density, urban density, and air pollution (see Figs. B1 to B3 in the supplementary material).

16. Cross-sectional augmented IPS (CIPS) unit root test (Pesaran, 2007) allows for cross-sectional dependence by augmenting the Im-Pesaran-Shin (IPS) unit root test (Im et al., 2003) with a cross-section average. The IPS and CIPS tests relax the assumption of a common autoregressive parameter in the augmented Dickey-Fuller (ADF) specification contrary to other standard tests such as the Levin-Lin-Chu, Harris-Tzavalis or Breitung tests.

17. The county distances are great-circle distances calculated using the Haversine formula based on internal points in the geographic area. The Haversine formula is given by

$$d = 2r\arcsin\left(\sqrt{\sin^2\left(\frac{\Phi_2 - \Phi_1}{2}\right) + \cos\Phi_1\cos\Phi_2\sin^2\left(\frac{\Lambda_2 - \Lambda_1}{2}\right)}\right).$$

d is the distance between the two points along a great circle of the sphere (Earth). It is the spherical distance (i.e., the shortest distance between two points on the surface of a sphere). r is the radius of the sphere (637.8137 km for Earth). Φ_1 and Φ_2 are the latitudes of points 1 and 2 in radians, respectively. Likewise, Λ_1 and Λ_2 are the longitudes of points 1 and 2 in radians, respectively.

18. For instance, choosing the 5 nearest neighbors does not allow to take into account sky glows with a diameter greater than 213 km. Consequently, choosing a number of neighbors that does not include a radius of 400 km risks impacting the estimates and yield unlikely marginal effects. Our specification is not very sensitive to the choice of 15 or 20 neighbors as long as we take into account the maximum observed distances of sky glows. Conversely, if we restrict the spatial matrix to few neighbors (and therefore to shorter distances), the estimates of the marginal effects are strongly biased. Estimates based on 5 and 20 neighbors confirm this and are available upon request.

19. In our case, the $X = \left[x_t, W_N x_t\right]$ matrix contains both unspatialized (x_t) and spatialized ($W_N x_t$) exogeneous variables where $x_t = \left[\log Q_t, urban\ rate_t, \log P_t\right]$.

20. For an $(N \times T)$ matrix H_T:

$$\min_{F_T,\tilde{\Gamma}} \operatorname{tr}\left(\left(H_T - \tilde{\Gamma}F_T'\right)\left(H_T - \tilde{\Gamma}F_T'\right)'\right) = \sum_{i=r+1}^{N} \varpi_i\left(H_T H_T'\right)$$

where $\varpi_i(A)$ denotes the ith largest eigenvalue of an $(N \times N)$ symmetric matrix A with eigenvalues listed in a decreasing order such that $\varpi_N(A) \leq \varpi_{N-1}(A) \leq \cdots \leq \varpi_1(A)$.

21. See Ditzen and Reese (2023) for a recent synthesis. Shi and Lee (2017) have proposed to start by consistently estimating the regression coefficients and then to determine the number of factors from the residuals. This ensures the number is estimated consistently.

22. The DSAR and DSDM specifications correspond to:

$$DSAR: Y_t = \lambda W_N Y_t + \phi Y_{t-1} + \rho W_N Y_{t-1} + x_t \beta + \xi + \varepsilon_t$$
$$DSDM: Y_t = \lambda W_N Y_t + \phi Y_{t-1} + \rho W_N Y_{t-1} + x_t \beta + W_N x_t \gamma + \xi + \varepsilon_t,$$

where ξ is the $(N \times 1)$ vector of fixed effects (see Lee & Yu, 2015). The QML estimation methods of the DSDM and DSAR models are available in the R library *SDPDmod.* The Matlab code of the QML estimation method of Shi and Lee (2017) is available on Wei Shi's web page (https://sites.google.com/view/wei-shi). His Matlab code was executed within our R code using the *matlabr* library, an interface that allows system calls to Matlab.

23. For the sake of brevity, we do not report the estimates of the two common factors, f_t, nor of the matrix of the factor loadings, Γ.

24. We tested different specifications in which the introduction of the variable log (population/km^2) ($\log L$) always proved irrelevant whether the urban rate was present or not.

25. We have used the CD_W test instead of the *CD* test proposed by Pesaran (2004) because Juodis and Reese (2022) have shown that the *CD* test tends to over reject the null in the presence of latent factors. Juodis and Reese (2022) have instead proposed a randomized test statistic to correct for over-rejection (see also Pesaran & Xie, 2021).

26. While all three specifications fit the data relatively well, the DGNSP-CCE provides yet a better fit for counties with values such as those of the District of Columbia: The estimated quantiles are closer to the observed quantiles and the normal Q-Q plot of residuals highlights the very good fit of the DGNSP-CCE model (see Fig. D6 in the supplementary material).

27. As Campos et al. (2005, p. 3) rightly points out, *"in general-to-specific modeling, empirical analysis starts with a general statistical model that captures the essential characteristics of the underlying dataset, i.e., that general model is congruent. Then, that general model is reduced in complexity by eliminating statistically insignificant variables, checking the validity of the reductions at every stage to ensure congruence of the finally selected model".*

28. https://www.aiddata.org/geoquery.

29. The steradian (sr) is a unit derived from the meter (m). Its expression, in base units, is $sr = m^2 \cdot m^{-2}$. It is thus a dimensionless unit. The energy intensity is expressed in watt per steradian and the radiance, in watt per square meter steradian. The original data in the AidData geoquery tool was in $nano\,Watt/cm^2/sr$ and has been converted in $Watt/km^2/sr$.

30. Fig. 3.1 represents the continental United States at night and is a composite assembled from data acquired by the Suomi NPP satellite in April and October 2012. The image was made possible by the satellite's "Day/Night Band" of the Visible Infrared Imaging Radiometer Suite (VIIRS), which detects light in a range of wavelengths from green to near-infrared and uses filtering techniques to observe dim signals such as city lights, gas flares, auroras, wildfires and reflected moonlight. Credit: NASA Earth Observatory/ NOAA NGDC.

31. See http://Aiddata.org/geoquery and https://www.esa-landcover-cci.org.

ACKNOWLEDGMENTS

The authors would like to thank the two referees for their constructive comments and suggestions. The authors confirm they have not received any funding for this research and that they have no conflicts of interest to report.

REFERENCES

Addison, D. M., & Stewart, B. (2015). *Nighttime lights revisited: The use of nighttime lights data as a proxy for economic variables*. [Technical Report 7496. World Bank Policy Research Working Paper].

Ahn, S. C., & Horenstein, A. R. (2013). Eigenvalue ratio test for the number of factors. *Econometrica*, *81*, 1203–1227.

Aysheshim, K. D., Hinson, J. R., & Panek, S. D. (2020). A primer on local area gross domestic product methodology. *Survey of Current Business*, *100*, 1–13.

Bai, J., & Ng, S. (2002). Determining the number of factors in approximate factor models. *Econometrica*, *70*, 191–221.

Bailey, N., Kapetanios, G., & Pesaran, M. H. (2016). Exponent of cross-sectional dependence: Estimation and inference. *Journal of Applied Econometrics*, *31*, 929–960.

Blundell, R., Bond, S., & Meghir, C. (1996). Econometric models of company investment. In L. Matyas & P. Sevestre (Eds.), *The econometrics of panel data. A handbook of the theory with applications* (2nd revised ed., pp. 685–710). Springer.

Bresson, G., Kramarz, F., & Sevestre, P. (1996). Dynamic labour demand models. In L. Matyas & P. Sevestre (Eds.), *The econometrics of panel data. A handbook of the theory with applications* (2nd revised ed., pp. 660–684). Springer.

Brueckner, J. K. (2003). Strategic interaction among governments: An overview of empirical studies. *International Regional Science Review*, *26*, 175–188.

Burns, A. C., Saxena, R., Vetter, C., Phillips, A. J., Lane, J. M., & Cain, S. W. (2021). Time spent in outdoor light is associated with mood, sleep, and circadian rhythm-related outcomes: A cross-sectional and longitudinal study in over 400,000 UK Biobank participants. *Journal of Affective Disorders*, *295*, 347–352.

Cain, S. W., McGlashan, E. M., Vidafar, P., Mustafovska, J., Curran, S. P., Wang, X., Mohamed, A., Kalavally, V., & Phillips, A. J. (2020). Evening home lighting adversely impacts the circadian system and sleep. *Scientific Reports*, *10*, 1–10.

Campos, J., Ericsson, N. R., & Hendry, D. F. (2005). *General-to-specific modeling: An overview and selected bibliography*. [Technical Report 838. FRB International Finance Discussion Paper].

Cattell, R. B. (1966). The scree test for the number of factors. *Multivariate Behavioral Research*, *1*, 245–276.

Chen, X., & Nordhaus, W. D. (2011). Using luminosity data as a proxy for economic statistics. *Proceedings of the National Academy of Sciences*, *108*, 8589–8594.

CIRES. (2011). Bright city lights exacerbate air pollution. *Spheres*, 4–5. http://www.jstor.org/stable/24352775.

Coate, P., & Mangum, K. (2021). *Fast locations and slowing mobility*. [Technical Report. Federal Reserve Bank of Philadelphia].

da Silva, D. F. C., Elhorst, J. P., & Silveira Neto, R.d.M. (2017). Urban and rural population growth in a spatial panel of municipalities. *Regional Studies*, *51*, 894–908.

Debarsy, N., Ertur, C., & LeSage, J. P. (2012). Interpreting dynamic space–time panel data models. *Statistical Methodology*, *9*, 158–171.

Ditzen, J., & Reese, S. (2023). xtnumfac: A battery of estimators for the number of common factors in time series and panel-data models. *The Stata Journal*, *23*, 438–454.

Dizon, E., & Pranggono, B. (2022). Smart streetlights in smart city: A case study of Sheffield. *Journal of Ambient Intelligence and Humanized Computing*, 1–16.

Duriscoe, D. M., Anderson, S. J., Luginbuhl, C. B., & Baugh, K. E. (2018). A simplified model of all-sky artificial sky glow derived from VIIRS day/night band data. *Journal of Quantitative Spectroscopy and Radiative Transfer*, *214*, 133–145.

Duriscoe, D. M., Luginbuhl, C., & Elvidge, C. (2014). The relation of outdoor lighting characteristics to sky glow from distant cities. *Lighting Research & Technology*, *46*, 35–49.

Elhorst, J. P. (2014). Spatial panel data models. In J. P. Elhorst (Ed.), *Spatial econometrics, from cross-sectional data to spatial panels* (pp. 37–93). Springer.

Elhorst, J. P. (2021). The dynamic general nesting spatial econometric model for spatial panels with common factors: Further raising the bar. *Review of Regional Research*, 1–19.

Elhorst, J. P., Gross, M., & Tereanu, E. (2021). Cross-sectional dependence and spillovers in space and time: Where spatial econometrics and global VAR models meet. *Journal of Economic Surveys*, *35*, 192–226.

Elvidge, C. D., Baugh, K., Zhizhin, M., Hsu, F. C., & Ghosh, T. (2017). VIIRS nighttime lights. *International Journal of Remote Sensing*, *38*, 5860–5879.

Elvidge, C. D., Zhizhin, M., Ghosh, T., Hsu, F. C., & Taneja, J. (2021). Annual time series of global VIIRS nighttime lights derived from monthly averages: 2012 to 2019. *Remote Sensing*, *13*, 922.

European Commission. (2021). *A European Green Deal. Striving to be the first climate-neutral continent*. European Commission.

Falchi, F., Cinzano, P., Duriscoe, D. M., Kyba, C. C., Elvidge, C. D., Baugh, K., Portnov, B. A., Rybnikova, N. A., & Furgoni, R. (2016). The new world atlas of artificial night sky brightness. *Science Advances*, *2*, e1600377.

Gallaway, T., Olsen, R. N., & Mitchell, D. M. (2010). The economics of global light pollution. *Ecological Economics*, *69*, 658–665.

Ganong, P., & Shoag, D. (2017). Why has regional income convergence in the US declined? *Journal of Urban Economics*, *102*, 76–90.

Glaeser, E. L., & Gottlieb, J. D. (2009). The wealth of cities: Agglomeration economies and spatial equilibrium in the United States. *Journal of Economic Literature*, *47*, 983–1028.

Glaeser, E. L., Scheinkman, J., & Shleifer, A. (1995). Economic growth in a cross-section of cities. *Journal of Monetary Economics*, *36*, 117–143.

Goldblatt, R., Heilmann, K., & Vaizman, Y. (2020). Can medium-resolution satellite imagery measure economic activity at small geographies? Evidence from Landsat in Vietnam. *The World Bank Economic Review*, *34*, 635–653.

Gonzalez-Navarro, M., & Turner, M. A. (2018). Subways and urban growth: Evidence from earth. *Journal of Urban Economics*, *108*, 85–106.

Goodman, S., BenYishay, A., Lv, Z., & Runfola, D. (2019). Geoquery: Integrating HPC systems and public web-based geospatial data tools. *Computers & Geosciences*, *122*, 103–112.

Goulet, G., Mongrain, V., Desrosiers, C., Paquet, J., & Dumont, M. (2007). Daily light exposure in morning-type and evening-type individuals. *Journal of Biological Rhythms*, *22*, 151–158.

Henderson, V., Storeygard, A., & Weil, D. N. (2011). A bright idea for measuring economic growth. *American Economic Review*, *101*, 194–99.

Henderson, V., Storeygard, A., & Weil, D. N. (2012). Measuring economic growth from outer space. *American Economic Review*, *102*, 994–1028.

Hendry, D. F., Pagan, A. R., & Sargan, J. D. (1984). Dynamic specification. In Z. Griliches, & M. D. Intriligator (Eds.), *Handbook of Econometrics* (Vol. 2, pp. 1023–1100).

Hu, Y., & Yao, J. (2022). Illuminating economic growth. *Journal of Econometrics*, *228*, 359–378.

Im, K. S., Pesaran, M. H., & Shin, Y. (2003). Testing for unit roots in heterogeneous panels. *Journal of Econometrics*, *115*, 53–74.

Jewett, M. E., Kronauer, R. E., & Czeisler, C. A. (1994). Phase-amplitude resetting of the human circadian pacemaker via bright light: A further analysis. *Journal of Biological Rhythms*, *9*, 295–314.

Juodis, A., & Reese, S. (2022). The incidental parameters problem in testing for remaining cross-section correlation. *Journal of Business & Economic Statistics*, *40*, 1191–1203.

Kennan, J. (1979). The estimation of partial adjustment models with rational expectations. *Econometrica*, 1441–1455.

Keola, S., Andersson, M., & Hall, O. (2015). Monitoring economic development from space: Using nighttime light and land cover data to measure economic growth. *World Development*, *66*, 322–334.

Kyba, C. C., Kuester, T., Sánchez de Miguel, A., Baugh, K., Jechow, A., Hölker, F., Bennie, J., Elvidge, C. D., Gaston, K. J., & Guanter, L. (2017). Artificially lit surface of Earth at night increasing in radiance and extent. *Science Advances*, *3*, e1701528.

Lee, L. F., & Yu, J. (2015). Spatial panel data models. In B. H. Baltagi (Ed.), *The Oxford handbook of panel data* (pp. 363–401). Oxford University Press.

LeSage, J., & Pace, R. (2009). *An introduction to spatial econometrics*. CRC Press, Taylor-Francis.

Martinez, L. R. (2022). How much should we trust the dictator's GDP growth estimates? *Journal of Political Economy*, *130*, 2731–2769.

Martinez-Nicolas, A., Martinez-Madrid, M. J., Almaida-Pagan, P. F., Bonmati-Carrion, M. A., Madrid, J. A., & Rol, M. A. (2019). Assessing chronotypes by ambulatory circadian monitoring. *Frontiers in Physiology*, *10*, 1396.

Onatski, A. (2010). Determining the number of factors from empirical distribution of eigenvalues. *The Review of Economics and Statistics*, *92*, 1004–1016.

Parent, O., & LeSage, J. P. (2011). A space-time filter for panel data models containing random effects. *Computational Statistics & Data Analysis*, *55*, 475–490.

Pesaran, M. H., & Xie, Y. (2021). *A bias-corrected CD test for error cross-sectional dependence in panel data models with latent factors*. [Technical Report. arXiv preprint arXiv:2109.00408].

Pesaran, M. H. (2004). *General diagnostic tests for cross section dependence in panels*. [Technical Report. Institute for the Study of Labor (IZA) Discussion Paper No. 1240].

Pesaran, M. H. (2006). Estimation and inference in large heterogeneous panels with a multifactor error structure. *Econometrica*, *74*, 967–1012.

Pesaran, M. H. (2007). A simple panel unit root test in the presence of cross-section dependence. *Journal of Applied Econometrics*, *22*, 265–312.

Sager, L. (2019). Estimating the effect of air pollution on road safety using atmospheric temperature inversions. *Journal of Environmental Economics and Management*, *98*, 102250.

Ścieżor, T., & Czaplicka, A. (2020). The impact of atmospheric aerosol particles on the brightness of the night sky. *Journal of Quantitative Spectroscopy and Radiative Transfer*, *254*, 107168.

Shi, W., & Lee, L. F. (2017). Spatial dynamic panel data models with interactive fixed effects. *Journal of Econometrics*, *197*, 323–347.

Stark, H., Brown, S., Wong, K., Stutz, J., Elvidge, C., Pollack, I., Ryerson, T., Dube, W., Wagner, N., & Parrish, D. (2011). City lights and urban air. *Nature Geoscience*, *4*, 730–731.

Van Dingenen, R., Dentener, F., Crippa, M., Leitao, J., Marmer, E., Rao, S., Solazzo, E., & Valentini, L. (2018). TM5-FASST: A global atmospheric source–receptor model for rapid impact analysis of emission changes on air quality and short-lived climate pollutants. *Atmospheric Chemistry and Physics*, *18*, 16173–16211.

Yowell, T., & Devine, J. (2013). *Evaluating current and alternative methods to produce 2010 county population estimates*. [Census Bureau Working Paper Number POP-WP100].

Yu, J., De Jong, R., & Lee, L. F. (2008). Quasi-maximum likelihood estimators for spatial dynamic panel data with fixed effects when both n and T are large. *Journal of Econometrics*, *146*, 118–134.

Zhao, M., Zhou, Y., Li, X., Cao, W., He, C., Yu, B., Li, X., Elvidge, C. D., Cheng, W., & Zhou, C. (2019). Applications of satellite remote sensing of nighttime light observations: Advances, challenges, and perspectives. *Remote Sensing*, *11*, 1971.

APPENDIX. DATA SOURCES

A.1. NIGHTTIME LIGHT & AIR POLLUTION

The physical data used in the paper were extracted using the AidData Geoquery tool (Goodman et al., 2019).[28] The dependent variable, nighttime light, comes from the Visible Infrared Imaging Radiometer Suite (VIIRS) Day/Night Band lights data. It corresponds to the average monthly radiance (or energy luminance) measured in watt per square kilometer steradian ($Watt/km^2/sr$) (see Elvidge et al., 2017, 2021).[29] The Federal Information Processing System (FIPS) is used to map the VIIRS data at the county level. Satellite data are provided several times a day and are filtered so as to obtain detailed point estimates of light pollution.[30] VIIRS high-resolution lighting data are updated monthly and have the potential to create a new surge in nighttime light-based studies that focus on social and economic activities. See NOAA Earth Observation Group (VIIRS Nighttime Lights).

Urban area data are drawn from European Space Agency land cover program.[31] As many as 22 land cover classes per pixel, including urban areas, are defined using the Land Cover Classification System (LCCS) developed by the United Nations Food and Agriculture Organization. The LCCS categories were grouped according to their Intergovernmental Panel on Climate Change (IPCC) classes. The full name of each class can be found from land cover map user guide: http://maps.elie.ucl.ac.be/CCI/viewer/. The underlying data has a resolution of roughly 350 meters (defined in degrees, not meters). The data extracted from GeoQuery corresponds to the count of pixels in each unit (county) associated with each land cover class. One can then multiply each count by the resolution (350m × 350m) to get an approximate coverage estimate in square meters.

Particulate matter ($PM_{2.5}$) estimates are based on prediction models that combine satellite-based estimates and simulations based on the TM5-FASST model, an atmospheric source–receptor model that analyses emission changes of air quality and short-lived climate pollutants (see Van Dingenen et al., 2018).

A.2. COUNTY GDP & POPULATION

Data on yearly county-level domestic product (GDP) were extracted from the Bureau of Economic Analysis' website: GDP by County, Metro, and Other Areas. GDP is measured by the income approach, i.e. as the sum of compensation of employees, taxes on production and imports less subsidies (SUB), and gross operating surpluses. Details of the procedure can be found in Aysheshim et al. (2020).

Yearly county-level population estimates were drawn from the Census Bureau's website: https://www.census.gov/data/datasets/time-series/demo/popest/2010s-counties-total.html. Naturally, intercensal population counts are not available and must be estimated. The Census Bureau uses a procedure that has been shown to be very accurate in the past (see Yowell & Devine, 2013). The details of the procedure can be found in https://www2.census.gov/programs-surveys/popest/technical-documentation/methodology/2010-2019/natstcopr-methv2.pdf.

CHAPTER 4

WIND ENERGY, CO_2 ABATEMENT, AND THE ENVIRONMENTAL KUZNETS CURVE IN DENMARK

Federico Carlini[a], Bent Jesper Christensen[b], Nabanita Datta Gupta[c], and Paolo Santucci de Magistris[a]

[a]*Department of Economics and Finance, Luiss University, Italy*
[b]*Department of Economics and Business Economics, Aarhus Center for Econometrics and Aarhus University, Denmark*
[c]*Department of Economics and Business Economics, Aarhus University, Denmark*

ABSTRACT

The authors show that the adoption of wind energy reduces CO_2 emissions from energy production in Denmark, based on monthly data covering the period from January, 2005, through December, 2019. The effect is robust to 2SLS estimation, hence indicating that the effect is causal, using wind speed for exogenous variation in the instrumentation of wind energy, as suggested by Novan (2015). Unlike the latter study, the authors find that the instrumentation matters, hence indicating endogeneity of the wind adoption policy. The concavity of the emissions-output relation predicted by the environmental Kuznets curve (EKC) hypothesis turns insignificant when controlling for wind adoption, with or without instrumentation for the latter, hence indicating that the emissions reductions following economic development (output) are explained by clean energy production. Furthermore, emissions are reduced by higher temperature, corresponding to lower heating demand. Our methodological and substantive

Econometrics of Climate, Energy, and Green Transition
Advances in Econometrics, Volume 47A, 119–146

ISSN: 0731-9053/doi:10.1108/S0731-90532026000047A005

results on the value of the wind speed instrument for wind generation, and on the latter driving the EKC for Denmark, supplement results from higher-frequency generator-level and lower-frequency cross-country studies, respectively. The results are robust to control for possible long memory of the emissions and wind energy series. Marginal emissions avoided (MEA) are estimated at 0.25 tonnes of CO_2 per MWh of energy produced by wind and significant in the resulting fractional cointegration model, where wind speed increases wind generation and the EKC remains insignificant.

Keywords: CO_2 abatement; emissions; renewable energy; causal effect; environmental Kuznets curve; fractional cointegration

JEL Classifications: Q20; Q54; C50

1. INTRODUCTION

The recent synthesis report from the Intergovernmental Panel on Climate Change (IPCC, 2023) supports the hypothesis that global warming and climate change observed over recent decades mainly are caused by greenhouse gas (GHG) emissions. The largest component of GHG emissions is carbon dioxide (CO_2) emissions,[1] stemming mainly from the combustion of fossil fuels such as coal, oil, and natural gas for the purpose of energy generation. In an attempt to address the challenges of climate change, the 2015 Paris Agreement joined by most countries of the world advocates limiting the global temperature rise to 1.5 °C above pre-industrial levels. According to IPCC (2023), this will require cutting global CO_2 emissions to net zero by 2050. One of the potential policy tools toward meeting these demands is the adoption of clean and renewable energy sources, such as wind, solar, geothermal, hydro, ocean, or bioenergy.

We focus on CO_2 emissions from energy production in Denmark. This country has been a pioneer in the wind power industry going back to the 1970s, and with policy makers announcing further investments in large-scale adoption of wind energy around the time of the implementation of the European Union Emissions Trading Scheme (EU ETS) and the Kyoto Protocol in 2005. Today, Denmark is the world leader in wind energy, with production corresponding to 47% of domestic electricity consumption in 2019, compared to 2% in 1990, and 19% in 2005. Following the literature on the impact of clean energy adoption on emissions, we examine whether the adoption of wind energy, the main clean and renewable energy source in Denmark, has served to reduce emissions, controlling for the potential endogeneity of the adoption policy choice. Furthermore, following the literature on the EKC, we examine whether emissions depend in a concave manner on economic development (output). The idea is that a stronger economy should afford more environmentally friendly policies, as the demand for environmental quality increases with income, leading emissions to increase at a decreasing rate as output increases. After a certain point, further increases in output can even lead to reductions in emissions, a phenomenon known as decoupling of emissions and growth.

As the environmentally friendly policies include the adoption of wind energy, we investigate whether any EKC effect remains after controlling for wind energy adoption. This analysis serves to identify the policy generating the EKC.

The literature on the impact of wind energy adoption on emissions has controlled for demand, weather conditions, etc., using regression methods. In an early study, Cullen (2013) uses conventional power production as the dependent variable and includes wind generation, demand, temperature, and lags among the independent variables. Production data at 15-minute frequency for each generator on the ERCOT (Electricity Reliability Council of Texas) electricity grid in Texas over a two-year period from 2005 to 2007 are regressed on aggregated (across generators) independent variables. The model predicts the conventional (coal, natural gas, nuclear, etc.) production offset by wind, and emissions offset are obtained through multiplication by emissions factors. As wind is allowed to enter nonlinearly, MEA are derived in terms of partial derivatives, and estimated at 0.43.[2]

Several studies consider relevant variations to the basic regression framework from Cullen (2013). Kaffine et al. (2013) and Novan (2015) similarly consider ERCOT data, with a focus on heterogeneity across generation portfolios. Novan (2015) applies an instrumental variable (IV) correction for the potential endogeneity of wind production in the regression, using wind speed as an instrument generating exogenous variation in wind production, but finds that results are unaltered by IV. These studies report MEA below hypothetical reductions based on an average emissions analysis, i.e., the marginal generator replaced by wind pollutes less than the average generator.[3] Similar studies for other regions include Amor et al. (2014), with a focus on congestion effects in the Ontario grid, Thomson et al. (2017) for Great Britain, and a number of studies for Ireland, including Wheatley (2013), Di Cosmo and Valeri (2018), O'Mahoney et al. (2018), and Oliveira et al. (2019), who account for serial correlation using Newey and West (1987) standard errors, following Kaffine et al. (2013) and Novan (2015). Although system dependent, MEA estimates tend to range between 0.3 and 0.7.

In our analysis, we similarly compute emissions by applying emissions factors to conventional production, and derive MEA in terms of partial derivatives. We control for demand by including the EKC, and for temperature, precipitation, and other climate variables, as well as lagged independent variables. We further investigate the potential value of the wind speed instrument for wind generation suggested by Novan (2015). Instead of high-frequency (e.g., 15-minute in Cullen, 2013) panel observations on production at the individual generator level over a short calendar period, we conduct a long-run monthly-frequency analysis at the aggregate level. Whereas regression using high-frequency short-span data identifies the marginal generator replaced by wind in the existing system at the data frequency (say, within the day), estimated emissions reductions from our long-span aggregate analysis reflect replacement over the month, and the change in generation portfolio over time. In contrast to Novan (2015), we find that IV correction using the wind speed instrument matters, consistent with the notion that wind energy production is a decision variable, and endogenous in the emissions regression, with wind speed inducing exogenous variation in wind production. Other variation in wind production can be induced by endogenous decisions, such as the addition of windmills, possibly in response to emissions changes.

The literature on the EKC is mainly based on annual-frequency cross-country panel analysis (Grossman & Krueger, 1995; Holtz-Eakin & Selden, 1995), typically using a quadratic specification to capture the predicted concave (inverse U-shaped) emissions-output relation. For simplicity, we focus on the quadratic, while expanding with wind generation and climate variables.[4] Focusing on Denmark, we are able to base the analysis on a long, monthly series, covering the period January, 2005, through December, 2019 ($T = 180$), thus adding information by increasing the observation frequency rather than the cross-section dimension. This way, we relate to both literatures, controlling for wind generation and increasing observation frequency, relative to the EKC literature, while lowering frequency and expanding time span and aggregation level, relative to the emissions-wind energy literature. Regarding the EKC, the main question we address is whether the concave emissions-output relation remains after controlling for wind energy in Denmark.

In our earlier work, Christensen et al. (2021) (henceforth CDS), we used similar data for Denmark as in the present paper, but only through November 2017, and we only had access to data on wind speed through 2010. We documented a structural break in 2005, coinciding in time with the implementation of the EU ETS and the Kyoto Protocol, as well as announcements by policy makers about further investments in wind power, and so likely policy driven, with faster rate of reduction in emissions and increase in wind power after 2005 than before. Therefore, in the present study, we use 2005 as the starting year of our analysis data set. In CDS, we found that wind generation reduces emissions in OLS regression, but IV correction for potential endogeneity of wind adoption could only be implemented for the subperiod 2005 through 2010 for which wind speed data were available. The results indicated that IV correction made a difference, in contrast to the findings of Novan (2015), whereas the EKC was insignificant in both OLS and IV regressions. These results give rise to some questions, which we address in the present paper. First, are the results on the value of the wind speed instrument reliable, given that they are based on a short subperiod, and contradict those of Novan (2015)? Second, is the insignificant EKC similarly a result of data limitations? Third, what is the relation between any potential EKC effect and wind generation? Does the former remain after control for the latter?

In the present paper, we add about two years of observations, as our series are updated through December 2019, as opposed to November 2017 in CDS. Importantly, we now have access to wind speed data throughout. Furthermore, we include emissions from combustion of waste for energy production in our emissions measure, in addition to the emissions from combustion of fossil fuels for energy production considered in CDS. We investigate whether wind adoption remains significant for emissions in the extended sample, whether IV correction indicates endogeneity of wind adoption after more than doubling the period length, from 6 to 15 years of monthly wind speed observations for the instrumentation, whether an EKC in fact exists for Denmark, and whether it remains after control for wind energy in the extended sample. Further, we consider the impact of the climate variables on the relations, as well as the resulting MEA estimates for Denmark.

In the analysis, we account for additional covariates, including controls for seasonality, given our monthly data frequency, alongside the local climate variables. Local climatic conditions clearly impact the amount of CO_2 emitted, as well as the relation between emissions and wind power production. Temperature matters both for energy demand, with a direct effect on emissions unrelated to wind energy, and for efficiency in wind generation. The effect of temperature on demand stems mainly from demand for heating and cooling. Global warming in the Northern hemisphere, improved housing materials, and better insulation have reduced heating demand and increased demand for air conditioning (Stocker et al., 2013), with a negative net effect on energy demand in cold countries. In Denmark, most heating is generated from the burning of coal, oil, natural gas, and waste, with only a small fraction covered via by-products (excess heat) from electricity production, implying a negative direct demand effect of higher temperature on emissions. The efficiency effect works in the opposite direction, because higher temperature makes the air less dense, hence reducing the efficiency of the thermodynamic cycle used to drive turbines (Cullen, 2013). The total impact of temperature on emissions is a combination of the negative direct demand and positive indirect efficiency effects.

Wind generation is affected by other local climatic conditions, too, including turbulence, oscillations, precipitation, and sunshine. On stormy days, more wind power is generated, while on calm, sunny days, the opposite occurs, implying that a mix of wind and solar energy can complement each other (Jacobson & Delucchi, 2011). Similarly, precipitation, including ice and snow, can damage or slow down wind turbines, hence reducing efficiency of wind generation (Pieralli et al., 2015), and can increase heating demand, too, in both cases potentially increasing emissions. Therefore, we analyze the impact of climate variables on the relation between emissions, wind energy, and the EKC variables. We include the local climate variables as predetermined explanatory variables, the assumption being that while local weather affects local emissions, it is caused by global conditions, including global emissions, rather than by local emissions. For example, local temperature is not affected by local emissions, but rather by cumulated global emissions (Leduc et al., 2016).

Our empirical results indicate a significantly negative relation between CO_2 emissions and wind energy production. The effect is robust to instrumentation of wind generation by wind speed, suggesting that the effect is causal. The result that the instrumentation matters, hence indicating endogeneity of the wind adoption policy, holds up over the extended sample period. The EKC provides a reasonable fit to emissions for Denmark, which is on the downward sloping portion of the curve, i.e., decoupling applies to this country. As in Carlini et al. (2023), the EKC is most significant when based on growth rates, possibly due to the unit root property of output. However, we show in the present paper that it turns insignificant when controlling for wind adoption, with or without instrumentation for the latter. This result indicates that the emissions reductions following economic development (output) are explained by clean energy production. Further, temperature matters more for emissions in its capacity as a driver of demand for heating than through its effect on generation efficiency, as emissions decline with rising temperature. Our methodological and substantive results on the value of the wind speed instrument for wind generation, and on the latter driving the EKC for Denmark, supplement results from the higher-frequency generator-level and lower-frequency cross-country studies, respectively.

As noted by CDS, the emissions and wind energy series are strongly persistent, with possible long-memory properties, although not unit roots. Therefore, in a final analysis, we verify that our results are robust to control for possible long memory. Thus, MEA is estimated at 0.25 and significant in the resulting fractional cointegration relation between emissions and wind energy, where wind speed increases wind generation and the EKC remains insignificant. This fractional analysis follows the methodology of Carlini et al. (2023). However, that study did not use data on wind speed, and hence found a lower MEA estimate, at 0.16, as well as an indication that wind generation increases with industrial production growth, an effect that turns insignificant upon control for wind speed in our analysis.

The chapter is laid out as follows. Section 2 presents the data, including the emissions, wind generation, EKC, and climate measures. Section 3 discusses the empirical analysis, based on ordinary and 2SLS regression, as well as fractional cointegration. Section 4 concludes.

2. DATA

Our analysis is based on monthly data over the period January 2005 through December 2019. For emissions, we focus on those from energy production, thus bypassing those from transportation, agriculture, and other sources. The energy sector is the largest source of CO_2 emissions in Denmark (see the National Inventory Report, Nielsen et al., 2016, p. 82). We construct the series for CO_2 emissions from energy production in month t as

$$CO_{2,t} = \sum_{i=1}^{K} C_{i,t} IEF_{i,t}, \tag{1}$$

where $C_{i,t}$ is consumption of the ith fuel type, and $IEF_{i,t}$ the associated implied emissions factor. We consider $K = 4$ fuels, namely, coal, oil, natural gas, and waste. Monthly data on $C_{i,t}$ are obtained from the Danish Energy Agency (DEA) under the Ministry for Energy, Utilities and Climate.[5] For $IEF_{i,t}$, the EU ETS conducts fuel analysis to construct IEFs that are used in Denmark's National Inventory Reports (see Nielsen et al., 2016), prepared annually by the Danish Center for Environment and Energy (DCE), which is responsible for submitting Denmark's national emission inventory under the United Nations Framework Convention on Climate Change (UNFCCC) and the Kyoto Protocol. Average IEF (including the oxygenation factor) over the period is 94.17 kg CO_2 per GJ for coal,[6] 79.49 kg/GJ for oil, 57.381 kg/GJ for natural gas, and 39.06 kg/GJ for waste burning. In our empirical analysis, we focus on log emissions,

$$E_t = \log CO_{2,t}, \tag{2}$$

with $CO_{2,t}$ from (1).

Monthly data on production of electricity, $Prod_t$, and electricity production from wind energy (net of electricity used in electricity production), $Wind_t$, both measured in GWh, are obtained from DEA. The original source is a national database known as the "Stamdataregisteret," which contains information about production for all electricity-producing wind power production facilities. The monthly wind share, or wind penetration, is therefore

$$w_t = \frac{Wind_t}{Prod_t}. \tag{3}$$

The focus on electricity allows isolating the wind share. Our regression specifications use

$$W_t = \log\left(\frac{w_t}{1-w_t}\right), \tag{4}$$

the logit transform of wind share from (3). Wind share or production mix is preferred over level of wind generation for interpretation and policy purposes. The log transforms in (2) and (4) avoid truncated error distributions. Further, the distribution of changes in emissions depends on the level, and the log transform has a stabilizing effect on this.

As an indicator of demand, and to allow for an EKC, aggregate output and its square are included in the model. Industrial production is used as a proxy for output, since GDP is not available at monthly frequency. The monthly industrial production index for Denmark is retrieved from Eurostat, with base year 2010. To be sure, industrial production generates emissions beyond those from energy production, but serves in the EKC analysis as a measure of development and, hence, preferences for environmentally friendly policies, such as the adoption of wind energy. Therefore, we investigate whether any EKC effect (with respect to our output proxy) remains in emissions from energy production (the portion of total emissions that the adoption policy may have an impact on) after controlling for wind generation. If not, the indication is that any EKC (or development) effect in emissions from energy production is generated by the adoption policy, consistent with the interpretation that development fosters preferences for environmental quality.

Monthly data on temperature (in °C), precipitation (in mm), sunshine (in hours), and wind speed (in m/s) are obtained from DMI historic records (Cappelen, 2018), which have been maintained consistently since 1874 (cf. Cappelen & Jørgensen, 2011). Wind speed is measured as a monthly average across three weather stations (Thyborøn, Esbjerg Airport, and Holbæk Airport). Furthermore, we use the North Atlantic Oscillation Index (NAOI) to capture atmospheric variability patterns affecting Northern Europe. NAOI is highly correlated with other measures of atmospheric circulation, such as the interdiurnal pressure-variability index, dp(abs)24, and with wind speed and storminess (Hanna et al., 2008). Monthly NAOI levels are obtained from the Climate Prediction Center of the US Government National Weather Service.[7]

Table 4.1. Summary Statistics. The Table Reports Summary Statistics for the Monthly Data Series Over the Period January 2005 Through December 2019. ADF Regressions Include a Linear Trend, and a Number of Lagged First Differences Selected by AIC (Maximum 3 Lags). In the ADF Regressions, CO_2 and Industrial Production (*ip*) Are Measured in Logarithms, and Wind Share by the Logit Transform (4). The Ljung-Box (LB) Tests Are Computed with 6 Lags.

Variable	Unit	Mean	Std.Dev.	ADF	*p*-val	Ljung-Box	*p*-value
CO_2 emissions	1,000 tonnes	3820.7	815.05	−11.059	< 0.0010	354.13	0.0000
wind share, w	Share in energy prod.	0.3285	0.1536	−5.3836	< 0.0010	690.70	0.0000
wind speed	Meters per second (m/s)	5.2697	0.8472	−6.5895	< 0.0010	38.419	0.0000
industrial production, ip	Index	98.594	9.5090	−2.5039	0.3440	850.17	0.0000
(log *ip*)^2	Index	21.042	0.9176	−2.4938	0.3490	852.83	0.0000
temp	Degrees C°	8.9239	5.8530	−16.297	< 0.0010	466.41	0.0000
precip	mm	64.498	31.279	−6.9294	< 0.0010	27.575	0.0001
sunshine	Hours	144.27	81.867	−11.525	< 0.0010	375.99	0.0000
NAOI	Index	−0.0399	1.1338	−6.3710	< 0.0010	34.042	0.0000

Summary statistics are given in Table 4.1. Sample size is $T = 180$. Wind penetration (3) averages 33% over the period, and wind speed 5.3 m/s. From the Ljung-Box (LB) tests, all series exhibit strong serial dependence, so augmented Dickey-Fuller (ADF) regressions are implemented, with CO_2 emissions and industrial production measured in logarithms, and wind share by the logit transform (4). From the results, the EKC variables, industrial production and its square, exhibit unit roots, so we will compare with results using instead these variables in log-differences (growth rates). For all other variables, the unit root is rejected.

Fig. 4.1 shows the evolution of the series. Seasonal patterns are evident in all, as is the negative trend in emissions, E_t from (2), and the positive trends in wind energy, W_t from (4), and industrial production, $\log ip_t$. The climate variables, exhibits (c) and (e) through (h), show the well-known predictable, highly seasonal, and stationary behavior.

3. EMPIRICAL ANALYSIS

We consider the regression specification

$$E_t = b_0 + b_1 \sin(2\pi t / 12) + b_2 \cos(2\pi t / 12) + b_w W_t + b_x' X_t + \varepsilon_t. \tag{5}$$

The inclusion of seasonals is important, given our monthly data frequency.[8] The coefficient b_w on W_t determines the impact of wind energy on emissions E_t. The effects of EKC and climate variables are studied by including these variables and lags among the covariates X_t. The use of wind energy, demand, temperature, and lags as regressors to explain emissions follows Cullen (2013) and the subsequent regression literature.

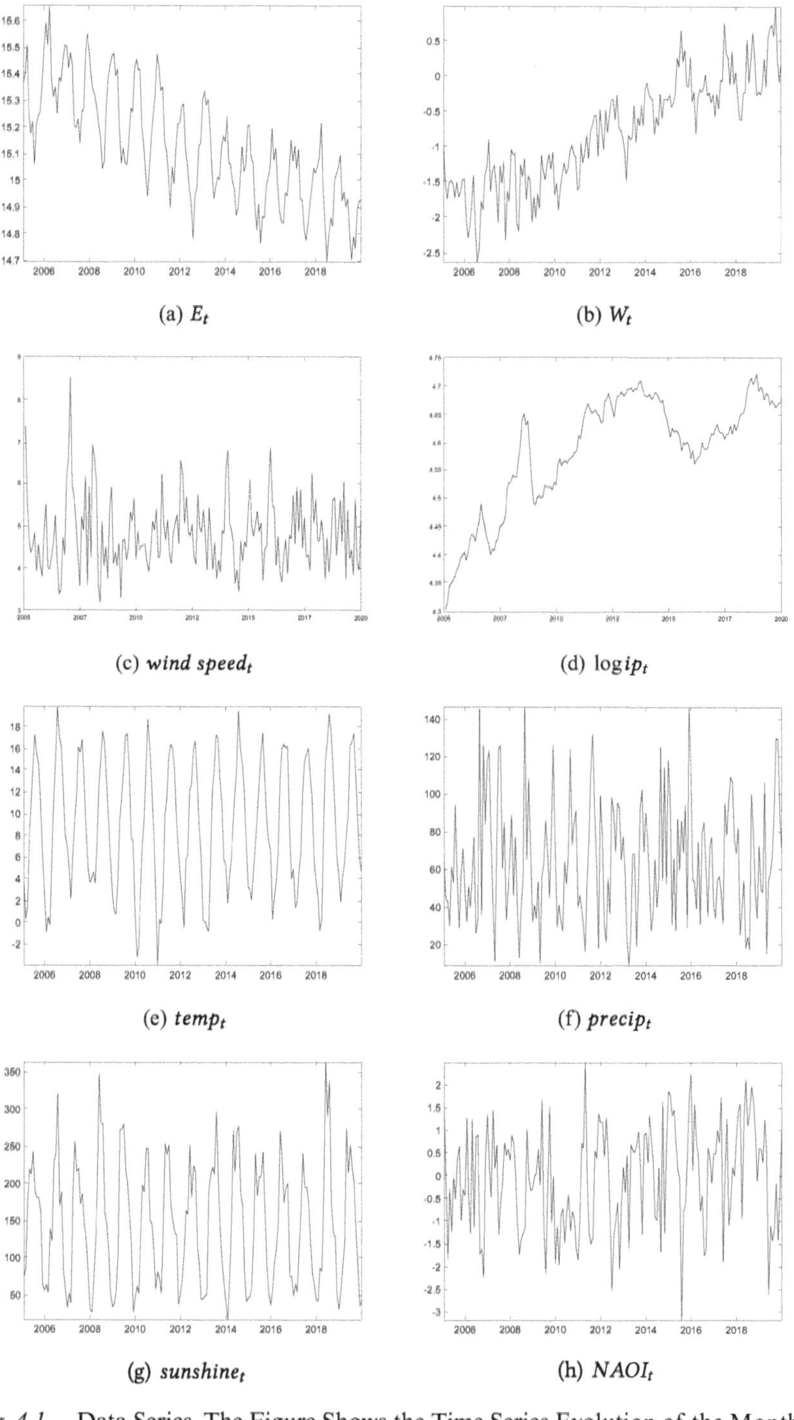

Fig. 4.1. Data Series. The Figure Shows the Time Series Evolution of the Monthly Data Series, Covering the Period January 2005 Through December 2019.

Results for various specifications using climate and demand variables in X_t in (5) appear in Table 4.2. The first specification, Model 1, excludes wind energy, W_t, and includes the EKC variables, log industrial production and its square, as explanatory variables. Consistent with the EKC hypothesis, the coefficient on the quadratic term is negative, i.e., the emissions-output relation is concave. Fig. 4.2 shows the estimated relation, after control for seasonals. Evidently, Denmark is on the downward sloping portion of the EKC. This situation, which has been described as decoupling of emissions and growth (Zhang, 2000), is as expected in the EKC literature for a developed country, although it has been challenging to establish empirically (Richmond & Kaufmann, 2006; Uçak et al., 2015).

While Fig. 4.2 demonstrates a reasonably good EKC fit for Denmark, with adjusted R^2 at 63% in Model 1 in Table 4.2, the coefficients on the EKC variables are insignificant at conventional levels (robust HAC standard errors below estimates). Considering the unit root property of log industrial production and its square, cf. Table 4.1, we also consider a specification with industrial production in log differences (growth rates), Model 3, Table 4.2. The coefficients in the quadratic retain the signs from Model 1, positive on the linear term, and negative on the quadratic, but are an order of magnitude larger in Model 3, and now significant at the 5% level. The results are indicative of the usefulness of the growth version of the EKC.[9]

Models 2 and 4 correspond to Models 1 and 3, respectively, but include wind energy, W_t, as an additional regressor. In this case, the EKC coefficients are an order of magnitude smaller, statistically insignificant, and even switch signs in Model 2. In contrast, the coefficient b_w on wind generation is strongly significant, with a robust t-statistic of around 20 in both models, and negative, consistent with the notion that wind generation reduces emissions. In Model 5, we include the climate variables, as well as lagged values of both climate and EKC variables. Wind energy remains strongly significant for emissions, whereas the EKC coefficients switch signs and are insignificant. Comparing across all models in the table, the explained portion of emissions, as measured by $\bar{R}^2$, is highest when wind generation is included. The results suggest that the EKC effect is explained by wind energy adoption. When controlling for wind energy, this enters significantly, $\bar{R}^2$ increases, and the EKC disappears.

In Model 5, the significance of the seasonal controls drops drastically, from both terms significant at level 1% to only one of them significant, and only at level 10%, hence indicating that seasonality in the relation between emissions, wind energy, and the EKC is driven by climate. Temperature gets a significantly negative coefficient, consistent with the notion that the direct demand effect dominates the indirect efficiency effect, and that the demand effect is determined by the demand for heating to a larger extent than by the demand for cooling. Precipitation increases emissions, presumably due to less efficient energy generation, and increased heating demand. The other climate variables and lagged controls are insignificant for emissions, which is a result in itself.

Table 4.2. Regression Results. The Table Reports Parameter Estimates (and Robust HAC Standard Errors) from Regression (5) using Monthly Data from January 2005 through December 2019. The Dependent Variable is $E_t = \log CO_{2,t}$. Superscripts *a*, *b* and *c* Denote Significance at the 1%, 5%, and 10% Significance Level, Respectively.

Coeff.	Variable	Model 1	Model 2	Model 3	Model 4	Model 5
b_1	$\sin(2\pi t/12)$	0.0645[a]	0.0455[a]	0.0724[a]	0.0464[a]	0.0268
		(0.0209)	(0.0080)	(0.0276)	(0.0077)	(0.0438)
b_2	$\cos(2\pi t/12)$	0.1415[a]	0.1348[a]	0.1554[a]	0.1316[a]	0.0694[c]
		(0.0195)	(0.0090)	(0.0270)	(0.0099)	(0.0390)
b_w	W_t	–	−0.1839[a]	–	−0.2125[a]	−0.2127[a]
			(0.0092)		(0.0104)	(0.0121)
b_x	$\log ip_t$	10.3616	−1.4208	–	–	–
		(14.3975)	(4.9780)			
	$(\log ip_t)^2$	−1.2701	0.1228	–	–	–
		(1.5860)	(0.5477)			
	$\Delta \log ip_t$	–	–	118.255[b]	2.1232	−7.8669
				(58.6399)	(27.0428)	(24.3550)
	$(\Delta \log ip_t)^2$	–	–	−12.7158[b]	−0.3077	0.7620
				(6.3595)	(2.9365)	(2.6559)
	$temp_t$	–	–	–	–	−0.0140[a]
						(0.0044)
	$precip_t$	–	–	–	–	0.0004[a]
						(0.0002)
	$sunshine_t$	–	–	–	–	0.0001
						(0.0002)
	$NAOI_t$	–	–	–	–	0.0013
						(0.0059)
	$\Delta \log ip_{t-1}$	–	–	–	–	4.6031
						(18.6318)
	$(\Delta \log ip_{t-1})^2$	–	–	–	–	−0.4788
						(2.0277)
	$temp_{t-1}$	–	–	–	–	0.0061[c]
						(0.0038)
	$precip_{t-1}$	–	–	–	–	0.0000
						(0.0002)
	$sunshine_{t-1}$	–	–	–	–	0.0000
						(0.0001)
	$NAOI_{t-1}$	–	–	–	–	−0.0033
						(0.0053)
$\bar{R}^2$		0.63	0.89	0.35	0.90	0.89
BP p-value		0.68	0.60	0.93	0.26	0.48
LB(6) p-value		0.00	0.00	0.00	0.00	0.00
BG(6) p-value		0.00	0.00	0.00	0.01	0.00
JB p-value		0.04	0.90	0.03	0.73	0.41
ARCH(6) p-value		0.00	0.99	0.00	0.80	0.83
S-ARCH(6,11) p-value		0.00	0.79	0.00	0.48	0.79

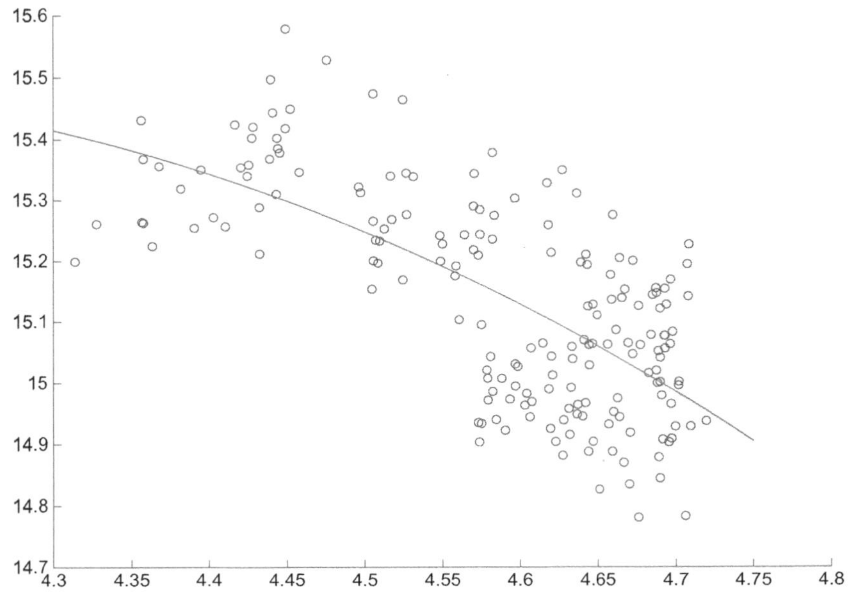

Fig. 4.2. E_t^* (second axis) and $\log ip_t^*$ (first), Emissions and Output After Control for Seasonality, $\sin(2\pi t/12)$ and $\cos(2\pi t/12)$, Along with the Fitted EKC.

The Breusch-Pagan (BP) heteroskedasticity test is insignificant throughout Table 4.2. Due to the time series nature of the data series, the table includes an LM test for residual ARCH effects, too, computed as TR^2 from a regression of squared residuals on six own lags, and asymptotically χ_6^2 under the null of homoskedastic errors. Similarly, due to potential seasonality in volatility clustering, a seasonal ARCH test (S-ARCH) including in addition 11 monthly dummies and thus asymptotically χ_{17}^2 is computed. From the results, when wind energy W_t is included (Models 2, 4, and 5), there is no residual ARCH effect (seasonal or otherwise), and errors appear normal, by the Jarque-Bera (JB) test. When W_t is excluded (Models 1 and 3), residuals appear non-Gaussian at the 5% level, and exhibit ARCH effects. The results reinforce the relevance of wind energy for explaining the evolution of emissions.

The reported results in Table 4.2 exclude lagged emissions as explanatory variables, which follows the regression literature. However, emissions, wind generation, and output are strongly serially dependent (Table 4.1 and Fig. 4.1). As a result, the fitted residuals exhibit serial correlation, with significant Ljung-Box (LB) and Breusch-Godfrey (BG) statistics, hence indicating possible misspecification.

For improved residual behavior, we consider in Table 4.3 an extended specification including four lags of the dependent emissions variable, E_t. Each model from Table 4.2 is reestimated, now including $E_{t-1},\ldots,E_{t-4}$ as additional controls (unreported) in X_t in (5). Thus, Model 1b corresponds to Model 1, but with lagged dependent variable control, and similarly for the subsequent models. Based on the LB and BG statistics in Table 4.3, residual autocorrelation is largely gone, except in Models 1b and 2b, using the EKC variables in levels, possibly due to their unit

Table 4.3. Regression Results. The Table Reports Parameter Estimates (and Robust HAC Standard Errors) from Regression (5) Using Monthly Data from January 2005 Through December 2019. The Dependent Variable Is $E_t = \log(CO_{2,t})$. Superscripts *a, b,* and *c* Denote Significance at the 1%, 5%, and 10% Significance Level, Respectively. The Models in This Table Include Four Lags of E_t (Unreported).

Coeff.	Variable	Model 1b	Model 2b	Model 3b	Model 4b	Model 5b	Model 6b
b_1	$\sin(2\pi t/12)$	−0.0653[a]	−0.0195[c]	−0.0721[a]	−0.0253[b]	−0.0972[a]	−0.0822[a]
		(0.0110)	(0.0100)	(0.0099)	(0.0102)	(0.0240)	(0.0219)
b_2	$\cos(2\pi t/12)$	0.1195[a]	0.1164[a]	0.1235[a]	0.1171[a]	0.0288	0.0345
		(0.0162)	(0.0117)	(0.0125)	(0.0119)	(0.0236)	(0.0210)
b_w	W_t	–	−0.1085[a]	–	−0.1092[a]	−0.0915[a]	−0.0931[a]
			(0.0099)		(0.01174)	(0.0117)	(0.0101)
b_x	$\log ip_t$	−0.1557	−1.8692	–	–	–	–
		(5.7357)	(4.7679)				
	$(\log ip_t)^2$	0.0027	0.1932	–	–	–	–
		(0.6294)	(0.5208)				
	$\Delta \log ip_t$	–	–	31.426[b]	3.5914	2.3392	1.2935
				(15.591)	(13.0297)	(14.573)	(12.314)
	$(\Delta \log ip_t)^2$	–	–	−3.3315[c]	−0.3966	−2.7947	−0.1815
				(1.7010)	(1.4253)	(13.024)	(1.349)
	$temp_t$	–	–	–	–	−0.0184[a]	−0.0171[a]
						(0.0034)	(0.0029)
	$precip_t$	–	–	–	–	0.0002	–
						(0.0002)	
	$sunshine_t$	–	–	–	–	0.0002	–
						(0.0002)	
	$NAOI_t$	–	–	–	–	−0.0011	–
						(0.0049)	
	$\Delta \log ip_{t-1}$	–	–	–	–	−2.7947	3.6625
						(13.024)	(13.311)
	$(\Delta \log ip_{t-1})^2$	–	–	–	–	0.3183	−0.3916
						(1.4213)	(1.4523)
	$temp_{t-1}$	–	–	–	–	0.0040	0.0047[c]
						(0.0029)	(0.0027)
	$precip_{t-1}$	–	–	–	–	0.0002	–
						(0.0002)	
	$sunshine_{t-1}$	–	–	–	–	−0.0001	–
						(0.0001)	
	$NAOI_{t-1}$	–	–	–	–	0.0050	–
						(0.0042)	
$\bar{R}^2$		0.89	0.92	0.81	0.92	0.94	0.93
BP p-value		0.79	0.26	0.49	0.20	0.46	0.62
LB(6) p-value		0.40	0.11	0.35	0.17	0.30	0.24
BG(6) p-value		0.01	0.04	0.19	0.10	0.12	0.09
JB p-value		0.30	0.26	0.16	0.10	0.23	0.34
ARCH(6) p-value		0.05	0.51	0.00	0.17	0.49	0.15
S-ARCH(6,11) p-value		0.12	0.45	0.01	0.20	0.47	0.22

root properties, cf. Table 4.1. Residuals appear normally distributed throughout the table. Again, the ARCH and S-ARCH tests are only significant when wind energy is excluded, Models 1b and 3b, with $\bar{R}^2$ slightly lower for these two models, as well. In Model 1b, the coefficients on the level EKC variables switch signs, relative to the expected concave shape, and remain insignificant. In Model 3b, the growth variables are significant and indicate concavity, but coefficients are again an order of magnitude smaller and significance lost when wind energy is entered, Model 4b. When the climate variables are included, along with lagged climate and growth variables, Model 5b, wind energy remains significant at the 1% level, with a negative coefficient, i.e., wind energy reduces emissions, whereas the growth variables remain insignificant. As in Table 4.2, temperature gets a significantly negative coefficient. The other climate variables are insignificant, and if they are dropped, Model 6b, the qualitative results on the remaining variables carry over.[10]

From the analysis, proper specification requires allowance for dynamics (four lags of wind energy in Table 4.3). The EKC is more significant in growth than in level variables, and the growth specification mitigates signs of misspecification. However, the EKC turns insignificant when controlling for wind energy, which is strongly significant, with a negative coefficient. Further ADF tests (as in Table 4.1) for E_t and W_t are significant (p-values 0.0000), with the linear trend significant in the ADF regressions (again, p-values 0.0000). This is consistent with the impression from Fig. 4.1 of emissions and wind energy being trend stationary, in turn implying that specification (5) is a balanced co-trended regression, provided W_t is included and X_t involves the EKC growth (as opposed to level and hence unit root) variables – i.e., Models 4b, 5b, 6b. Fitted residuals $\hat{\varepsilon}_t$ are shown in Fig. 4.3 for Model 5b, and appear well-behaved, consistent with the LB and BG statistics in Table 4.3. The results suggest that wind energy reduces emissions, and drives the EKC phenomenon.

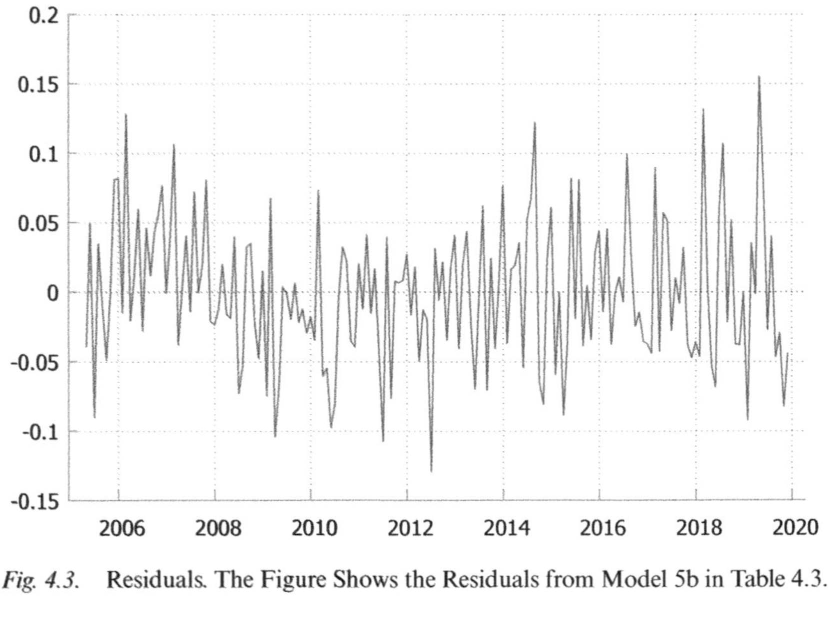

Fig. 4.3. Residuals. The Figure Shows the Residuals from Model 5b in Table 4.3.

3.1. Marginal Emissions Avoided

The estimates allow an assessment of the magnitude of the impact of wind energy on emissions. As in Cullen (2013), since the relation is nonlinear, this is done in terms of partial derivatives. To this end, as $W = \log(w/(1-w))$, from (4), with w the wind share in energy production, we have

$$\frac{\partial W}{\partial w} = \frac{1}{w(1-w)}. \tag{6}$$

It follows that, to a first order of approximation, a change in wind share is associated with a proportional change in CO_2 emissions given by

$$\frac{\partial \mathrm{CO}_2/\partial w}{\mathrm{CO}_2} = \frac{\partial E}{\partial W}\cdot\frac{\partial W}{\partial w} = \frac{\partial E/\partial W}{w(1-w)}, \tag{7}$$

or $b_w/[(w(1-w)]$ in the regression model. For an assessment in absolute terms, write wind share as $w = \omega/\varpi$, where ω and ϖ are wind energy and total energy production, respectively, so that

$$\frac{\partial \mathrm{CO}_2}{\partial \omega} = \frac{\partial \mathrm{CO}_2/\partial w}{\mathrm{CO}_2}\cdot\frac{\partial w}{\partial \omega}\cdot\mathrm{CO}_2 = \frac{\partial \mathrm{CO}_2/\partial w}{\mathrm{CO}_2}\cdot\frac{\mathrm{CO}_2}{\varpi}, \tag{8}$$

i.e., MEA by increasing wind energy production is estimated by multiplying the emissions intensity $\mathrm{EI} = \mathrm{CO}_2/\varpi$ onto the proportional impact (7). With EI at 1.399 tCO_2/MWh over the sample period, the resulting MEA estimate from both Models 5b and 6b in Table 4.3 is 0.06, with estimated standard error 0.003. This MEA estimate is modest, relative to those in the literature, which are typically between 0.3 and 0.7. Nevertheless, it is statistically significant, hence indicating a real abatement potential of wind adoption, whereas MEA is typically reported without associated standard error in the literature. The relatively moderate level could be due to the high wind penetration in Denmark, with further emissions reductions becoming increasingly harder to achieve.[11]

3.2. Instrumentation by Wind Speed

There are at least three reasons to expect that wind energy, W_t, may correlate with the shock to emissions, ε_t, and thereby be endogenous in (5), hence leaving OLS inconsistent. First, there may be endogeneity stemming from reverse causality. Indeed, high emissions may lead politicians and industry to shift to wind energy to reduce emissions. This is a political effect, driving a classical case of simultaneity. Since this effect induces a positive relation between emissions and wind energy, the resulting bias in the estimate of the expected (negative) effect of wind energy, b_w, i.e., the causal impact of wind adoption on emissions, is in the opposite (positive) direction, toward zero. Such attenuation effect could at least in part explain the modest magnitude of estimated MEA in Section 3.1.

Second, there could be omitted variables affecting both emissions and wind energy. For example, global warming increases the demand for air conditioning (Stocker et al., 2013), and reduces the need for heating in cold countries, with uncertain net effect on emissions, while at the same time leading governments to pursue clean energy sources to reduce warming. This is a second policy-induced effect. In this case, the resulting bias in the estimate of b_w would be negative, i.e., in the same direction as the expected main effect, if the drop in heating demand dominates the increase in air conditioning, as suggested by the results in Tables 4.2 and 4.3 (negative coefficient on temperature). To mitigate the possible bias from omitted global warming, we continue to include temperature among our controls X_t.

Third, there is likely a degree of measurement error in wind energy. DEA has become aware of a number of cases of imprecise or lacking data, and as a result has initiated a data quality control process, although not being financially liable for any losses incurred by users due to errors in data. Such errors imply a possible errors-in-variable (EIV) problem in W_t, and thus an additional potential attenuation bias toward zero in the estimate of b_w. The estimated standard error is biased toward zero, too, so the t-statistic for b_w is less biased than the parameter, but the EIV problem remains.

Beside including temperature as a control to mitigate possible omitted variable bias, we correct for possible endogeneity (stemming from simultaneity, omitted variables, EIV) by IV techniques, specifically, two-stages least squares (2SLS). The first stage regression is

$$W_t = a_0 + a_1 \sin(2\pi t / 12) + a_2 \cos(2\pi t / 12) + a_x' X_t + a_z' Z_t + u_t. \tag{9}$$

This includes the explanatory variables from (5), i.e., seasonals and X_t. In addition, following Novan (2015), wind speed is used as instrument for W_t. Based on a natural phenomenon, wind speed should be uncorrelated with shocks to CO_2 emissions,[12] but is expected to be highly correlated with wind energy production – stronger wind facilitates power generation. Furthermore, even with identical wind speeds, W_t can vary, such as through the addition of windmills. This is an endogenous policy decision, whereas the wind speed instrument generates exogenous variation in W_t. Given the strong dynamics, we include both current and lagged wind speed in the instrument vector, denoted by Z_t in (9), as well as four lagged dependent variables, as in Table 4.3. The second stage regression is based on equation (5), with predicted values $\widehat{W_t}$ from the first stage regression (9) replacing W_t.

Table 4.4 reports the parameter estimates from both first and second stage regressions. Models 2c, 4c, 5c, and 6c correspond to Models 2b, 4b, 5b, and 6b from Table 4.3, but with instrumentation. Second-stage robust heteroskedasticity and autocorrelation consistent (HAC) standard errors are computed using fitted residuals derived from the second-stage coefficient estimates, but with original W_t (as opposed to $\widehat{W_t}$) data. From the results, both the current and lagged wind speed instruments in Z_t are significant in the first stage (wind energy) regression, specification (9), throughout the table. Trend stationarity of W_t potentially leaves the coefficients on the stationary Z_t inflated, but estimates remain modest in magnitude, within the range (–0.25, 0.35), and the asymptotic t-statistics should be reliable. The level EKC remains insignificant in the second stage (emissions) regression upon instrumentation of wind energy, Model 2c. Using the growth variables instead, an unexpected convexity pattern emerges in the second stage,

Table 4.4. 2SLS Results. The Table Reports Parameter Estimates (and Robust HAC Standard Errors) from 2SLS Regressions Using Monthly Data from January 2005 through December 2019. The Dependent Variable Is W_t in the First Stage, and $E_t = \log(CO_{2,t})$ in the Second. The First Stage Regressions Include Four Lags of W_t, and the Second Stage Regressions Include Four Lags of E_t (Unreported). Superscripts *a, b*, and *c* Denote Significance at the 1%, 5%, and 10% Significance Level, Respectively.

	Model 2c		Model 4c		Model 5c		Model 6c	
	First stage	Second stage	First stage	Second stage	First stage	Second stage	First stage	Second stage
Endogenous								
(b_w)								
W_t	–	-0.0645^a	–	-0.0553^a	–	-0.0483^b	–	-0.0559^a
		(0.0161)		(0.0187)		(0.0191)		(0.0171)
Exogenous								
(a_x, b_x)								
$\sin(2\pi t/12)$	0.1113^b	-0.0009	0.1264^a	-0.0114^a	0.3977^a	-0.1049^a	0.0322	-0.0898^a
	(0.0435)	(0.0147)	(0.0421)	(0.0137)	(0.0930)	(0.0286)	(0.0849)	(0.0264)
$\cos(2\pi t/12)$	-0.3078^a	0.11193^a	-0.3096^a	0.1240^a	-0.6690^a	0.0262	-0.1551^a	0.0364^a
	(0.0479)	(0.0129)	(0.0415)	(0.0128)	(0.0657)	(0.02636)	(0.0519)	(0.0213)
$\log ip_t$	4.1920	-3.1616	–	–	–	–	–	–
	(12.1153)	(4.6961)						
$[\log(ip_t)]^2$	-0.4258	0.3316	–	–	–	–	–	–
	(1.3283)	(0.5131)						
$\Delta \log ip_t$	–	–	-2.5846^a	0.4562	-2.1010^b	0.1575	-2.0728^b	-0.0454
			(0.9734)	(0.3194)	(0.9696)	(0.2882)	(1.0224)	(0.3150)
$(\Delta \log ip_t)^2$	–	–	-55.280	20.047^c	-46.406	17.594^c	-47.680	18.384^c
			(38.816)	(11.789)	(33.286)	(10.351)	(38.3090)	(10.866)
$temp_t$	–	–	–	–	0.0310^a	-0.0180^a	0.0274^a	-0.0172
					(0.0086)	(0.0036)	(0.0076)	(0.0031)
$precip_t$	–	–	–	–	0.0000	0.0001	–	–
					(0.0005)	(0.0001)		
$sunshine_t$	–	–	–	–	0.0001	0.0001	–	–
					(0.0004)	(0.0001)		
$NAOI_t$	–	–	–	–	-0.0155	-0.0002	–	–
					(0.0134)	(0.0001)		
$\Delta \log ip_{t-1}$	–	–	–	–	0.0348	0.1677	0.1801	0.1620
					(1.0044)	(0.3086)	(0.9769)	(0.3106)
$(\Delta \log ip_{t-1})^2$	–	–	–	–	-24.896	2.5980	-13.282	-1.8933
					(25.828)	(9.9271)	(24.817)	(9.8167)
$temp_{t-1}$	–	–	–	–	0.0103	0.0026	0.0049	0.0028
					(0.0080)	(0.0030)	(0.0087)	(0.0029)
$precip_{t-1}$	–	–	–	–	-0.0007	0.0001	–	–
					(0.0006)	(0.0001)		
$sunshine_{t-1}$	–	–	–	–	0.0002	-0.0002	–	–
					(0.0001)	(0.0002)		
$NAOI_{t-1}$	–	–	–	–	-0.0285^b	0.0058	–	–
					(0.0132)	(0.0045)		

(*Continued*)

Table 4.4. (*Continued*)

	Model 2c		Model 4c		Model 5c		Model 6c	
	First stage	Second stage	First stage	Second stage	First stage	Second stage	First stage	Second stage
Instruments (a_z)								
wind speed$_t$	0.3497[a]	–	0.3327[a]	–	0.3332[a]	–	0.3247[a]	–
	(0.0193)		(0.0208)		(0.0217)		(0.0221)	
wind speed$_{t-1}$	0.2542[a]	–	−0.2419[a]	–	−0.2279[a]	–	−0.2453[a]	–
	(0.0241)		(0.0223)		(0.0234)		(0.0224)	
$\bar{R}^2$	0.95	0.92	0.95	0.92	0.95	0.93	0.95	0.93
PT(6) p-val.	–	0.51	–	0.86	–	0.15	–	0.50
BG(6) p-val.	0.11	0.03	0.11	0.10	0.39	0.12	0.20	0.08
JB p-val.	0.41	0.60	0.39	0.20	0.67	0.93	0.53	0.48
First-stage F-stat.	137.54	–	77.69	–	135.27	–	129.55	–
Sargan p-val.	–	0.03	–	0.19	–	0.04	–	0.09
Wu-Hausman p-val.	–	0.00	–	0.00	–	0.00	–	0.00
ARCH(6) p-val.	–	0.38	–	0.02	–	0.04	–	0.22
S-ARCH(6,11) p-val.	–	0.34	–	0.03	–	0.14	–	0.08

Models 4c, 5c, and 6c. In Model 5c, temperature again gets a significant negative coefficient, whereas the other climate variables and lagged covariates are insignificant. In Model 6c, dropping the insignificant climate variables, precipitation, sunshine hours, NAOI, and lags,[13] the quadratics in growth are insignificant at the 5% level, whereas wind energy W_t remains significant at the 1% level after instrumentation by wind speed. The results indicate the existence of a causal effect of wind energy production on CO_2 emission reductions. The negative sign common throughout the table confirms that wind energy reduces emissions.

In the IV case, the Pesaran and Taylor (1999) (PT) test is preferred over the BP test, and shows no sign of heteroskedasticity in Table 4.4. The BG test shows no residual autocorrelation at the 5% level in either the first or the second stage, i.e., no sign of misspecification, except for the level EKC, Model 2c. The JB test indicates Gaussian errors in both stages, and the ARCH and S-ARCH tests show only mild signs of volatility clustering, and not in Model 6c. Fig. 4.4 shows the distribution of the second-stage residuals from Model 6c. Consistent with the JB test, they appear relatively close to normal, given the sample size ($T = 180$).

Table 4.4 includes a battery of statistics relevant for the 2SLS analysis, namely, first-stage F, and p-values from Sargan and Wu-Hausman tests. As a guideline, a first-stage F-statistic of at least 10 indicates that the instruments Z_t are relevant, i.e., they have adequate explanatory power for W_t (Staiger & Stock, 1997). The results confirm that wind speed meets this relevance criterion essential for a robust instrument for wind energy, with first-stage F-statistics of more than 75 in all models. The Sargan J statistic (Hansen, 1982; Sargan, 1958) is a test of overidentifying restrictions, with the null indicating that the instruments are valid

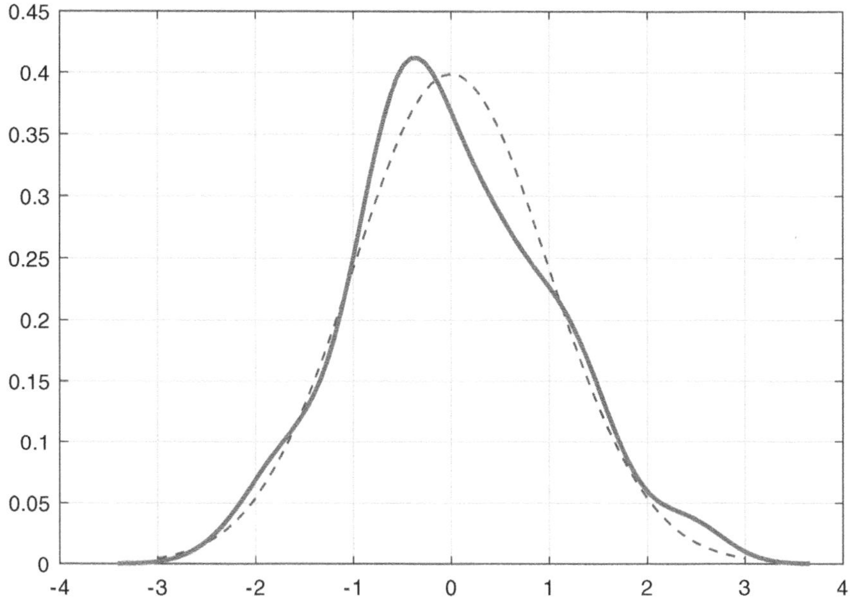

Fig. 4.4. Second-Stage Residuals. The Figure Shows the Kernel Density Function of the Standardized Second-Stage Residuals from Model 6c in Table 4.4, and the Standard Normal Density (Dotted).

(Z_t from (9) uncorrelated with ε_t from (5)). The results show only mild signs of invalid instruments, and not in Models 4c and 6c. The Wu-Hausman statistic (Hausman, 1978; Wu, 1973) is a test of whether instrumentation is needed, i.e., whether there is a significant difference between the original (OLS, Table 4.3) and instrumented (2SLS, Table 4.4) specifications. Our results indicate that instrumentation of wind adoption by wind speed matters throughout, which is in contrast to the result of Novan (2015), and suggests that wind energy is, indeed, endogenous in the emissions regression. Regardless trend stationarity of W_t, the correlation with the fitted residuals $\hat{\varepsilon}_t$ from (5) is –0.09, based on Model 6c, and the correlation between $\hat{\varepsilon}_t$ and $\hat{u}_t$, the fitted first-stage wind energy residuals from (9), is –0.12. Further, the estimated coefficients b_w on wind energy in Table 4.4 are of the order one half of the corresponding estimates without instrumentation in Table 4.3. The negative correlations and the differences in coefficients are consistent with the outcome of the Wu-Hausman test and, hence, endogeneity of wind energy. The results indicate a negative bias (away from zero) in OLS, consistent with an omitted global warming bias, but not with reverse causality (emissions spurring wind adoption), or with an EIV problem in wind energy (which would lead to attenuation bias toward zero). The smaller coefficient upon instrumentation implies a corresponding reduction in estimated MEA, whereas second-stage $\bar{R}^2$-values in Table 4.4 are on par with those for the corresponding models in Table 4.3.

Overall, the regression results indicate that wind energy is endogenous in the emissions regression, and has a causal negative effect, reducing emissions. Furthermore, wind speed is a relevant and valid instrument for wind energy, and this instrumentation matters for results, a finding in contrast to that of Novan (2015). Finally, the indication is that the EKC is driven by wind speed.

3.3. Fractional Integration

The analysis so far relies on regression of emissions, E_t, on wind energy, W_t, with and without instrumentation of wind energy by wind speed. The results in Table 4.1 that E_t and W_t are strongly persistent, but without unit roots, suggest that the series potentially exhibit long memory, i.e., that they are fractionally integrated. To investigate this possibility, also noted by CDS, Table 4.5 reports exact local Whittle (ELW; Shimotsu, 2010) estimates of the order d of fractional integration of each series. The analysis is carried out after removing a linear deterministic trend and seasonals, using a separate preliminary regression for each series, as the long-run stochastic properties are relevant for the question of long memory. Estimates of d are shown for two different bandwidths, m, associated with standard errors of 0.1053 and 0.0812 for $\hat{d}$.

From the results, E_t and W_t indeed exhibit long memory, with $\hat{d}$ significantly positive. The estimates are significantly below unity, too, i.e., no unit root, confirming the ADF results in Table 4.1. The findings are consistent with a common order of fractional integration d for E_t and W_t, i.e., they are integrated of order d, or $I(d)$, with $0 < d < 1$. In contrast, the EKC series possess unit roots, again consistent with the ADF results in Table 4.1, i.e., they are $I(1)$. Correspondingly, the industrial growth variables do not appear to exhibit long memory, and neither do the climate series, i.e., they are $I(0)$.

Fractional integration of common order of E_t and W_t suggests that they may be fractionally cointegrated, i.e., that their paths may be tied together in a long-run

Table 4.5. Exact Local Whittle (ELW) Estimates of the Fractional Parameter d, for Different Bandwidths m, Using Detrended and De-seasonalized Series. The Standard Error of $\hat{d}$ Is $1/(2\sqrt{m})$, or 0.1053 for Bandwidth $m = [T^{0.6}]$, and 0.0812 for $m = [T^{0.7}]$ ($T = 180$).

Variable	$m = [T^{0.6}]$	$m = [T^{0.7}]$
E_t	0.2571	0.3775
W_t	0.2651	0.2705
$wind\ speed_t$	0.0666	0.0195
$\log ip_t$	1.0091	1.0132
$(\log ip_t)^2$	1.0088	1.0181
$\Delta \log ip_t$	−0.0683	0.0636
$(\Delta \log ip_t)^2$	0.0457	0.0889
$temp_t$	0.1731	0.0307
$precip_t$	0.1342	−0.0656
$sunshine_t$	−0.2703	−0.1733
$NAOI_t$	0.0042	0.1272

equilibrium relation. In this case, a fractional cointegration analysis can be a suitable supplement the regression analysis, to examine the robustness of the results. Following Carlini et al. (2023), we consider an extension of the fractional vector error-correction model ($\text{FVECM}_{d,b}$) introduced by Granger (1986) and subsequently studied by Davidson (2002) and Johansen (2008) to accommodate $I(0)$ explanatory variables. In this analysis, we focus on the growth variables in place of the EKC level variables, to secure $I(0)$ covariates, and because the growth variables figured more prominently than the level variables in the regression analysis, in terms of significance, explanatory power, and residual behavior. Furthermore, beside the seasonal trend, climate, and EKC (growth) variables also considered by Carlini et al. (2023), we include wind speed in the analysis. We use the resulting model to investigate the relation between the emissions and wind energy series, and the role of the EKC.

The extended model, labeled $\text{FVECM-X}_{d,b,}$ is given by

$$\Delta^d Y_t = \alpha\beta'\Delta^{d-b} L_b Y_t + \sum_{j=1}^{k} \Gamma_j \Delta^d L_c^j Y_t + \varepsilon_t, \quad t = 1,\ldots,T, \tag{10}$$

where Δ^d is the fractional difference operator,

$$\Delta^d = (1-L)^d = \sum_{j=0}^{\infty} (-1)^j \binom{d}{j} L^j, \tag{11}$$

with L the (ordinary) lag operator, i.e., $L^j Y_t = Y_{t-j}$, whereas $L_b = 1 - \Delta^b$ is the *fractional lag operator*, with $L_b = L$ for $b = 1$, and similarly for L_c. In (10), ε_t is an independent and identically distributed p-dimensional error term with zero mean and positive definite covariance matrix $\Omega > 0$, and $Y_t = S_t - \mu_t$ contains the deviations between the original p-dimensional data vector S_t of endogenous system variables and the $p \times 1$ vector μ_t, which determines the dependence of S_t on the explanatory variables. The long-run dynamics are governed by the $p \times r$ matrices α and β, $0 \le r \le p$. Here, the columns of β are the equilibrium or cointegration vectors, α the speeds of error correction or adjustment to equilibrium, and r the cointegration rank. The coefficient $d \ge 0$ determines the order (degree) of long memory or fractional integration of Y_t, and b the *cointegration gap*, $0 \le b \le d$. Thus, while Y_t is $I(d)$, the departure from equilibrium or error-correction term $\beta' Y_t$ is $I(d-b)$. If $d > 0$, the series Y_t exhibit long memory, with autocorrelation functions decaying hyperbolically, as opposed to geometrically, as in the stationary ARMA case (in which $d = 0$). If, in addition, $b > 0$, then the long-memory series move together in the long run, in that a linear combination of them, given by the error-correction term, exhibits shorter memory than the original series. Finally, the short-run dynamics are governed by the $p \times p$ matrices Γ_j, $j = 1,\ldots,k$, and the scalar $c > 0$ (e.g., k ordinary lags of $\Delta^d Y_t$ enter for $c = 1$).

For the dependence on covariates, we focus on the specification

$$\mu_t = \mu + \zeta_0 t + \zeta_1 \sin(2\pi t/12) + \zeta_2 \cos(2\pi t/12) + \Lambda X_t, \tag{12}$$

where μ is a p-vector of constants capturing the influence of initial values, i.e., non-zero starting points for the first observation on the process (see Johansen &

Nielsen, 2012, and Nielsen & Shibaev, 2018, in the FCVAR$_{d,b}$ context). Further, ζ_i, $i=0,1,2$ are p-vectors of loadings on the deterministic terms (trend and seasonals), and Λ is a $p \times q$ matrix of loadings on the $q \times 1$ vector X_t containing the additional explanatory variables. In our application, we consider $S_t = (E_t, W_t)'$, the emissions and wind energy series, so $p = 2$, and X_t contains the EKC and climate variables.[14]

Relative to the FVECM-X$_{d,b}$ in (10), the classic cointegrated VECM model studied in Johansen (1991, 1995) corresponds to the special case $\mu_t = \mu$, $d=b=c=1$. The FVECM$_{d,b}$ specification of Granger (1986) is the special case with $\mu_t = \mu$, and using the ordinary lag operator in the short-run component for $k \geq 1$, i.e., imposing $c=1$, too, but with d, b free. The FCVAR$_{d,b}$ proposed by Johansen (2008) is similar to the FVECM$_{d,b}$, but uses L_b in the short-run component, hence imposing $c=b$. As outlined in Carlini and Santucci de Magistris (2019), imposing $c=1$ (the FVECM$_{d,b}$) rather than $c=b$ (the FCVAR$_{d,b}$) avoids certain identification problems stemming from an over-specified lag structure. Further identification issues related to the selection of lag length can be avoided by setting c to a suitable finite constant, as noted by Carlini and Santucci de Magistris (2022), who recommend a value $c=2$. All three specifications ($c=1, 2, b$) coincide for $k=0$ (no short-run component). The FVECM-X$_{d,b}$ in (10) includes the extension given by μ_t from (12), involving explanatory variables.

We conduct quasi Gaussian maximum likelihood (QML) inference in the FVECM-X$_{d,b}$ model (10)-(12). For the special case FCVAR$_{d,b}$, i.e., $\mu_t = \mu$, $c=b$, Johansen and Nielsen (2012) show consistency of the QML estimator, assuming only suitable moment conditions for ε_t, and Carlini and Santucci de Magistris (2022) show that analogous results carry over to the FVECM$_{d,b}$, i.e., $\mu_t = \mu, c=1,2$. Here, we extend the QML approach to the FVECM-X$_{d,b}$. In the empirical application, we fail to reject Gaussianity of the fitted residuals.

Results are shown in Table 4.6. The common order d of fractional integration of emissions and wind energy around μ_t is estimated at 0.62, and quite precisely so, with both the short-memory ($d=0$) and unit-root ($d=1$) alternatives rejected. We find $b=d$, and reported results are those obtained with this restriction imposed. Thus, the E_t and W_t series in deviations from μ_t from (12) fractionally cointegrate to a short-memory (order $d-b=0$) residual, as in standard $I(1)-I(0)$ cointegration, although the latter is rejected here, since $d<1$. The Johansen and Nielsen (2012) test of fractional cointegration rejects no cointegration (cointegration rank $r=0$) at level 5%, and fails to reject fractional cointegration with one cointegrating vector ($r=1$) at all conventional levels. The estimated cointegration vector is $\hat{\beta} = [1, 0.318]'$. In the long run, if W_t is high, relative to μ_t, the positive coefficient 0.318 shows that E_t must be low, to satisfy the cointegrating relation, consistent with low emissions levels accompanying high wind energy levels (note that $\hat{\beta}' S_t = E_t + 0.318 W_t$). From the reported estimates of α, it is emissions that significantly adjust toward the long-run equilibrium (robust t-statistic of –4.44), consistent with the notion that increases in wind energy drive emissions reductions. Reported results are for $k=2$ short-run dynamic terms, as selected by AIC, using $c=2$ in (10), with similar results obtained for $c=1, b$ (Γ_j unreported).

Table 4.6. FVECM-$X_{d,b}$ Results. The Table Reports the Parameter Estimates of the FVECM-$X_{d,b}$ with $k = 2$ Two Lags, as Selected by AIC, Using the Monthly Emissions and Wind Energy Series E_t and W_t Over the Period January 2005 through December 2019. The Johansen and Nielsen (2012) Test of Fractional Cointegration Takes the Value 10.760 (p-value = 0.029) for $r = 0$ and 2.142 (p-value = 0.948) for $r = 1$. The Estimated Cointegration Vector for $r = 1$ Is $\hat{\beta} = [1, 0.318]'$. Estimated MEA Is 0.2545, with Bootstrapped Standard Error 0.091.

		E_t				W_t			
		Est.	Std.Err.	*t*-stat	*p*-val	Est.	Std.Err.	*t*-stat	*p*-val
Par.	**Variable**								
d	Memory	0.6199	0.0849	7.3041	0.0000	0.6199	0.0849	7.3041	0.0000
α	error correction	−0.5252	0.1182	−4.4418	0.0000	−0.5484	0.3095	−1.7720	0.0764
μ	*intercept*	8.4026	0.0407	206.2055	0.0000	−1.6677	0.1319	−12.6470	0.0000
ζ_0	$trend_t$	−0.0025	0.0006	−4.4269	0.0000	0.0113	0.0018	6.2366	0.0000
ζ_1	$\sin(2\pi t/12)$	−0.0429	0.0177	−2.4261	0.0153	−0.0849	0.0532	−1.5945	0.1108
ζ_2	$\cos(2\pi t/12)$	0.0391	0.0227	1.7213	0.0852	−0.1677	0.0637	−2.6308	0.0085
Λ	$wind\ speed_t$	−0.0073	0.0050	−1.4613	0.1439	0.2708	0.0136	19.8591	0.0000
	$\Delta \log ip_t$	−0.0004	0.0046	−0.0923	0.9264	−0.0135	0.0127	−1.0643	0.2872
	$(\Delta \log ip_t)^2$	0.0066	0.0041	1.5943	0.1109	−0.0112	0.0127	−0.8812	0.3782
	$temp_t$	−0.1272	0.0184	−6.9192	0.0000	0.0870	0.0506	1.7195	0.0855
	$precip_t$	−0.0045	0.0057	−0.7870	0.4313	0.0184	0.0151	1.2237	0.2211
	$sunshine_t$	0.0124	0.0121	1.0214	0.3071	−0.0081	0.0318	−0.2537	0.7997
	$NAOI_t$	−0.0024	0.0054	−0.4394	0.6604	−0.0001	0.0139	−0.0065	0.9948
Misspecification tests									
LB(5)		7.1197	–	–	0.2119	2.8303	–	–	0.7261
LB(10)		9.8830	–	–	0.4508	11.5738	–	–	0.3146
DH		3.1330	–	–	0.5358				

Wind speed is the only variable in X_t that is significant for wind generation, W_t, at the 5% level (robust t-statistic close to 20; the time trend and one of the seasonals are significant, too). Wind speed increases wind generation, and the result is consistent with wind speed being a relevant instrument for wind energy in the 2SLS analysis. At the same time, temperature reduces emissions (t-statistic of −6.92), in line with the regression results (the trend and one of the seasonals are significant for emissions, too). The EKC growth variables show no sign of concavity and are insignificant. The loss of concavity is consistent across the regression and fractional analyses, although the results are not directly comparable, as a linear trend is taken out in the latter case (ζ_0 from (12) is strongly significant for both E_t and W_t in Table 4.6).

As in the instrumented regression analysis, Section 3.2, wind energy W_t is included as one of the endogenous variables in the model, in the fractional case via $S_t = (E_t, W_t)'$, where $Y_t = S_t - \mu_t$. In contrast to the EKC variables, wind energy enters prominently, as seen in the fractional case by the strength of cointegration ($b = d > 0$), and the estimated β-coefficient, at 0.32, considerably larger in magnitude than the b_w-coefficients from the regression analysis. Correspondingly, the impact of wind energy on emissions is stronger, with MEA based on the impulse-response function (IRF) from the model (following Carlini et al., 2023) estimated at 0.25 and significant (bootstrapped standard error 0.09). This value is considerably larger than in the regression analysis, and larger than the estimate in Carlini et al. (2023), at 0.16, presumably because our analysis includes wind speed among the explanatory variables. Further, the Carlini et al. (2023) analysis suggested that wind energy W_t is increasing in industrial production growth, but our results show that this effect is an artefact, and turns insignificant when controlling for wind speed (p-value 0.29 in Table 4.6).

Given the high wind penetration in Denmark, our MEA estimate, at 0.25, is broadly consistent with estimates for other countries in the regression literature, typically in the range 0.3 to 0.7. The significance reinforces the abatement potential of wind energy, whereas MEA estimates in the literature typically are reported without standard errors, and do not account for long memory or endogeneity of wind energy. Finally, the LB tests and the Doornik and Hansen (2008) (DH) test of multivariate normality in Table 4.6 show no signs of misspecification or non-Gaussianity of errors.[15]

Overall, the fractional analysis confirms the main conclusions from the regression analysis, namely, that wind energy reduces emissions, that this effect is causal, i.e., it remains when accounting for endogeneity of wind adoption, and that when wind energy is included, the EKC disappears.

4. CONCLUSION

We relate to two literatures, namely, the emissions-wind generation literature, typically using relatively high frequency data at the disaggregated level, and the EKC literature, based on lower frequency cross-country panel analysis. Our intermediate (monthly) frequency analysis for Denmark allows combining elements from both literatures, leading to a number of new contributions. On the methodological side, we demonstrate the value of the wind speed instrument for wind generation. The finding that instrumentation matters, consistent with endogeneity of the policy choice, is in contrast to that of Novan (2015), who reports an insignificant difference between OLS and IV estimates of the effect of wind generation on emissions. On the substantive side, we establish a causal effect of wind energy adoption on emissions, hence demonstrating the abatement potential of the adoption policy. We find that Denmark is on the downward sloping portion of the EKC, so decoupling applies, as expected for a developed country, although the phenomenon has been challenging to establish empirically. Furthermore, we show that wind generation drives the EKC for Denmark. The EKC effect turns insignificant when controlling for wind energy, with or without instrumentation of the latter, hence indicating that the emissions reduction following economic development (output) is explained by clean energy production. In addition, we find that emissions are reduced by higher temperature, corresponding to lower heating demand. This is clearly a local effect, whereas (cumulated) emissions and temperature (global warming) are expected to move together on the global scale. Finally, we verify the robustness of the results to possible long memory (fractional integration) in the emissions and wind energy series. MEA are estimated at 0.25 tonnes of CO_2 per MWh of energy produced by wind and significant in the resulting fractional cointegration relation between emissions and wind energy, where wind speed increases wind generation and the EKC remains insignificant.

The finding of a causal impact of wind energy adoption on emissions is important. In recent years, CO_2 emissions have been declining in a number of countries, including Denmark. This decline could be associated with several factors, such as warming (reduced heating demand), beside adoption of clean energy sources, in particular wind, in place of fossil fuels. This underscores the importance of reliable tests to assess whether the observed correlation between rising fossil-free power generation methods and decreasing emissions is mainly spurious or, indeed, reflects causality running from clean energy technologies to CO_2 emissions abatement. Precise information on the potential for reducing CO_2 by substituting wind for other generation methods is valuable to policy makers choosing among energy production technologies while facing increasing environmental challenges stemming from continuing reports on GHG emissions and global warming.

The result that wind generation drives the EKC is important, as well. The idea behind the EKC is that a stronger economy should afford more environmentally friendly policies. Information on which policies reduce emissions is valuable to decision makers. Beside wind generation and other emissions reducing policies in the energy sector, environmentally friendly policies in other sectors could be considered, such as changes of fodder in agriculture, adoption of electric vehicles in transportation, electrification of manufacturing, and replanting of vegetation in forestry and land use. An empirical analysis would require data on such policies, and on emissions from the relevant sectors, beside energy (emissions from agriculture, transportation, manufacturing, forestry and land use, etc.). Our result is conservative in that other environmentally friendly policies may be additional drivers of the EKC. We leave a full analysis of this possibility as an exciting avenue for future research.

NOTES

1. Other GHG emissions include methane (CH_4) and nitrous oxide (N_2O).
2. Henceforth, MEA is stated in tCO_2/MWh, i.e., tonnes of CO_2 emissions avoided per MWh of energy produced by wind.
3. Siler-Evans et al. (2012) consider more US regions and find that in some, the marginal effect is below the average (in the region), while in others, the reverse applies.
4. Alternatives to the quadratic considered in the literature include splines (Auffhammer & Steinhauser, 2012; Schmalensee et al., 1998), and kernel regression (Millimet et al., 2003).
5. https://ens.dk/service/statistik-data-noegletal-og-kort/maanedlig-og-aarlig-energistatistik.
6. 1 kg $CO_2/GJ = 0.0036$ tCO_2/MWh.
7. See http://www.cpc.ncep.noaa.gov/data/teledoc/nao.shtml.
8. With t counting months, $t/12$ counts years, so the Fourier terms in (5) capture the annual cycle. Higher-order terms ($\sin(2\pi t/3)$, $\cos(2\pi t/3)$ for a quarterly cycle, etc.) were insignificant.
9. Similarly, Carlini et al. (2023) find that the EKC variables are insignificant in levels, but that the squared growth rate enters significantly (they exclude contemporaneous wind energy throughout).
10. The reduction is not rejected in joint Wald and F-tests.
11. Limited storability of power renders sole reliance on wind energy impossible.
12. Local weather phenomenons such as wind are driven by global climate and, thus, cumulated global emissions, rather than local emissions (Leduc et al., 2016).
13. The reduction is not rejected in joint Wald and F tests.
14. As both emissions and wind energy are endogenous variables in the cointegration model, so that instrumentation is unnecessary, wind speed is included directly among the explanatory variables X_t in (12).
15. The QML approach does not require Gaussianity.

ACKNOWLEDGMENTS

We are grateful to the editors, the anonymous referees, and participants in the Conference on Climate Change, Carbon Emissions, and the Green Transition, Novembre Nordico, Accademia di Danimarca, Rome, for useful comments, to John Cappelen, Danish Meteorological Institute, and Ole-Kenneth Nielsen, Department of Environmental Science. Emission Modeling and Environmental Geography, Aarhus University, for providing access to some of the data used in this study, and to Aarhus Center for Econometrics (ACE), funded by the Danish National Research Foundation, grant number DNRF186, and Center for Research on Energy (CoRE), funded by InCommodities, for research support. The authors declare no competing interests, financially or otherwise, with any organizations or individuals.

REFERENCES

Amor, M. B., de Villemeur, E. B., Pellat, M., & Pineau, P.-O. (2014). Influence of wind power on hourly electricity prices and GHG (greenhouse gas) emissions: Evidence that congestion matters from Ontario zonal data. *Energy*, *66*, 458–469.

Auffhammer, M., & Steinhauser, R. (2012). Forecasting the path of US CO_2 emissions using state-level information. *Review of Economics and Statistics*, *94*(1), 172–185.

Cappelen, J. (2018). *Denmark: DMI historical climate data collection 1768–2017*. Danish Meteorological Institute.

Cappelen, J., & Jørgensen, B. (2011). *Dansk vejr siden 1874–måned for måned med temperatur, nedbør og soltimer samt beskrivelser af vejret – with English translations*. [Technical Report 11-02, DMI Teknisk Rapport].

Carlini, F., & Santucci de Magistris, P. (2019). On the identification of fractionally cointegrated VAR models with the F(d) condition. *Journal of Business & Economic Statistics, 37*, 135–146.

Carlini, F., & Santucci de Magistris, P. (2022). *Beyond the co-fractional model of Granger (1986)*. [Technical report, CREATES WP series].

Carlini, F., Christensen, B. J., Gupta, N. D., & Santucci de Magistris, P. (2023). Climate, wind energy, and CO_2 emissions from energy production in Denmark. *Energy Economics, 125*, 106821.

Christensen, B. J., Datta Gupta, N., & Santucci de Magistris, P. (2021). Measuring the impact of clean energy production on CO_2 abatement in Denmark: Upper bound estimation and forecasting. *Journal of the Royal Statistical Society: Series A (Statistics in Society), 184*(1), 118–149.

Cullen, J. (2013). Measuring the environmental benefits of wind-generated electricity. *American Economic Journal: Economic Policy*, 5(4), 107–133.

Davidson, J. (2002). A model of fractional cointegration, and tests for cointegration using the bootstrap. *Journal of Econometrics*, 110(2), 187–212.

Di Cosmo, V., & Valeri, L. M. (2018). How much does wind power reduce CO_2 emissions? Evidence from the Irish single electricity market. *Environmental and Resource Economics, 71*(3), 645–669.

Doornik, J. A., & Hansen, H. (2008). An omnibus test for univariate and multivariate normality. *Oxford Bulletin of Economics and Statistics, 70*, 927–939.

Granger, C. W. J. (1986). Developments in the study of cointegrated economic variables. *Oxford Bulletin of Economics and Statistics, 48*(3), 213–228.

Grossman, G. M., & Krueger, A. B. (1995). Economic growth and the environment. *The Quarterly Journal of Economics, 110*(2), 353–377.

Hanna, E., Cappelen, J., Allan, R., Jónsson, T., Le Blancq, F., Lillington, T., & Hickey, K. (2008). New insights into North European and North Atlantic surface pressure variability, storminess, and related climatic change since 1830. *Journal of Climate, 21*(24), 6739–6766.

Hansen, L. P. (1982). Large sample properties of generalized method of moments estimators. *Econometrica, 50*(4), 1029–1054.

Hausman, J. A. (1978). Specification tests in econometrics. *Econometrica, 46*(6), 1251–1271.

Holtz-Eakin, D., & Selden, T. M. (1995). Stoking the fires? CO_2 emissions and economic growth. *Journal of Public Economics, 57*(1), 85–101.

IPCC. (2023). *Climate change 2023: Synthesis report*. [Technical report, Intergovernmental Panel on Climate Change].

Jacobson, M. Z., & Delucchi, M. A. (2011). Providing all global energy with wind, water, and solar power, part i: Technologies, energy resources, quantities and areas of infrastructure, and materials. *Energy Policy, 39*(3), 1154–1169.

Johansen, S. (1991). Estimation and hypothesis testing of cointegration vectors in Gaussian vector autoregressive models. *Econometrica, 56*, 1551–1580.

Johansen, S. (1995) *Likelihood-based inference in cointegrated vector autoregressive models*. Oxford University Press.

Johansen, S. (2008). A representation theory for a class of vector autoregressive models for fractional processes. *Econometric Theory, 24*(3), 651–676.

Johansen, S., & Nielsen, M. Ø. (2012). Likelihood inference for a fractionally cointegrated vector autoregressive model. *Econometrica, 80*(6), 2667–2732.

Kaffine, D. T., McBee, B. J., & Lieskovsky, J. (2013). Emissions savings from wind power generation in Texas. *The Energy Journal, 34*(1), 155–175.

Leduc, M., Matthews, H. D., & de Elía, R. (2016). Regional estimates of the transient climate response to cumulative CO_2 emissions. *Nature Climate Change, 6*(5), 474–478.

Millimet, D. L., List, J. A., & Stengos, T. (2003). The environmental Kuznets curve: Real progress or misspecified models? *Review of Economics and Statistics, 85*(4), 1038–1047.

Newey, W. K., & West, K. D. (1987). A simple, positive semi-definite, heteroskedasticity and autocorrelation consistent covariance matrix. *Econometrica*, *55*(3), 703–708.

Nielsen, M. Ø., & Shibaev, S. S. (2018). Forecasting daily political opinion polls using the fractionally cointegrated vector auto-regressive model. *Journal of the Royal Statistical Society Series A: Statistics in Society*, *181*(1), 3–33.

Nielsen, O.-K., Plejdrup, M. S., Winther, M., Nielsen, M., Gyldenkærne, S., Mikkelsen, M. H., Albrektsen, R., Thomsen, M., Hjelgaard, K., Fauser, P., Bruun, H. G., Johannsen, V. K., Nord-Larsen, T., Vesterdal, L., Callesen, I., Schou, E., Suadicani, K., Rasmussen, E., Petersen, S. B., ..., Hansen, M. G. (2016). *Denmark's National Inventory Report 2015 and 2016: Emission inventories 1990-2014 - Submitted under the United Nations Framework Convention on Climate Change and the Kyoto Protocol*. [Technical report, DCE-Danish Center for Environment and Energy].

Novan, K. (2015). Valuing the wind: Renewable energy policies and air pollution avoided. *American Economic Journal: Economic Policy*, *7*(3), 291–326.

O'Mahoney, A., Denny, E., Hobbs, B. F., & O'Malley, M. (2018). The drivers of power system emissions: An econometric analysis of load, wind and forecast errors. *Energy Systems*, *9*(4), 853–872.

Oliveira, T., Varum, C., & Botelho, A. (2019). Wind power and CO_2 emissions in the Irish market. *Energy Economics*, *80*, 48–58.

Pesaran, H. M., & Taylor, L. W. (1999). Diagnostics for IV regressions. *Oxford Bulletin of Economics and Statistics*, *61*(2), 255–281.

Pieralli, S., Ritter, M., & Odening, M. (2015). Efficiency of wind power production and its determinants. *Energy*, *90*, 429–438.

Richmond, A. K., & Kaufmann, R. K. (2006). Is there a turning point in the relationship between income and energy use and/or carbon emissions? *Ecological Economics*, *56*(2), 176–189.

Sargan, J. D. (1958). The estimation of economic relationships using instrumental variables. *Econometrica, 26*(3), 393–415.

Schmalensee, R., Stoker, T. M., & Judson, R. A. (1998). World carbon dioxide emissions: 1950–2050. *Review of Economics and Statistics*, *80*(1), 15–27.

Shimotsu, K. (2010). Exact local Whittle estimation of fractional integration with unknown mean and time trend. *Econometric Theory*, *26*(2), 501–540.

Siler-Evans, K., Azevedo, I. L., & Morgan, M. G. (2012). Marginal emissions factors for the US electricity system. *Environmental Science & Technology*, *46*(9), 4742–4748.

Staiger, D., & Stock, J. H. (1997). Instrumental variables regression with weak instruments. *Econometrica, 65*(3), 557–586.

Stocker, T. F., Qin, D., Plattner, G.-K., Tignor, M., Allen, S. K., Boschung, J., Nauels, A., Xia, Y., Bex, V., & Midgley, P. M. (2013). *Climate change 2013: The physical science basis*. Technical report, Contribution of Working Group I to the Fifth Assessment Report of the Intergovernmental Panel on Climate Change. Cambridge Univ. Press.

Thomson, R. C., Harrison, G. P., & Chick, J. P. (2017). Marginal greenhouse gas emissions displacement of wind power in Great Britain. *Energy Policy*, *101*, 201–210.

Uçak, H., Aslan, A., Yucel, F., & Turgut, A. (2015). A dynamic analysis of CO_2 emissions and the GDP relationship: Empirical evidence from high-income OECD countries. *Energy Sources, Part B: Economics, Planning, and Policy*, *10*(1), 38–50.

Wheatley, J. (2013). Quantifying CO_2 savings from wind power. *Energy Policy*, *63*, 89–96.

Wu, D.-M. (1973). Alternative tests of independence between stochastic regressors and disturbances. *Econometrica, 41*(4), 733–750.

Zhang, Z. (2000). Decoupling China's carbon emissions increase from economic growth: An economic analysis and policy implications. *World Development*, *28*(4), 739–752.

CHAPTER 5

PERSISTENT CYCLES AND LONG-RUN COVARIABILITY IN PALEOCLIMATE TIME SERIES

Vasco J. Gabriel[a,b], Luis F. Martins[c,d], and Anthoulla Phella[e]

[a]*University of Victoria, Canada*
[b]*NIPE, Portugal*
[c]*Instituto Universitário de Lisboa (ISCTE-IUL, BRU-IUL), Portugal*
[d]*CIMS, UK*
[e]*University of Glasgow, UK*

ABSTRACT

Motivated by the presence of a strong cyclical component in paleoclimate data, this chapter considers the problem of conducting cointegration inference when the data contains very large and persistent cycles. Our first contribution is to show, analytically and through Monte Carlo simulations, that while point estimation remains consistent, commonly applied tests are no longer valid when the data contains persistent cycles. Our second contribution is empirical: the authors propose the use of the long-run covariability approach of Müller and Watson (2018) to quantify low-frequency comovement amongst a range of paleoclimate times series over the last 800,000 years. These methods allow us to focus on the long run properties of the data, bypassing short and medium run fluctuations, while being agnostic regarding the order of integration of the time series. The authors provide new estimates for the long-run relationship between temperatures and CO_2 atmospheric concentration, concluding that in the long-run a 100 ppm increase in CO_2 concentration levels would raise temperatures by around 1°C. Finally, the authors illustrate how joint modeling of

Econometrics of Climate, Energy, and Green Transition
Advances in Econometrics, Volume 47A, 147–190

ISSN: 0731-9053/doi:10.1108/S0731-90532026000047A006

this set of paleoclimate time series can be carried out by factor analysis and how long-term projections about temperature increases and ice-sheet retreat can be constructed.

Keywords: Paleoclimate data; glaciar cycles; low frequency analysis; cointegration; long-term projections

JEL Classification: C22; C53; Q54

1. INTRODUCTION

The analysis of paleoclimate data has played an important role in informing the debate around the causes of climate change and in quantifying the long run relationship between global temperatures and greenhouse gases, namely atmospheric carbon dioxide (CO_2) concentration.[1] Indeed, the correct determination of the time series properties of paleoclimate data is crucial to ascertain the long term drivers of Earth's climate and, through appropriate (formal) statistical procedures, to establish a baseline for its evolution, therefore providing a useful contrast with recent anthropogenic-driven climate change (see Covey et al., 1996; Lea, 2004; Knutti et al., 2017; *inter alia*). In this regard, and focusing on the last 800,000 years, we argue that Milankovitch cycles (i.e., the role played by Earth's orbital movements, which affects solar radiation), while important in explaining the complex dynamics of glacial/interglacial cycles, may present non-negligible challenges for the study of the long-run features of climate data.

A strand of the literature has focused on the application of cointegrated vector autoregressions, making use of inherent error-correction mechanisms to model long-run relationships between climate and orbital geometry; for example, Kaufmann and Juselius (2013) and Kaufmann and Pretis (2020, 2021) find support for a long-run equilibrium driven by solar insolation, but disturbed by interactions among components of the climate system (see also Miller, 2019 for measurement issues associated with paleoclimate data). However, evidence for the presence of stochastic trends in the relevant time series is mixed at best. Several papers report results that are consistent with the presence of a stochastic trend (Gordon, 1991; Woodward & Gray, 1993; Woodward & Gray, 1995; Gordon et al., 1996; Kärner, 1996). Conversely, many other studies suggest that the data is consistent with the presence of a deterministic trend with possibly highly persistent noise (Bloomfield & Nychka, 1992; Bloomfield, 1992; Baillie & Chung, 2002; Fomby & Vogelsang, 2002). The results in Davidson et al. (2016), for example, do not support the hypothesis of integrated behavior.

The consequences of uncertainty around the order of integration of the series of interest for the purpose of cointegration analysis are well known in the literature.[2] Elliott (1998) discusses the robustness of cointegration methods when the regressors are near-unit processes, finding that while point estimation remains consistent, hypothesis testing based on the assumption of exact unit roots may lead to highly misleading results under slight deviations from the unit root benchmark.

Furthermore, Pesaran et al. (2001) propose a cointegration test that bypasses pre-testing for unit roots, therefore allowing for uncertainty about whether regressors are stationary or nonstationary. More recently, Dou and Müller (2021) generalize the local-to-unity framework, showing that it can approximate well a large class of models that generate substantial persistence not dissimilar to $I(1)$ processes. On the other hand, Duffy and Simons (2023) characterize cointegration based on impulse response functions in a way that long run relationships are identified even if the series are not exact unit roots.

Our focus is on how the presence of strong persistent cycles may affect cointegration inference. Earlier literature considered the possibility of unit roots and cointegration at recurring frequencies such as seasonal ones, see Hylleberg et al. (1990). Moreover, Engle and Kozicki (1993), Vahid and Engle (1993), and Vahid and Engle (1997) develop tests for common features, which may include "cycles." However, cyclical behavior here is understood as the stationary remainder after removing nonstationary terms (Vahid & Engle, 1993, footnote 1, p. 341), which does not generate the sort of very persistent and pronounced cycles observed in ice-age data.

On the other hand, processes with complex unit roots add some flexibility to the $I(0)$ / $I(1)$ knife-edge dichotomy of previous literature, as they display persistent cyclical behavior (see Bierens, 2001). In this context, Nielsen (2001) and Del Barrio Castro et al. (2013, 2015) show analytically and through simulations that standard unit root tests have considerable size distortions, for finite samples and asymptotically, in the presence of complex unit roots.

Against this background, and inspired by the nature of paleoclimatic time series, we examine the consequences of the presence of large, persistent cycles for cointegration inference. We do so analytically and by means of Monte Carlo simulations, demonstrating that, under a variety of Data Generating Processes (DGPs) for persistent cycles in a vector error correction model (VECM) setting, maximum likelihood (ML) point estimation remains consistent, but converging at rate-$\sqrt{T}$, not at a rate-T as in the standard cointegration approach. Moreover, the trace and max-eigenvalue cointegration tests will also diverge, therefore suggesting that the data is stationary and the variables should be modeled in levels rather than in first-differences. These results are, to some extent, akin to the problem of cointegration with non-unit root regressors.

Indeed, the importance of modeling persistent cycles in climate time series has long been recognized in the climate literature, see Mitchell (1976). Several papers attempt to decompose the variability of the paleoclimate data in the frequency domain, see Mann and Lees (2019), Muller and MacDonald (1997), Wunsch (2008), Meyers et al. (2008), and Ditlevsen et al. (2020), *inter alia*. More recently, Proietti and Maddanu (2024) propose an alternative parametric approach through the fractional sinusoidal waveform process.

Furthermore, given that persistent cycles have the potential to lead to misleading cointegration inference, we propose to study the long-run comovement between temperatures and CO_2 atmospheric concentration by employing recently developed methods that highlight low-frequency covariability of time series; see Müller and Watson (2018) and Müller and Watson (2024), MW henceforth.

Indeed, we suggest that variation in paleoclimate time series is dominated by glaciation cycles and therefore contain only limited information about the very long-run relation between temperatures and CO_2. Using the procedures of MW allows us to isolate a small number of low-frequency trigonometric weighted averages, which are then used to conduct inference about the long-run (co)variability of temperatures and CO_2. Moreover, in order to attenuate "curse-of-dimensionality" issues, we allow for a group of drivers to be "partialled out," so that we are able to hone in on the long-run relationship between temperatures and CO_2 while controlling for orbital forcing.

This approach is quite novel and distinctive in this literature and there are several advantages in using these low-frequency techniques. First, they allow us to focus on time spans that go beyond cyclical dynamics and thus obtain better estimates of long-run coefficients that are uncontaminated by short or medium run variations. Second, the methodology is flexible in that we can conduct inference on bivariate or multivariate low-frequency features of several climate variables. Third, these methods are fairly robust to the persistence patterns of paleoclimate data, permitting combinations of nonstationary, near-nonstationary or stationary series, thus circumventing the need to (pre)test for unit roots and cointegration. Indeed, the data transformations are approximately Gaussian and therefore standard inference tools and confidence intervals can be employed. Finally, the construction of long horizon forecasts is relatively straightforward, thus allowing us to complement the scenario analysis in Castle and Hendry (2020).

Put simply, the method consists in obtaining low-frequency weighted averages of the data by using trigonometric projections that ensure approximate Gaussianity of the transformed series. Inference is then based on a (relatively) small number q of low-frequency averages, whereby correlation or regression coefficients (and respective standard errors) can be computed in the usual way. The choice of q determines the cyclicality that the researcher wishes to study. In our case, we are agnostic about the choice of q and suggest selecting q such that covariability is maximized. As it turns out, in our case q ranges from 16 to 20, which indicates spans of data between 80,000 and 100,000 years, consistent with the cyclicality in paleoclimate data.

Thus, we start by obtaining measures of long-run covariability between temperatures and levels of CO_2, with our results suggesting that correlation is indeed strong and quite significant, with a 90% confidence interval of $[0.90, 0.98]$, while the long-run regression coefficient is estimated at around 0.09. Given that the exclusively bivariate focus is likely to lead to overestimation, we use an extension of the MW approach that allows us to control for measures capturing orbital forcing, i.e., a selection of control variables is "partialled out" prior to the application of low-frequency projections. The resulting confidence intervals for the regression coefficient of temperatures on CO_2 range between 0.048 and 0.106, and therefore not too dissimilar to the results found in Castle and Hendry (2020).

We also pursue the alternative approach of summarizing relevant exogenous information by extracting a common factor driving orbital forcing and CO_2 levels, with these results confirming our previous findings. Finally, emulating Castle and Hendry (2020), we present long-term forecasts for temperatures and ice-volume that can be constructed from low-frequency (multivariate) factor models, conditioning on (anthropogenically determined) current levels of CO_2 concentration, which are far higher than those typical during previous glaciar cycles. Our results suggest a steady increase in temperatures, coupled with a substantial decline in ice volumes well below historical minima for the sample period under study, pointing toward an ice-free planet under current CO_2 levels.

The chapter is organized as follows. Section 2 provides a brief description of the data and a set of models that generate persistent cycles, used in Section 3 to analyze the implications for cointegration inference within a VECM setup. In Section 4, we explore the low-frequency inference procedures of MW using paleoclimate data, presenting baseline results for the simple bivariate relationship between temperatures and CO_2 levels, as well estimations considering additional controls, which can either be "partialled out" or encapsulated into a common factor extracted via principal component analysis. Furthermore, we discuss multivariate low-frequency analysis and forecasting of paleoclimate time series, while Section 5 offers some concluding remarks.

2. DATA, RELATED LITERATURE, AND MODELS

To motivate the discussion, we begin this section with an overview of the paleoclimatic data, highlighting the main features, namely persistent cyclicality and comovement. We then consider simple models that generate marked cyclical components, which will be used in Section 3 to study their effects on cointegration analysis.

2.1. Data

We focus on three paleoclimate time series: Antarctic land surface temperature, atmospheric CO_2 concentration levels, and ice volume. The relationship between temperatures and CO_2 has received particular attention in the literature. Indeed, CO_2 concentrations are widely recognized as the primary anthropogenic factor driving recent temperature changes. Given its relatively long atmospheric persistence compared to other greenhouse gases, CO_2 is also expected to influence future temperature trends. Additionally, Kaufmann and Juselius (2013) found one of ten cointegrating relationships specifically between these two variables. If their findings are reliable, similar patterns should emerge when analyzing just these two series. The estimates in Castle and Hendry (2020) are used here as a benchmark, but see also McMillan and Wohar (2013), Davidson et al. (2016), Miller (2019), and Blazsek and Escribano (2023).

Temperature data were sourced from Jouzel et al. (2007) as part of the European Project for Ice Coring in Antarctica (EPICA), using deuterium measurements from deep ice cores in combination with other paleoclimate records and climate model simulations – as in other studies, we use temperature anomalies in °C with respect to mean temperature in the last millennium. Equally from this project, atmospheric CO_2 concentration levels (in parts per million, ppm, by volume) were obtained from Lüthi et al. (2008), based on air trapped in ice cores extracted in Antarctica. These measurements suggest that atmospheric CO_2 varied between 170 ppm and 300 ppm during the period considered here (see Lüthi et al., 2008). On the other hand, ice volume estimates come from Lisiecki and Raymo (2005), using benthic $\delta^{18}O$ records derived from calcium carbonate shells of foraminifera found in seafloor sediments from a wide range of latitudes, longitudes, and depths. In addition, and following Kaufmann and Juselius (2013), we consider standard orbital drivers, namely Eccentricity (*Ec*), Obliquity (*Ob*), and Precession (*Pr*).

The period comprises 800,000 years (800 kyr), with all observations adjusted to the common EDC3 time scale and linearly interpolated for missing observations. The total sample size in 1000 year intervals is thus $T = 801$ with the last 100 observations (i.e., 100,000 years, ending 1000 years before the present) used to evaluate the predictive ability of our models (see Kaufmann & Juselius, 2013; Davidson et al., 2016; Castle & Hendry, 2020; Blazsek & Escribano, 2023, for further details on the construction of the data, as well as Miller, 2019 for the consequences of interpolation on subsequent statistical analysis).

The most striking feature of the paleoclimate series is their cyclicality, i.e., significant recurring comovements, such that temperature and CO_2 levels stay below their mean for long periods during glaciations (see Fig. 5.1), with the opposite pattern for ice volume. As extensively discussed in Davidson et al. (2016), this behavior makes it difficult to reconcile with the cointegration approach used to study long-run relationships and followed in much of the literature. In fact, it could be argued that glacial cycles are the long-run movements in the data, as they play the most prominent role, recurring every 80,000–100,000 years (although not in a completely regular fashion).

Modeling paleoclimatic data is an inherently difficult task because the structural relationship between orbitally-induced insolation and seasons in the paleoclimate rests on semi-quantitative arguments. For example, using filtered data, Lisiecki (2010) and Kawamura et al. (2010) present evidence that strongly suggests a relationship between orbital variables based on their frequency spectra. On the other hand, Rial (1999) suggests that the eccentricity signal acts as a frequency modulator for ice volume and argues why therefore certain peaks in the ice volume spectrum are missing. These approaches do not establish a direct relationship between variables by means of a statistical model, but rather focus on the potential physical mechanisms in favor of one. In contrast, Imbrie and Imbrie (1980) establish a formal, albeit deterministic, model which, to date, offers the cleanest direct relationship between orbital variables and ice volume on Earth, with a broad consensus in the literature regarding the likely non-linear nature of the relationship.

Aside from the role of orbital variation in driving ice ages, considerable attention has been devoted to the interplay of temperatures, ice volume, and atmospheric concentration of CO_2. The treatment of the latter and, in particular, whether it should be treated as a forcing variable or an endogenous response, has been the subject of some debate. Lea (2004) and Jaccard et al. (2016), for example, suggest that orbital forcings drive variations in temperatures, which in turn affect

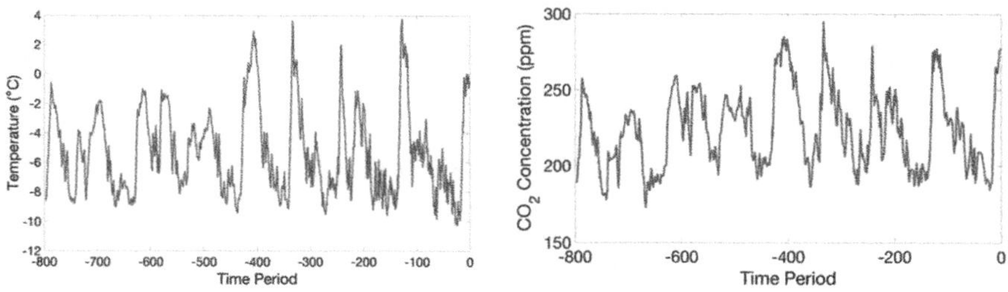

(a) Temperature (b) CO_2

Fig. 5.1. Temperatures and CO_2 Concentration Levels.

ice volume and how much trapped CO_2 is released into the atmosphere. In turn, Davidson et al. (2016) find that CO_2 and other greenhouse gases are Granger-caused by temperatures.

Consequently, Castle and Hendry (2020) model these variables as a jointly endogenous system, with orbital forcing variables deemed to be strongly exogenous. They find evidence of an endogenous response of CO_2 to orbital forcing, as well as support for a "weak" form of the Milankovitch hypothesis, i.e., in order to account for all aspects of glacial cycles, one needs to also consider nonlinear interactions between the different orbital components (in line with the physics literature cited above).

Nevertheless, the features in the data remarked above raise the following questions:

1. To what extent the strong dynamics of persistent cycles (such as those displayed in Fig. 5.1) impair cointegration analysis?
2. Once these (exogenous) cycles are taken into account, how can one quantify with precision the relationship between temperatures and CO_2?

This section and the next attempt to provide an answer to the first question, while Section 4 deals with 2. Given its importance for accurate climate projections, our focus is on inference about the long-run relationship between temperature and gas concentrations, so in order to abstract from the admittedly difficult-to-model cyclical component, we propose using the low-frequency "filtering" procedures of MW.

2.2. Simple Models for Persistent Cycles

As discussed in the preceding sub-section and in the wider literature, orbital variables (and, to a large extent, paleoclimatic variables) possess very persistent cycles. Proietti and Maddanu (2024) recently proposed the fractional sinusoidal waveform process to model the strong cyclical component, such that parameters that regulate the amplitude and the cycle phase follow fractional noise processes. We present alternative, potentially simpler, models, distinguishing deterministic from stochastic laws.

2.2.1. Periodic Deterministic and Stochastic Cycles

As a simple way to capture the data properties, we first consider the following model:

$$y_t = \mu + \delta_t \cos\left(\lambda\pi \frac{t}{T}\right) + \theta u_t, \text{ with } u_t = \rho u_{t-1} + \varepsilon_t,\ t = 2,\ldots,T, \tag{1}$$

where $\lambda > 2$ is constant, δ_t can be time-varying and ε_t is a white noise (WN) with unit variance.[3] The number of cycles $\lambda / 2$, each with periodicity $2T / \lambda$, is assumed to be constant, whereas the expected cycle's range $[\mu - \delta_t, \mu + \delta_t]$ can vary over time, both properties being present in the data reviewed in Section 2.1. The parameters θ and ρ control the amount and persistence of noise around the cycle, respectively, and are assumed to follow an AR(1) process, possibly a near-unit root process.

The component that is left with the most general specification as possible is δ_t, which controls the cycle's range. This can be deterministic or stochastic, and with different orders of convergence. For data that remains relatively stable around μ, such that δ_t is of the same order of u_t, it is assumed that, as $T \to \infty$, $\frac{1}{\sqrt{T}} \sum_{t=1}^{\lfloor rT \rfloor} \delta_t \to \tilde{\delta}(r)$, i.e., $\sum_{t=1}^{\lfloor rT \rfloor} \delta_t = O(\sqrt{T})$ or $O_p(\sqrt{T})$ for any $r \in [0,1]$. In this case, the scaled demeaned partial sum

$$T^{-1/2} \sum_{t=1}^{\lfloor rT \rfloor} (y_t - \mu) \Rightarrow \cos(\lambda\pi r)\tilde{\delta}(r) + (\lambda\pi r)\int_0^1 \sin(\lambda\pi rs)\tilde{\delta}(s)\,ds + \sigma_u W(r), \tag{2}$$

as $T \to \infty$, for $r \in [0,1]$ (see Bierens, 1994, Lem 9.6.3, p. 200). If δ_t is deterministic, one can consider $\delta_t = \frac{\delta}{\sqrt{T}}$, where $\tilde{\delta}(r) = \delta \lfloor r \rfloor$, or a linear time trend $\delta_t = \delta \frac{t}{T^{3/2}}$, with $\tilde{\delta}(r) = \delta \frac{1}{2} r^2$. If δ_t is stochastic, it can be assumed, for example, that $\delta_t = \frac{1}{T} \sum_{j=1}^{t} \epsilon_j$, where ϵ_t is a $\mathrm{WN}\left(0, \sigma_\epsilon^2\right)$, so that $\tilde{\delta}(r) = \sigma_\epsilon \int_0^r W(s)\,ds$.

The paleoclimatic data possesses cycles with wider ranges and therefore $\sum_{t=1}^{\lfloor rT \rfloor} \delta_t = O(\sqrt{T})$ or $O_p(\sqrt{T})$ is not a reasonable assumption to make in this case.

For example, if δ_t is a constant ($\delta_t = \delta$), we have $\sum_{t=1}^{T} \delta_t = O_p(T)$ and $T^{-1/2} \sum_{t=1}^{T} (y_t - \mu) = O(\sqrt{T}) + T^{-1/2} \sum_{t=1}^{T} u_t$ because

$$\frac{1}{T} \sum_{t=1}^{T} \cos\left(\frac{\lambda\pi}{T} t\right) \to \frac{\sin(\lambda\pi)}{\lambda\pi}, \text{ as } T \to \infty. \tag{3}$$

For integer $\lambda > 2$, $\frac{1}{T}\sum_{t=1}^{T}\cos\left(\frac{\lambda\pi}{T}t\right) \to 0$, as $T \to \infty$. Hence, $\delta_t \cos\left(\lambda\pi\frac{t}{T}\right)$ dominates over θu_t and the normalization is the first moment of the series

$$\frac{1}{T}\sum_{t=1}^{T}(y_t - \mu) \xrightarrow{p} \delta\frac{\sin(\lambda\pi)}{\lambda\pi}. \tag{4}$$

Similarly, for deterministic $\delta_t = \delta_0\left(1 - \delta_1\frac{t}{T}\right)$ we have $\frac{1}{T}\sum_{t=1}^{T}\delta_t \to \delta_0\left(1 - \delta_1\frac{1}{2}\right)$, and for stochastic (scaled random walk) $\delta_t = \delta_0 + \frac{1}{T}\sum_{j=1}^{t}\epsilon_j, \delta_0 \neq 0$, we have $\frac{1}{T}\sum_{t=1}^{T}\delta_t \to \delta_0$.

2.2.2. *Persistent Cycle-Near-Unit Root Decomposition*

An alternative model to capture persistent cycles is a simple cycle/noise decomposition where, instead of a cosine function, the cyclical component follows a latent AR(2) process with complex unit roots. Specifically,

$$y_t = \mu + z_t + \gamma u_t, \quad t = 1,\ldots,T, \tag{5}$$

with

$$z_t = \phi_1 z_{t-1} + \phi_2 z_{t-2} + \eta v_t, \tag{6}$$

$$u_t = \rho u_{t-1} + \varepsilon_t, \tag{7}$$

where v_t and ε_t are two mutually independent $\text{WN}(0,1)$. Here, μ controls for the level and γ for the amount of noise in the data. z_t is a nonstationary AR(2) process where ϕ_1 and ϕ_2 control for the (time-invariant) frequency of the cycles (following Bierens, 2001, $\phi_2 = -1$ and $\phi_1 = 2\cos(\phi)$ so that the cycle lasts $2\pi / \phi$ periods). The parameter η controls for the time-variability of the cycle's range (if $\eta = 0$ the cycle has constant range; the larger the η, the larger the variability the cycle exhibits) and z_1, z_2 are constants with probability 1: for the sake of simplicity, z_2 controls for the cycle's range after, assuming $P(z_1 = 0) = 1$. Finally, u_t is a stationary near-unit root AR(1) process that smoothly fluctuates around the cycle component.[4]

From Bierens (2001), imposing $\phi_2 = -1$, $\phi_1 = 2\cos(\phi)$ and $\eta = 1$, equation (6) implies

$$z_t = \frac{1}{\sin(\phi)}\sum_{j=1}^{t}\sin(\phi(t+1-j))v_j + d_t; \tag{8}$$

$$d_t = A\cos(\phi t) + B\sin(\phi t) + C, \tag{9}$$

where A, B, C depend on initial conditions. Thus, y_t is explained through

$$y_t = \mu + d_t + \frac{1}{\sin(\phi)} \sum_{j=1}^{t} \sin(\phi(t+1-j)) v_j + \gamma \left(\rho^t u_0 + \sum_{j=0}^{t-1} \rho^j \varepsilon_{t-j} \right), \tag{10}$$

which may include a trend d_t.

3. COINTEGRATION ANALYSIS IN THE PRESENCE OF PERSISTENT CYCLES

In this section, we study the properties of standard cointegration inference for models with $I(1)$ variables when the true data includes persistent cycles. We use

Monte Carlo simulations for a variety of models and derive analytical results for a toy model.

3.1. Monte Carlo Simulations

For the sake of simplicity, and following the existing literature, we consider the bivariate VECM

$$\begin{pmatrix} \Delta y_t \\ \Delta x_t \end{pmatrix} = \begin{pmatrix} \alpha_1 \\ \alpha_2 \end{pmatrix} (1, \beta_2) \begin{pmatrix} y_{t-1} \\ x_{t-1} \end{pmatrix} + \begin{pmatrix} u_{1t} \\ u_{2t} \end{pmatrix}, \quad t = 2, \ldots, T, \tag{11}$$

the corresponding Maximum Likelihood Estimator (MLE) for $\alpha_1, \alpha_2, \beta_2$ and the trace eigenvalue test for cointegration. We study the bias of the MLE (empirical mean and standard deviation) and for $\hat{\beta}_2$ we compute distributional quantiles ($\tau \in [0,1]$ with empirical quantiles $\tau = 0.05, 0.50$, and 0.95) for two convergence rates, $T(\hat{\beta}_2 - \beta_2)$ and $\sqrt{T}(\hat{\beta}_2 - \beta_2)$, to address the typical cases of nonstationary and stationary data. For the trace test, we compute the percentage of times there is evidence of stationary data, $r = 2$ (rejections of spurious and cointegration regressions). The sample sizes are $T = 50, 100, 800, 10000$ to cover the cases of small samples, our paleoclimate application, as well as larger samples. The number of replications is set to 5,000.

To better understand the consequences of estimating the model described in (11) when the data $\{x_t, y_t\}_{t=1}^{T}$ includes persistent cycles, we begin by presenting the results for the standard cointegration case where variables are nonstationary unit root processes. Let $x_t = x_{t-1} + u_{xt}$, where u_{xt} is a Gaussian WN(0,1), and $y_t = x_t + v_t$, where v_t is also a Gaussian WN(0,1), independent of u_{xt}. That is, the true coefficients are $\alpha' = (\alpha_1, \alpha_2) = (-1, 0)$ and $\beta' = (1, \beta_2)$ with $\beta_2 = -1$. The results are in Table 5.1.

As expected, because model (11) is well specified for cointegrated nonstationary unit root processes, the trace test has the correct size for any T – even for small $T = 50$ the empirical size is almost 0.05. The MLE for β is unbiased and

Table 5.1. Estimation of the Bivariate ECM – Nonstationary Unit Root Processes.

	trace	β_2		$T(\beta_{2+1})$			$\sqrt{T}(\beta_2+1)$			α_1		α_2	
T	mean	mean	st. dev.	$\tau=0.05$	$\tau=0.5$	$\tau=0.95$	$\tau=0.05$	$\tau=0.5$	$\tau=0.95$	mean	st. dev.	mean	st. dev.
50	0.049	−1.000	0.051	−3.901	−0.012	3.896	−0.551	−0.001	0.551	−0.534	0.872	−0.008	0.145
100	0.047	−1.000	0.024	−3.965	0.003	3.862	−0.396	3.8e-04	0.386	−0.483	0.890	−0.010	0.101
800	0.051	−1.000	0.003	−3.837	0.063	3.708	−0.135	0.002	0.131	−0.397	0.917	−0.003	0.035
10,000	0.054	−1.000	2.3e-04	−3.839	−0.028	3.729	−0.038	−2.8e-04	0.037	−0.330	0.944	−0.001	0.009

Note: Model (11); *trace* is the percentage of rejections of spurious and cointegration regressions using the trace test.

the distribution has the correct order of convergence, getting closer to the asymptotic one as T increases. In particular, the MLE for β_2 has mean equal to the true one (−1) and the standard deviation approaches zero as T increases. The MLE is T-consistent since the distribution, as given by the quantiles, of $T(\beta_2+1)$ does not collapse to zero, as it does for $\sqrt{T}(\beta_2+1)$. The MLE for α_2 is unbiased, but not for α_1. These findings help in understanding the issues with the trace test statistic and the MLE once we keep the (now) misspecified model (11) for DGPs that possess different types of persistent cycles.

Next, we consider distinct models for x_t with persistent cycles, keeping the same specification as before, where $y_t = x_t + v_t$, so that $\alpha' = (-1,0)$ and $\beta_2 = -1$. In the first case, $x_t = \delta_t \cos\left(\lambda\pi \frac{t}{T}\right) + \varepsilon_t$ where ε_t is a Gaussian WN$(0,\sigma_\varepsilon^2)$, with a deterministic δ_t. Regarding the model in equation (1), we assume $\mu = \rho = 0$ and $\theta = 1$. For constant $\delta_t = \delta$, by visual inspection of temperatures and CO_2 concentration, where T is around 800, we consider the following parameterization: $\delta = 7$ or $\delta = 80$, $\lambda = 6$ or $\lambda = 16$, and $\sigma_\varepsilon = 1$ or $\sigma_\varepsilon = 7$. For time-varying δ_t, the scaled linear trend is $\delta_t = \delta_0\left(1 - \delta_1 \frac{t}{T}\right)$ for $\delta_0 = 7$, and $\delta_1 = -1$ or $\delta_1 = -2$, for fixed $\lambda = 16$ and $\sigma_\varepsilon = 1$.

The results are reported in Table 5.2. Three main findings stand out. First, the MLE is not biased, with $\hat{\beta}_2$ converging faster to the true value than $\hat{\alpha}_1, \hat{\alpha}_2$, as T increases. Second, the rate at which $\left(\hat{\beta}_2 - \beta_2\right)$ converges in distribution is not the T-rate, but rather the $\sqrt{T}$-rate, because the extreme quantiles increase with T, and, as expected, the *5th* and *95th* quantiles depend on the model's specification. Putting these two findings together and contrasting with the results in Table 5.1, we conclude that fitting a standard VECM with data that follows the model in equation (1) leads to unbiased estimates, but with erroneous standard errors, confidence sets, and therefore overall inference. The third finding pertains to the trace test for cointegration: clearly, by testing for cointegration in the standard VECM, one will conclude that the data is stationary because the percentage of rejections is 1 (the exception being the case of $T = 50,100$ when $\delta = 7, \lambda = 6, \sigma_\varepsilon = 1$, where there is evidence for cointegrated $I(1)$ data). Therefore, if the data is stationary, one should model variables in levels instead of first-differences. In general, these main conclusions are robust to the particular specification of the deterministic δ_t.

In Table 5.3, we present results for the same model for x_t, but with $\sigma_\varepsilon = 1$ and with a stochastic δ_t. We consider a scaled random walk $\delta_t = \gamma + \delta_{t-1} + \frac{1}{T}\xi_t$, with $\xi_t \sim \mathrm{WN}\left(0,\sigma_\xi^2\right)$, both with no drift ($\gamma = 0$ and with a drift ($\gamma = 0.01$). Moreover, from the AR(1) specification $\delta_t = \phi_0 + \phi_1\delta_{t-1} + \xi_t$, we have the cases of a $\mathrm{WN}\left(\phi_0,\sigma_\xi^2\right)$, a stationary AR(1) with $\phi_1 = 0.5$, and a near-unit root process, where $\phi_1 \equiv \phi_{1,T} = 1 - \frac{1}{T}$. The conclusions are the same as those obtained for a deterministic δ_t, with the exceptions of the scaled random walk with a drift and of the near-unit root process – in these two cases, the range of the cycles is not stable, which goes against what is observed in the paleoclimatic data.

Table 5.2. Estimation of the Bivariate ECM – Periodic Deterministic Cycle.

	trace	β_2		$T(\beta_2+1)$			$\sqrt{T}(\beta_2+1)$			α_1		α_2	
T	mean	mean	sd	$\tau=0.05$	$\tau=0.5$	$\tau=0.95$	$\tau=0.05$	$\tau=0.5$	$\tau=0.95$	mean	sd	mean	sd
$\delta=7;\lambda=6;\sigma_\varepsilon=1$													
50	0.005	−1.000	0.029	−2.488	0.030	2.413	−0.351	0.004	0.341	−0.572	0.899	−0.053	0.335
100	0.012	−1.000	0.020	−3.484	0.019	3.376	−0.348	0.002	0.337	−0.583	0.837	−0.042	0.168
800	1	−1.000	0.007	−9.346	−0.125	9.082	−0.330	−0.004	0.321	−0.623	0.783	−0.017	0.048
10,000	1	−1.000	0.002	−34.035	−0.086	34.259	−0.340	−8.6e-04	0.342	−0.924	0.381	−0.002	0.014
$\delta=7;\lambda=16;\sigma_\varepsilon=1$													
50	1	−0.999	0.031	−2.581	0.050	2.599	−0.365	0.007	0.367	−0.614	1.041	−0.075	0.669
100	1	−1.000	0.020	−3.489	−0.016	3.412	−0.348	−0.001	0.341	−0.551	0.886	−0.055	0.284
800	1	−1.000	0.007	−9.280	0.090	9.420	−0.328	0.003	0.333	−0.648	0.763	−0.017	0.049
10,000	1	−1.000	0.002	−32.642	−0.471	33.478	−0.326	−0.004	0.334	−0.923	0.384	−0.002	0.014
$\delta=80;\lambda=16;\sigma_\varepsilon=7$													
50	1	−0.999	0.002	−0.219	0.004	0.221	−0.031	6.4e-04	0.031	−0.895	7.298	0.024	7.290
100	1	−1.000	0.001	−0.303	−0.002	0.295	−0.030	−2.0e-04	0.029	−0.809	3.046	0.008	2.997
800	1	−1.000	6.1e-04	−0.800	0.005	0.817	−0.028	2.0e-04	0.028	−0.576	0.896	−0.092	0.362
10,000	1	−1.000	1.7e-04	−2.837	−0.042	2.905	−0.028	−4.2e-04	0.029	−0.481	0.883	−0.040	0.091
$\delta_0=7;\delta_1=-1;\lambda=16;\sigma_\varepsilon=1$													
50	1	−0.999	0.019	−1.611	0.031	1.612	−0.227	0.004	0.228	−0.595	1.256	−0.028	0.960
100	1	−1.000	0.013	−2.255	−0.010	2.166	−0.225	−0.001	0.216	−0.475	0.969	−0.023	0.401
800	1	−1.000	0.004	−5.971	0.102	6.091	−0.211	0.003	0.215	−0.492	0.872	−0.018	0.049
10,000	1	−1.000	0.001	−21.236	−0.161	21.748	−0.212	−0.001	0.217	−0.731	0.682	−0.004	0.013
$\delta_0=7;\delta_1=-2;\lambda=16;\sigma_\varepsilon=1$													
50	1	−0.999	0.014	−1.168	0.018	1.152	−0.165	0.002	0.163	−0.632	1.499	−0.008	1.279
100	1	−1.000	0.009	−1.625	−0.014	1.575	−0.162	−0.001	0.157	−0.463	1.032	0.013	0.528
800	0	−1.000	0.003	−4.351	0.081	4.445	−0.153	0.002	0.157	−0.448	0.895	−0.015	0.052
10,000	1	−1.000	9.6e-04	−15.476	−0.086	15.988	−0.154	−8.6e-04	0.159	−0.598	0.801	−0.005	0.013

Notes: Model (1) with δ_t deterministic; *trace* is the percentage of rejections of spurious and cointegration regressions using the trace test.

Table 5.3. Estimation of the Bivariate ECM – Periodic Stochastic Cycles.

	trace	β_2		$T(\beta_2+1)$			$\sqrt{T}(\beta_2+1)$			α_1		α_2	
T	mean	mean	sd	$\tau=0.05$	$\tau=0.5$	$\tau=0.95$	$\tau=0.05$	$\tau=0.5$	$\tau=0.95$	mean	sd	mean	sd
$\gamma=0;\delta_0=7;\lambda=16;\sigma_\xi=1$													
50	1	–0.999	0.031	–2.560	0.014	2.643	–0.362	0.002	0.373	–0.641	1.040	–0.076	0.678
100	1	–0.999	0.020	–3.332	–0.006	3.532	–0.333	–6.8e-04	0.353	–0.557	0.879	–0.053	0.282
800	1	–0.999	0.007	–9.189	0.130	9.372	–0.324	0.004	0.331	–0.649	0.764	–0.018	0.048
10,000	1	–1.000	0.002	–33.230	0.192	33.205	–0.332	0.001	0.332	–0.925	0.378	–0.001	0.014
$\gamma=0.01;\delta_0=7;\lambda=16;\sigma_\xi=1$													
50	1	–0.999	0.030	–2.465	0.015	2.547	–0.348	0.002	0.360	–0.611	1.070	–0.083	0.696
100	1	–0.999	0.019	–3.091	–0.004	3.294	–0.309	–4.4e-04	0.329	–0.556	0.884	–0.044	0.298
800	0.999	–0.999	0.004	–5.605	0.079	5.784	–0.198	0.002	0.204	–0.498	0.870	–0.018	0.050
10,000	0	–1.000	2.2e-04	–3.636	–0.006	3.701	–0.036	–6.5e-05	0.037	–0.270	0.962	–0.004	0.013
$\phi_0=7;\phi_1=0;\lambda=16;\sigma_\xi=1$													
50	1	–0.999	0.031	–2.497	0.015	2.618	–0.353	0.002	0.370	–0.632	1.049	–0.085	0.681
100	1	–0.999	0.021	–3.389	0.002	3.526	–0.338	2.5e-04	0.352	–0.563	0.883	–0.064	0.300
800	1	–0.999	0.007	–9.172	0.197	9.343	–0.324	0.007	0.330	–0.662	0.788	–0.023	0.059
10,000	1	–1.000	0.002	–33.441	0.084	33.153	–0.334	8.4e-04	0.331	–0.871	0.490	–0.003	0.017
$\phi_0=7;\phi_1=0.5;\lambda=16;\sigma_\xi=1$													
50	1	–0.999	0.015	–1.236	0.008	1.284	–0.174	0.001	0.181	–0.589	1.484	–0.021	1.229
100	1	–0.999	0.010	–1.663	–0.002	1.739	–0.166	–2.0e-04	0.174	–0.451	1.026	–0.021	0.509
800	0.999	–0.999	0.003	–4.526	0.045	4.663	–0.160	0.001	0.164	–0.524	0.856	–0.019	0.059
10,000	1	–1.000	9.9e-04	–16.558	–0.013	16.350	–0.165	–1.3e-04	0.163	–0.623	0.782	–0.005	0.015
$\phi_0=7;\phi_1=\left(1-\frac{1}{T}\right);\lambda=16;\sigma_\xi=1$													
50	1	–1.000	0.001	–0.120	0.002	0.120	–0.017	3.1e-04	0.017	–1.032	12.229	–0.082	12.224
100	0.899	–1.000	4.9e-04	–0.080	–5.1e-04	0.083	–0.008	–5.1e-05	0.008	–0.869	9.833	0.078	9.831
800	0	–1.000	2.1e-05	–0.027	1.0e-04	0.028	–9.7e-04	3.8e-06	0.001	–0.981	3.607	–0.017	3.597
10,000	1	–1.000	4.9e-07	–0.008	–3.9e-05	0.008	–8.1e-05	–3.9e-07	8.2e-05	–1.007	1.029	–0.018	1.016

Notes: Model (1) with δ_t stochastic; *trace* is the percentage of rejections of spurious and cointegration regressions using the trace test.

Finally, we study the properties of the standard VECM of equation (11) with $\alpha' = (-1,0)$ and $\beta' = (1,-1)$ when x_t follows the persistent cycle-near-unit root decomposition.[5] The cycle component is defined by equation (6) where x_t evolves as a non-stationary AR(2) process with complex unit roots and, for comparability, we also consider x_t as following the fractional sinusoidal waveform process of Proietti and Maddanu (2024). In the first case, $\mu = 0, z_1 = 0, z_2 = 0.25, \gamma = 1, \eta = 0.001, \rho = 0.95$ and $\phi_1 = 1.9960534, \phi_2 = -1$.[6] In the AR(2) model, $x_t = 0.02 + \phi_1 x_{t-1} + \phi_2 x_{t-2} + 0.01 u_t$, where $u_t = 0.2 u_{t-1} + \varepsilon_t$, $\varepsilon_t \sim \text{WN}(0,1)$, and we allow (ϕ_1, ϕ_2) to take three different combinations to capture distinct cycle lengths: $(1.9960534,-1)$, $(1.411423,-0.5)$, and $(1.6355457,-0.7)$.[7] The two fractional sinusoidal waveform processes are generated according to the model and the estimated coefficients for paleoclimatic temperatures and CO_2 concentrations (we refer the reader to Proietti & Maddanu, 2024 for details). The results are in Table 5.4. Once again, the main conclusions obtained earlier hold true for these DGPs (c.f. Tables 5.2 and 5.3). Noticeably, from the trace test there is a switch from cointegration to stationary data as T gets large because the percentage of rejections switch from around 0 to 1 as T increases.

3.2. A Theoretical Result

The Monte Carlo simulations suggest that the estimation of the standard VECM when the data has persistent cycles provides unbiased estimators, a different rate of convergence in distribution and, consequently, erroneous inference, as well as cointegration tests that identify variables as being stationary. We now show this result analytically for a simple model.

Consider as the true DGP the following bivariate vector time series process:

1. **Assumption 1**: Let $z_t = (y_t, x_t)'$, where $y_t = x_t + u_{yt}$ and $x_t = \delta \cos\left(\lambda\pi \frac{t}{T}\right) + u_{xt}$, with $u_t = (u_{yt}, u_{xt})$ following a bivariate standard normal distribution, and u_{yt} and u_{xt} are mutually independent with variances σ_y^2 and σ_x^2, respectively.

   That is, in first differences the models are

$$\Delta y_t = \delta\left[\cos\left(\lambda\pi \frac{t}{T}\right) - \cos\left(\lambda\pi \frac{(t-1)}{T}\right)\right] + \left(\Delta u_{xt} + \Delta u_{yt}\right) \tag{12}$$

$$\Delta x_t = \delta\left[\cos\left(\lambda\pi \frac{t}{T}\right) - \cos\left(\lambda\pi \frac{(t-1)}{T}\right)\right] + \Delta u_{xt} \tag{13}$$

and, equivalently, as the bivariate model

$$\Delta z_t = \mu_t \iota + \alpha\beta' z_{t-1} + \tilde{u}_t, t = 2,\ldots,T, \tag{14}$$

where

$$\mu_t \equiv \mu_t(\delta,\lambda) = \delta\left[\cos\left(\lambda\pi \frac{t}{T}\right) - \cos\left(\lambda\pi \frac{(t-1)}{T}\right)\right]; \tag{15}$$

Table 5.4. Estimation of the Bivariate ECM – Alternative Models with Stochastic Cycles.

	trace	β_2		$T(\beta_2+1)$			$\sqrt{T}(\beta_2+1)$			α_1		α_2	
T	mean	mean	sd	q_{05}	q_{50}	q_{95}	q_{05}	q_{50}	q_{95}	mean	sd	mean	sd
Persistent cycle-near unit root decomposition													
50	0.040	−1.000	0.051	−4.006	−0.005	3.991	−−0.566	-8.2e-04	0.564	−0.602	0.835	−0.034	0.147
100	0.055	−0.999	0.028	−4.406	−0.025	4.543	−0.440	−0.002	0.454	−0.634	0.791	−0.026	0.101
800	1	−0.999	0.008	−11.188	0.171	11.391	−0.395	0.006	0.402	−0.819	0.573	−0.006	0.035
10,000	1	−1.000	0.002	−38.917	−0.228	39.253	−0.389	−0.002	0.392	−0.999	0.032	−3.1e-06	0.010
AR(2) process with complex unit roots: $\phi_1 = 1.9960534; \phi_2 = -1$													
800	6.0e-04	−1.000	0.005	−7.158	0.022	6.969	−0.253	7.7e-04	0.246	−0.920	0.394	7.7e-04	0.010
10,000	0.914	−1.000	0.001	−16.406	−0.389	16.825	−0.164	−0.003	0.168	−0.957	0.287	1.8e-04	0.006
AR(2) process with complex unit roots: $\phi_1 = 1.6355457; \phi_2 = -0.7$													
800	0	−0.999	0.112	−147.065	0.098	148.402	−5.199	0.003	5.246	−1.000	0.044	6.1e-06	5.9e-04
10,000	1	−1.000	0.031	−525.754	−6.460	534.869	−5.257	−0.064	5.348	−0.999	0.012	6.8e-07	1.6e-04
AR(2) process with complex unit roots: $\phi_1 = 1.411423; \phi_2 = -0.5$													
800	0	−0.999	0.156	−203.144	0.339	204.569	−7.182	0.012	7.232	−1.000	0.044	4.8e-06	4.7e-04
10,000	1	−1.000	0.043	−732.138	−11.932	737.315	−7.321	−0.119	7.373	−0.999	0.012	3.4e-07	1.3e-04
Fractional sinusoidal waveform process: Temperatures													
50	0	−0.999	0.048	−3.983	0.056	4.026	−0.563	0.008	0.569	−0.667	0.768	−0.001	0.017
100	0	−0.999	0.034	−5.598	0.027	5.709	−0.559	0.002	0.571	−0.854	0.536	−2.5e-04	0.012
800	0	−1.000	0.012	−16.210	−0.093	15.951	−0.573	−0.003	0.564	−1.000	0.043	−9.2e-05	0.004
10,000	1	−1.000	0.003	−55.627	0.496	56.793	−0.556	0.005	0.567	−0.999	0.012	3.5e-05	0.001
Fractional sinusoidal waveform process: CO_2 concentrations													
50	0.981	−0.942	7.321	−580.065	2.905	583.686	−82.033	0.410	82.545	−0.997	0.173	−6.1e-06	0.004
100	1	−0.940	4.503	−728.347	2.376	740.218	−72.834	0.237	74.021	−0.999	0.123	2.2e-05	0.002
800	1	−0.978	1.231	−1.6e+03	2.604	1.6e+03	−56.618	0.092	58.207	−0.999	0.042	−1.7e-05	9.9e-04
10,000	1	−1.003	0.297	−4.8e+03	−30.469	4.8e+03	−48.940	−0.304	48.541	−0.999	0.012	7.4e-06	2.7e-04

Notes: Model (5), AR(2) with complex unit roots, and fractional sinusoidal; *trace* is the percentage of rejections of spurious and cointegration regressions using the trace test.

$$\iota' = (1,1); \quad \alpha' = (-1,0); \quad \beta' = (1,-1); \quad \tilde{u}_t = (\Delta u_{xt} + u_{yt}, \Delta u_{xt})'. \tag{16}$$

From standard algebra,

$$\mu_t = \delta\left\{\cos\left(\lambda\pi\frac{t}{T}\right)\left[1-\cos\left(\lambda\pi\frac{1}{T}\right)\right] - \sin\left(\lambda\pi\frac{t}{T}\right)\sin\left(\lambda\pi\frac{1}{T}\right)\right\}, \tag{17}$$

showing that μ_t is a time-varying weighted function of cosines and sines, with weights $\left[1-\cos\left(\lambda\pi\frac{1}{T}\right)\right]$ and $\sin\left(\lambda\pi\frac{1}{T}\right)$, respectively.

The misspecified model is the standard bivariate cointegrated ECM with $y_t = x_t + u_{yt}$ and $x_t = x_{t-1} + u_{xt}$, that is,

$$\begin{pmatrix}\Delta y_t\\ \Delta x_t\end{pmatrix} = \begin{pmatrix}-1\\ 0\end{pmatrix}(1,-1)\begin{pmatrix}y_{t-1}\\ x_{t-1}\end{pmatrix} + \begin{pmatrix}u_{yt}\\ u_{xt}\end{pmatrix}, \quad t = 2,\ldots,T, \tag{18}$$

which ignores the time-varying intercept (cyclical component) $\mu_t(\delta,\lambda)$, and the errors are misspecified. From the standard Johansen (1988, 1991, 1995) approach, the model is

$$\Delta z_t = \alpha\beta' z_{t-1} + u_t, t = 2,\ldots,T, \tag{19}$$

where it is assumed that $u_t \sim i.i.d.N_2\left[0,\Omega\right]$, with Ω nonsingular, although we showed earlier that the errors are not *i.i.d.*, the log-likelihood for $r=1$ (cointegration) is

$$\hat{l}_T = -0.5T\ln\left(1-\hat{\theta}\right) - 0.5T\ln\left(\det\left(S_{00,T}\right)\right) \tag{20}$$

plus a constant, where $\hat{\theta}$ is the largest solution of the generalized eigenvalue problem

$$\det\left[\theta S_{11,T} - S_{10,T}S_{00,T}^{-1}S_{01,T}\right] = 0 \tag{21}$$

with

$$S_{00,T} = \frac{1}{T}\sum_{t=1}^{T}\Delta z_t \Delta z_t'; \quad S_{11,T} = \frac{1}{T}\sum_{t=1}^{T} z_{t-1}z_{t-1}'; \quad S_{01,T} = \frac{1}{T}\sum_{t=1}^{T}\Delta z_t z_{t-1}', \tag{22}$$

$S_{10,T} = S_{01,T}'$, and the ML estimator for β is the eigenvector associated with the largest eigenvalue $\hat{\theta}$:

$$S_{10,T}S_{00,T}^{-1}S_{01,T}\,\hat{\beta} = \hat{\theta}S_{11,T}\hat{\beta}. \tag{23}$$

The next Lemma provides the limiting result for the matrices $S_{ij,T}, i,j = 0,1$ when the data follows model (1) for a constant δ.

Lemma 1: Under Assumption 1, as $T \to \infty$,

$$S_{00,T} \xrightarrow{p} 2\Upsilon; \quad S_{11,T} \xrightarrow{p} \frac{1}{2}\delta^2\left(1+\frac{\sin(2\lambda\pi)}{2\lambda\pi}\right)\iota + \Upsilon; \quad S_{01,T}, S_{10,T} \xrightarrow{p} -\Upsilon, \tag{24}$$

where $\Upsilon = \begin{bmatrix} (\sigma_x^2+\sigma_y^2) & \sigma_x^2 \\ \sigma_x^2 & \sigma_x^2 \end{bmatrix}, \iota = \begin{bmatrix} 1 & 1 \\ 1 & 1 \end{bmatrix}$. For $\lambda > 2$ integer, $S_{11,T} \xrightarrow{p} \frac{1}{2}\delta^2\iota + \Upsilon$.

Proof.

See details in the Appendix.

From the previous Lemma, and following the Lemma 2 in Anderson et al. (1983), the ordered solutions $\hat{\theta}_1 \geq \hat{\theta}_2$ of the generalized eigenvalue problem in equation (21) converge in probability to the ordered solutions $\theta_1 \geq \theta_2$ of $\det\left[\theta\left(\frac{1}{2}\delta^2\left(1+\frac{\sin(2\lambda\pi)}{2\lambda\pi}\right)\iota+\Upsilon\right)-\Upsilon'(2\Upsilon)^{-1}\Upsilon\right]=0$. These are provided in the next Theorem. Contrary to the standard cointegration approach, there are no zero solutions and, in particular, the largest $\hat{\theta}$ converges in probability to $\frac{1}{2}$ for all admissible model parameters. Moreover, unlike the standard cointegration approach, since the smallest θ_2 is not zero, $T\hat{\theta}_2$ will not converge in distribution to a random variable, but rather grows to infinity and, therefore, the trace and the maximum eigenvalue tests will also diverge as $T \to \infty$. The implication of this is that the cointegration tests will provide evidence of $rank = 2$, i.e., suggesting that the data is stationary and therefore there is no need to take first differences, as it is assumed in the case of the VECM model.

Theorem 1: Under Assumption 1, as $T \to \infty$, the ordered solutions $\hat{\theta}_1 \geq \hat{\theta}_2$ of the generalized eigenvalue problem in equation (21) converge in probability to $\theta_1 = \frac{1}{2}$ and $\theta_2 = \dfrac{1}{\frac{\delta^2}{\sigma_x^2}\left(1+\frac{\sin(2\lambda\pi)}{2\lambda\pi}\right)+2} < \frac{1}{2}$, respectively. For $\lambda > 2$ integer, $\theta_2 = \dfrac{1}{\frac{\delta^2}{\sigma_x^2}+2}$. Moreover, $T\hat{\theta}_2 \to \infty$, as $T \to \infty$.

Proof.

The details are omitted, as the result is straightforward to obtain.

As a consequence of Theorem 1, the next Theorem shows that the MLE of $\hat{\alpha}$ is consistent and $\hat{\beta}$ is still consistent, but it converges at a rate-$\sqrt{T}$ and not at a rate-T, as in the standard cointegration approach. The main reason is because $S_{11,T}$ is $O_p(1)$, something distinct from the $I(1)$ case where $\frac{1}{T}S_{11,T} = O_p(1)$.

Theorem 2: Under Assumption 1, as $T \to \infty$, $\hat{\beta} \xrightarrow{p} b$, where the normalized b is given by $b = (1,-1)'$, and $\hat{\alpha} \xrightarrow{p} \alpha$, where $\alpha' = (-1,0)$. Moreover, as $T \to \infty$, $\sqrt{T}\hat{\beta} = O_p(1)$ and $T\hat{\beta} \to \infty$.

Proof.

See the details in the Appendix.

Moreover, while not covered in these, the Monte Carlo simulations suggest that both for δ_t not constant, and for other more general models, the MLE of $\hat{\beta}$ remains consistent, but the rate of convergence is $\sqrt{T}$, slower than T, the standard one.

4. LONG-RUN COVARIABILITY AND LOW-FREQUENCY INFERENCE

As discussed in the previous section, not accounting for the statistical properties of persistent cycles may lead to erroneous inferences within the cointegration framework, popularized in climate econometrics by Kaufmann et al. (2013) and Kaufmann and Juselius (2013). To overcome this issue, and with the objective of obtaining sensible (and testable) baseline estimates for the long run relationship between temperatures and CO_2, we propose to use the low-frequency "filtering" framework of MW.

Indeed, low-frequency variation can be extracted by using a relatively small number q of weighted averages, where the weights are deterministic (and known) low-frequency trigonometric series. Consider the simplest case of a single time series x_t observed over $t = 1,\ldots,T$, letting $\Psi_j(s) = \sqrt{2}cos(js\pi)$, so that $\Psi_j(t/T)$ has period $2T/j$, with $\Psi(s) = (\Psi_1(s), \Psi_2(s),\ldots,\Psi_q(s))'$ a $\mathbb{R}^q$ valued function, with $\Psi(T) = (\Psi((1-1/2)/T), \Psi((2-1/2)/T),\ldots,\Psi((T-1/2)/T))'$ a $T \times q$ matrix obtained by evaluating the function at $s = (t-1/2)/T$ for $t = 1,\ldots,T$. Then, for a given q,

$$x_t = \varkappa_0 + \varkappa_1\Psi_1(t/T) + \ldots + \varkappa_q\Psi_q(t/T) + e_t, \tag{25}$$

where $\varkappa_0, \varkappa_1, \ldots, \varkappa_q$ are the model's coefficients, $\Psi_j(t/T) = \sqrt{2}\cos(j\pi(t-1/2)/T), j = 1,\ldots,q$, and e_t is the model's error term, we can obtain low-frequency projections by obtaining the fitted values from running OLS regressions of x_t on $\Psi(T)$, such that $\hat{x}_t = \bar{x} + \Psi((t-1/2)/T)'X_T$, where $\bar{x}$ and X_T are OLS coefficients, the latter having the simple form $X_T = T^{-1}\sum_{t=1}^{T}\Psi((t-1/2)/T)'x_t$, such that the jth regression coefficient X_{jt} is the jth cosine transform of $(x_1, x_2, \ldots, x_T)'$.

Müller and Watson (2018) show that this approach can be extended to a multivariate setting, in a way that long-run correlation (which we will denote by ρ_L) or regression coefficients can be obtained in a standard way based on the q cosine projections. Considering the scarcity of low-frequency information in the data, it is natural that only a small number of projection coefficients are employed to capture low-frequency variability, in turn leading to a typical "small-sample" problem. An advantage of these procedures is that statistical inference is straightforward and is applicable to both weakly and highly persistent time series, with little requirements regarding error and model assumptions.

4.1. Long-Run Covariability

We examine the long-run covariability of temperatures and CO_2 concentrations by computing the low-frequency correlation ρ_L and the bivariate regression coefficient β_L measuring the long-run relationship between temperatures and CO_2. From visual inspection of both series, we will assume that our time span of interest is smaller than 150 (150,000 years) and greater than 75 (75,000 years) datapoints, as there is no consensus in climate science on how to define "long run." This then corresponds to a range of about $q=10$ to $q=21$ cosine transforms, respectively. The maximum span is by default 1,596,000 years. The dynamics of these two series are heavily influenced by Milankovitch cyclicality, with pronounced fluctuations with a periodicity of around 100,000 years, related to Earth's orbit eccentricity, while orbital obliquity and precession are associated with cycles of higher frequency and less pronounced magnitude. Nevertheless, we present results obtained for $q=10,...,21$ in Table 5.5.

From these results, we observe that there is strong evidence that CO_2 and temperature are highly correlated over the long run. Indeed, the in-sample long-run correlation $\hat{\rho}_L$ of the two series is positive and very large – always above 0.83, achieving a maximum of 0.95 with $q=16$ and remaining high thereafter, with the confidence intervals noticeably narrowing for $q>15$.[8] As expected, the estimated long-run regression coefficient $\hat{\beta}_L$ is positive, thus confirming that an increase in CO_2 concentration of 1ppm is associated with an estimated increase in temperatures in the long-run. Note, however, that the slope coefficient is somewhat sensitive to the choice of q, monotonically increasing from 0.068°C for $q=10$ to 0.095°C with $q=21$.

Even though the above results give us a reasonable range of values across the different q's, for the sake of simplicity, we will focus our analysis on results for $q=16$. We do so for several reasons. First, we should note that there is no established criterion for the choice of q. One could use an information criterion like the AIC and the BIC, which, together with the adjusted R^2 from the regression that follows from the previously defined low-frequency projections, are also presented in Table 5.5. According to these criteria, the selected q is at the upper bound, which makes little sense given the cyclicality of the data discussed above.[9] To further help compare between alternative specifications, one can employ a simple (asymptotically normal) Vuong (1989) closeness test, based on the Kullback-Leibler distance: testing the case of $q=21$ against $q=16$ delivers a Vuong statistic of –1.2458, which

Table 5.5 Long-Run (LR) Covariation Measures for CO_2 and Temperature.

q	AIC	BIC	AdjR^2	LR correlation (ρ_L)	LR regr. coeff. (β_L)	LR regr. s.e. (σ_L)
10	−10.803	−10.198	0.697	0.865 [0.450, 0.960]	0.068 [0.025, 0.090]	0.395 [0.279, 0.809]
11	−10.959	−10.163	0.658	0.828 [0.500, 0.947]	0.068 [0.026, 0.093]	0.447 [0.313, 0.811]
12	−13.235	−12.265	0.671	0.841 [0.450, 0.952]	0.069 [0.028, 0.094]	0.447 [0.317, 0.864]
13	−14.128	−12.998	0.666	0.841 [0.450, 0.947]	0.072 [0.028, 0.096]	0.464 [0.332, 0.866]
14	−14.425	−13.146	0.716	0.865 [0.550, 0.953]	0.077 [0.040, 0.100]	0.498 [0.364, 0.825]
15	−14.222	−12.806	0.749	0.877 [0.637, 0.959]	0.082 [0.048, 0.102]	0.516 [0.382, 0.874]
16	−14.799	−13.254	0.894	**0.945 [0.900, 0.980]**	**0.090 [0.069, 0.100]**	**0.533 [0.386, 0.921]**
17	−13.999	−12.333	0.887	0.937 [0.850, 0.974]	0.092 [0.073, 0.104]	0.621 [0.459, 1.013]
18	−15.180	−13.399	0.894	0.940 [0.850, 0.974]	0.093 [0.072, 0.105]	0.627 [0.455, 1.005]
19	−16.968	−15.079	0.895	0.943 [0.850, 0.974]	0.094 [0.072, 0.105]	0.628 [0.463, 1.029]
20	−18.566	−16.575	**0.897**	0.943 [0.850, 0.974]	0.095 [0.075, 0.106]	0.643 [0.475, 1.033]
21	**−19.676**	**−17.587**	0.892	0.937 [0.850, 0.974]	0.095 [0.074, 0.107]	0.663 [0.496, 1.123]

Notes: x is CO_2 and y is temperature; AIC is the Akaike information criterion; BIC is the Bayesian information criterion; AdjR^2 is the adjusted R^2; results based on the Posterior Median and a Coverage Probability of 0.90 in square brackets; ρ_L is the long-run correlation coefficient, β_L is the long-run slope coefficient and σ_L the standard error.

suggests that there is little difference between these models (similar results apply when comparing results with $q = 16$ with specifications for $q > 16$).

Second, this is further confirmed by Fig. 5.2, which plots the (scaled) projections of the data onto the low-frequency cosine terms in (25) for each q. While the results for $q = 11$ (in blue) suggest too long a periodicity (145,000 years) and excessive smoothing of the variations in temperatures and CO_2, the projections for $q = 16$ (in red) and $q = 21$ (in green) are very similar, capturing the main cyclical features of the data. Finally, we note that for $q = 16$ the estimated long-run correlation is the largest and the range for the 90% confidence set is the narrowest (in bold, Table 5.5). Although admittedly ad-hoc, the basic idea is to pick the q for which the data seems to be most informative. Note also that for $q < 16$, the 90% confidence sets for the correlation and the regression coefficient are substantially wider, therefore suggesting that this strategy is a sensible one.

Thus, when $q = 16$, the long-run correlation equals 0.945 with a corresponding 90% confidence set of *[*0.900, 0.980*]*, while the regression coefficient is 0.090, with a standard error 0.533. This value is somewhat large, especially when compared to the ones found in the literature – c.f. Castle and Hendry (2020), who estimated an impact of 0.060°C. The lower bound of the 90% confidence set [0.069, 0.100] is close to the Castle and Hendry (2020) estimate, but does not include it.

For the sake of completeness, we also computed the long-run measures for the bivariate relationships of ice volume with temperatures or CO_2 concentrations, in Table 5.6. As in the previous case, $q < 16$ delivers wide confidence sets for the pair {Ice, Temperature}. The in-sample long-term correlation for $q = 16$ equals −0.871 with a confidence set of [−0.946, −0.638] (similar results are obtained for $q > 16$) and an estimated long-run regression coefficient of −4.991. For {Ice, CO_2} the correlation is also large (−0.918 with an interval of [−0.945, −0.800]) and the regression coefficient is −55.343, highlighting the long-run association between higher CO_2 concentrations and reduced ice volumes.

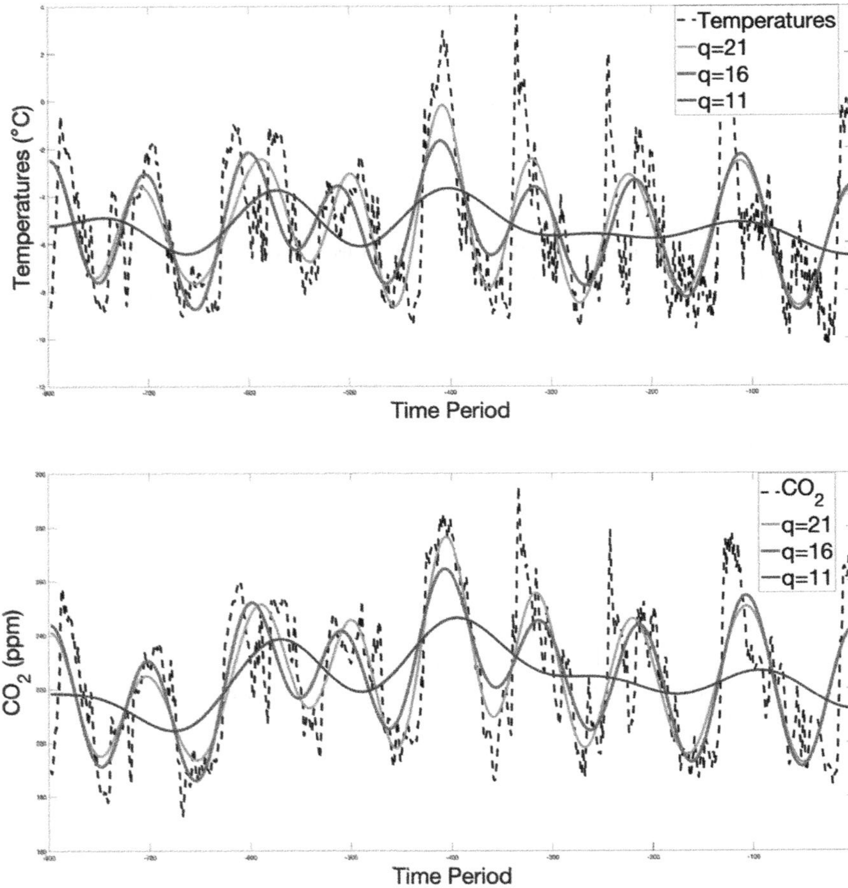

Fig. 5.2. Low Frequency Cycles for Temperatures and CO_2, $q = 11$, $q = 16$, $q = 21$.

Table 5.6. Long-Run Covariation Measures for Ice-Temperature and Ice-CO_2.

q	LR Correlation (ρ_L)	LR Regression Coefficient (β_L)	LR Regression st. Error (σ_L)
Ice and Temperature			
16	−0.871 [−0.946, −0.638]	−4.991 [−6.190, −3.745]	0.814 [0.608, 1.196]
Ice and CO_2			
22	−0.918 [−0.945, −0.800]	−55.343 [−66.609, −44.553]	9.891 [7.080, 14.917]

Notes: In the first row, x is Ice and y is temperature, in the second row x is Ice and y is CO_2; results based on the Posterior Median and a Coverage Probability of 0.90 in square brackets.

The value of 0.090 for the long run coefficient relating temperatures to CO_2 and the corresponding 90% confidence set are probably overestimated. The most likely explanation is that the standard bivariate Müller and Watson (2018) approach is not taking into account the effect of exogenous variables on temperatures, namely orbital forcing and non-linear functions thereof. Therefore, in order to be able to assess the long-run covariability between temperature and CO_2 concentrations without omitting orbital forcing, we extend the Müller and Watson (2018) approach so that these effects are partialled out – i.e., we first regress CO_2 on additional forcings z_t (i.e., $CO_{2t} = \theta' z_t + v_t$), then temperatures on residuals $\hat{v}_t$ for the first-stage partialling out.[10] We do so because of the "small sample" problem induced by using only a small number of trigonometric projections. To avoid compounding this problem by adding additional regressors, and given that in our application we can safely treat orbital forcing as exogenous, we suggest this approach as a convenient way of addressing this issue.

We therefore define the largest set of exogenous regressors z_t as:

$$z_t = (O_t, O_{t-1}), \tag{26}$$

where, following Castle and Hendry (2020),

$$O = (Ec, Ob, Pr, EcOb, EcPr, PrOb, Ec^2, Ob^2, Pr^2). \tag{27}$$

contains a range of non-linear impacts of the exogenous orbital variables. For robustness, we also consider smaller sets for z_t. Ultimately, we did not find important differences in the residuals $\hat{v}_t$, regardless of the chosen z_t, compared to the actual CO_2 concentrations.

Table 5.7 displays long-run covariability measures for temperatures and (distinct) CO_2 residuals for the "optimal" q, in the sense that the correlation is the largest and the range for the confidence set is the narrowest, as well as matching the required cyclicality.[11] First, we note that the selected q is always 16, the same

Table 5.7. Long-Run Covariation Measures for $\hat{v}_t$ and *Temperature*, $q = 16$.

LR Correlation (ρ_L)	LR Regression Coefficient (β_L)	LR Regression st. Error (σ_L)
$z_t = (O_t, O_{t-1})$		
0.744 [0.502, 0.917]	0.077 [0.048, 0.105]	1.009 [0.762, 1.479]
$z_t = O_t$		
0.744 [0.511, 0.917]	0.078 [0.048, 0.106]	1.012 [0.847, 1.245]
$z_t = \left(Ec, Ob, EcOb, EcPr, Ob^2\right)_t$		
0.804 [0.564, 0.918]	0.076 [0.048, 0.103]	0.980 [0.733, 1.425]
$z_t = (Ec_t, Ec_{t-1}, Ob_{t-1}, EcOb_{t-1}, Ob_t^2)$		
0.798 [0.512, 0.917]	0.075 [0.046, 0.102]	1.002 [0.752, 1.463]

Note: Results based on the Posterior Median and a Coverage Probability of 0.90 in square brackets or 0.67 in parentheses.

value as in the simple bivariate case. Second, the results are very consistent: estimated long-run correlations are large (between 0.74 and 0.8) and point estimates of the long-run regression coefficient vary between 0.067 and 0.078.

Overall, the main takeaways are that (1) regardless of whether or not orbital effects are partialled out, the long-run correlation between temperatures and CO_2 concentrations is very large (above 0.74); (2) with respect to the long-run impact of CO_2 concentrations on temperature levels, we obtain slightly larger point estimates than those reported in Castle and Hendry (2020), which can be rather interpreted as a lower bound. Castle and Hendry (2020) also obtain a solved long-run coefficient of 0.066°C increase in temperatures for a 1 ppm increase in the CO_2 concentration, whereas our long-run estimated impact ranges from about 0.070°C to 0.100°C, depending on the exact specification.

Moreover, as a complementary alternative to partialling out, we also consider long-run covariability measures between temperature and a common factor f_t^w capturing the main dynamics of all (or part of) the other variables in the model, i.e., CO_2, ice volume and orbital variables. Following Castle and Hendry (2020), we assume that temperatures in period t are explained by the set of variables $w_t = (Temp_{t-1}, CO_{2t}, Ec_t, EcOb_t, EcOb_{t-1}, EcPr_t)$ and formulate a factor model in which low-frequency measures of $Temp_t$ are related with the main common factor of w_t. In Table 5.8, we present the results for $\hat{f}_t^w$ extracted from w_t, also considering different subsets of its elements, using $q = 16$ as before (results are similar for any $q > 15$).

Table 5.8. Long-Run Covariation Measures for $\hat{f}_t^w$ and *Temperature*.

q	LR Correlation (ρ_L)	LR Regression Coefficient (β_L)	LR Regression st. Error (σ_L)
$w_t = (Temp_{t-1}, CO_{2t}, Ec_t, EcOb_t, EcOb_{t-1}, EcPr_t)$			
$PTV = 97.688$; $\hat{\lambda} = (0.999, 0.000, 0.003, 0.027)$			
16	0.945 [0.900, 0.980]	0.090 [0.069, 0.099]	0.528 [0.383, 0.912]
$w_t = (CO_{2t}, Ec_t, EcOb_t, EcPr_t)$			
$PTV = 97.914$; $\hat{\lambda} = (0.999, 0.000, 0.003, 0.027)$			
16	0.945 [0.900, 0.980]	0.090 [0.069, 0.100]	0.532 [0.386, 0.920]
$w_t = (CO_{2t-1}, CO_{2t}, Ice_{t-1}, Ice_t)$			
$PTV = 98.712$; $\hat{\lambda} = (0.706, 0.708, -0.010, -0.010)$			
16	0.943 [0.900, 0.974]	0.063 [0.048, 0.071]	0.558 [0.404, 0.962]
$w_t = (CO_{2t}, Ice_t)$			
$PTV = 99.999$; $\hat{\lambda} = (0.999, -0.015)$			
16	0.945 [0.900, 0.980]	0.090 [0.069, 0.100]	0.533 [0.387, 0.922]

Notes: Results based on the Posterior Median and a Coverage Probability of 0.90 in square brackets. PTV is the percentage of the total variance explained by the principal component. λ is the principal component coefficients (loadings).

We first note that the percentage of the variance (PTV) explained by the principal component is almost 100%, even for the largest of sets w_t. On the other hand, analyzing the corresponding factor loadings (displayed in $\hat{\lambda}$), the loading associated with CO_2t is essentially one, while the other loadings are quite small and close to zero. These two results together mean that the principal component $\hat{f}_t^w$ captures the dynamic features of CO_2t levels after extracting the information from the remaining variables. Thus, in essence, we accomplish the goal of obtaining low-frequency estimates of the relationship between temperatures and CO_2 levels in a much similar way to the partialling out procedure expounded above.

In sum, as far as the long run relationship between temperatures and CO_2 is concerned, the results in this section point to temperature increases between 6°C and 10°C. These are in the neighborhood of, but larger than, the estimates of Castle and Hendry (2020), Kaufmann and Juselius (2013), and Knutti et al. (2017).

4.2. Low-Frequency Factor Model and Long-Term Forecasts

In the previous section, we focused on the long-run relationship between temperatures and CO_2 concentration levels – first, a stripped down low-frequency bivariate analysis, followed by approaches that allow us to control for exogenous forcing. In this section, we turn our attention to modeling the joint dynamics of the whole climate system by employing the low-frequency factor models developed by Müller and Watson (2024), which, as a useful by-product, allow us to compute long-range forecasts.[12] Indeed, given the very low-frequency nature of our data, as well as the mixture of endogenous and exogenous variables we study, we deem this forecasting model to be more appropriate than a standard dynamic factor model. Next, we present the main features of the model and analyze the estimated factor loadings, after which we focus on long-horizon predictive distributions for the variables of interest, under relevant scenarios for CO_2 levels.

Following Müller and Watson (2024) and Müller et al. (2020), the model for the set of observables $x_t \in \mathbb{R}^n$ is

$$x_t = \mu + \lambda f_t^x + e_t, \tag{28}$$

where f_t^x denotes the single scalar unobserved common factor, $\lambda = (\lambda_1, \ldots, \lambda_n)$ contains the factor loadings, e_t represents a vector of mutually independent errors that captures the residual variability in x_t, and $\mu = (\mu_1, \ldots, \mu_n)$ is the intercept, while $e_{j,t}$, $j = 1, \ldots, n$, are stationary $I(d_j)$ and $\left\{ f_t^x, e_{1,t}, \ldots, e_{n,t} \right\}$ are independent. Moreover, the factor f_t^x follows a local-level model

$$f_t^x = v_t + \nu_t, \tag{29}$$

where $v_t \sim I(1)$ and $\nu_t \sim I(0)$, i.e., the local-level model is the sum of uncorrelated $I(0)$ and $I(1)$ processes with common long-run variance σ^2. The scale of f_t^x and λ are not separately identified and the factor loading λ_1 is normalized to unity. The estimation of the model is carried out by Bayesian methods, assuming the same priors for the parameters as in Müller and Watson (2024) (see paper for details). Once the posterior distribution is recovered, an additional advantage of this approach is that we can analyze how the relationships differ across quantiles - we consider the median, the tails at 5% and 95% and two intermediate quantiles, 17% and 83%.

We consider three specifications: (i) a simple bivariate one with the main variables $x_t = (Temp_t, CO_{2t})'$ with $n = 2$; (ii) a model that adds ice volume, i.e., $x_t = (Temp_t, CO_{2t}, Ice_t)'$, $n = 3$; and (iii) following Castle and Hendry (2020), we consider a model with exogenous orbital variables which includes significant non-linear interactions between the drivers, such that $x_t = (Temp_t, CO_{2t}, Ice_t, Ec_t, Ob_t EcPr_t, Ob_t^2)'$, $n = 7$.

The results for the posterior mean and posterior quantiles of the factor loadings (normalized with respect to the first observable variable) are displayed in Table 5.9. In the case where the number of observable variables is low (i.e., $n = 2$ or $n = 3$), the sole factor is highly correlated with CO_2. In fact, we can see that CO_2 is a very strong driver of low-frequency comovements with temperatures, particularly at the highest quantiles. With $n = 3$, and for a model with an intercept and normalized loadings, ice volume's loading is clearly less than one and has therefore a noticeably reduced importance when compared to CO_2. Interestingly, the salience of CO_2 remains strong even when orbital variables are included. Indeed, as expected and in accordance with the Milankovich hypothesis, orbital variables capture a significant proportion of the joint variation. In particular, note that the interaction $EcPr_t$ has a loading of 1.68 – the amount of solar energy is proportional (up to a phase) to $Ec \sin Pr$ and, to first order, $\sin x \approx x$, which explains the

Table 5.9. Factor Loadings for the Low-Frequency Factor Model.

Variables	*PostMean*	*PostQ*$_{0.05}$	*PostQ*$_{0.17}$	*PostQ*$_{0.50}$	*PostQ*$_{0.83}$	*PostQ*$_{0.95}$
$x_t = (Temp_t, CO_{2t})'$; $n = 2$						
Temp	1.00	1.00	1.00	1.00	1.00	1.00
CO_2	9.29	7.98	8.66	9.37	9.96	10.37
$x_t = (Temp_t, CO_{2t}, Ice_t)'$; $n = 3$						
Temp	1.00	1.00	1.00	1.00	1.00	1.00
CO_2	9.30	8.00	8.66	9.37	9.97	10.39
Ice	−0.15	−0.19	−0.17	−0.15	−0.12	−0.11
$x_t = (Temp_t, CO_{2t}, Ice_t, Ec_t, Ob_t, EcPr_t, Ob_t^2)'$; $n = 7$						
Temp	1.00	1.00	1.00	1.00	1.00	1.00
CO_2	1.50	−1.78	−0.40	1.50	3.42	4.79
Ice	1.36	−1.92	−0.56	1.33	3.35	4.71
Ec	1.35	−1.99	−0.66	1.37	3.33	4.65
Ob	0.78	−1.64	−0.62	0.56	2.32	3.76
EcPr	1.68	−1.70	−0.34	1.59	3.63	5.43
Ob^2	1.44	−1.85	−0.49	1.43	3.36	4.74

Notes: Factor loadings for the low frequency model, with different number of variables but a single extracted factor, for both the posterior mean and posterior quantiles (i.e., *PostQ* stands for posterior quantile). No sign restriction has been imposed on the distribution of factor loadings as that is indicated by posterior quantiles.

loading. Given the higher number of relevant observable variables we include, while still considering a single factor, the association between the factor with CO_2 diminishes, as expected. Nevertheless, CO_2 levels still have a non-negligible impact for quantiles 83 and 95. As anticipated, ice volume varies in the opposite direction, while the joint effects of (nonlinear interactions of) orbital variables appear to be the most significant contributors to low-frequency movements in the respective set of variables in x_t.

Having documented and quantified the low-frequency relationship between temperatures and CO_2 levels, and given the recent developments in the climate debate, it is important to understand how temperatures can evolve in the long-term for specific scenarios of CO_2 concentrations. Here, we follow Castle and Hendry (2020) by conditioning on the relatively stable path of orbital variables and on a stable level of 385 ppm for CO_2 to obtain long-term conditional forecasts for temperatures and ice volume using the low-frequency factor models estimated in the previous section.[13] We consider the horizon of 50 observations (50,000 years, half of the lowest period associated with the optimal q as explained in Section 4.1, which is a relatively long horizon period, given such extremely low frequency type of data.

In Fig. 5.3, we have the conditional forecasts for temperatures, while Fig. 5.4 displays projections for ice volumes, both in the case of $n = 7$. The projections for temperatures are close to the sample mean, but, crucially, predicted to increase. Turning to the long term of implications for ice volumes, we confirm the prediction that ice sheets will tend to reduce for high levels of CO_2 (naturally in tandem with the higher temperatures predicted above). See Diebold and Rudebusch (2022) for a discussion, albeit at shorter horizons.

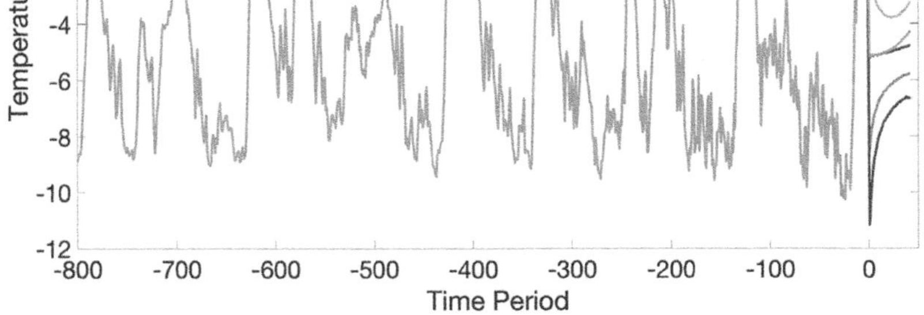

Fig. 5.3. Conditional Forecasts of Temperatures, for Different Quantile Levels τ.

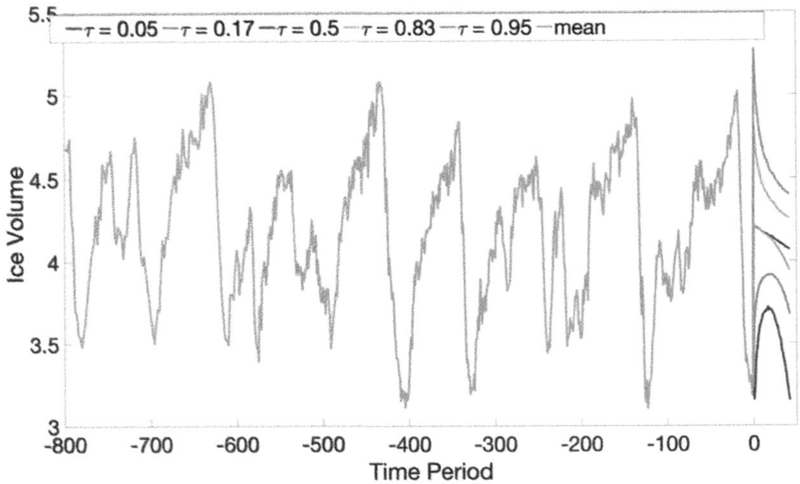

Fig. 5.4. Conditional Forecasts of Ice Volumes, for Different Quantile Levels τ.

5. CONCLUDING REMARKS

This chapter puts the spotlight on the cyclicality of paleoclimate data. On the one hand, we show that, despite point estimation remaining unaffected, ignoring persistent cycles leads to erroneous cointegration inference, a result akin to the issue of near-integrated regressors well known in the cointegration literature. On the other hand, if one is interested in long-range equilibrium estimates, we suggest using the low-frequency filtering procedures of Müller and Watson (2018) and Müller and Watson (2024), which circumvent some of the pitfalls regarding the presence of persistent cycles, spurred mainly by orbital forcings, and the uncertainty around the correct order of integration of the data.

Our results confirm the strong relationship between temperatures and CO_2 for a periodicity of around 100,000 years. The long-run coefficient thus obtained validates, to a large extent, previous long run climate equilibrium studies conducted by several authors. If anything, our findings suggest that the recent simulations of Castle and Hendry (2020) are a lower bound, indicating that warming due to the increase of CO_2 concentration levels can be even more substantial. This holds even when orbital forcings are taken into account, either by partialling out or by means of an extracted common factor. Joint modeling of all time series allows us to consider a long-term scenario exercise, in which we show the extent of acceleration in temperature increases, as well as ice-sheet recession.

In this setup, the choice of q is usually left at the researchers' discretion. In combination with visual inspection of the data, we proposed a "data-driven" approach, whereby we picked q such that the target long-run correlation is maximized. An interesting issue to consider is the choice of q when two or more time series display different cyclicality – it is not clear whether different q's should be selected for each series, or whether a common q would be preferable. We leave this for future research.

We should acknowledge the shortcomings of our approach. Indeed, by focusing narrowly on the long-run relationship between temperatures and CO_2, we make no attempt to model the mechanisms that link orbital forcing to temperatures, which is obviously important from a theoretical and an empirical point of view. Our first set of results suggest that orbital variables play a role, albeit minor compared to CO_2, in driving temperatures, at least in a linear setting, despite the inclusion of non-linear orbital terms. Reassuringly, the multivariate factor model of Section 4 reveals a stronger association between temperature and orbital variables, with the posterior mean estimates confirming that certain orbital variables help explain temperature variation, especially the interaction between eccentricity and precession.

Naturally, there are alternative approaches that the applied researcher may wish to consider. For instance, work by Friedrich et al. (2023), studying the relationship between radiative forcings and global temperatures, employs a high-dimensional VAR that, much like in our empirical analysis, allows for the order of integration to be ignored. Still in a (structural) VAR setting, Duffy and Simons (2023) characterize cointegration through impulse response functions, thus allowing long-run relationships to be identified even if the data does not contain exact unit roots – it would certainly be interesting to analyze how paleoclimate data fares with this method. Another work that is in spirit very similar to the approach we propose here is the paper by Blazsek and Escribano (2022), who use score-driven ice-age models, which control for omitted exogenous variables and extreme events and report results very similar to Castle and Hendry (2020) (and not too distinct from our own).

Moreover, while we highlight the issue of persistent cyclicality for cointegration inference, the cyclical models we study are fairly simple and a great deal more work is required to embed them into a VECM framework. In ongoing work, we study the properties of the noise-decomposition framework presented in Section 2.2.2. An alternative approach that certainly deserves further attention is the recent work by Kang and Marmer (2024), which considers highly persistent stochastic cycles, potentially spanning substantial fractions of the sampling period, and therefore very close to the characteristics exhibited by paleoclimate data.

NOTES

1. For the avoidance of doubt, all mentions to CO_2 refer to its atmospheric concentration.
2. The literature on near-unit roots is extensive, see the recent survey by Phillips (2021).
3. Alternative models for u_t could have been considered. For the purpose of this paper, we assume the AR(1) specification but, in general, u_t is such that $\frac{1}{\sqrt{T}}\sum_{t=1}^{\lfloor rT \rfloor} u_t \Rightarrow \sigma_u W(r), r \in [0,1]$ where σ_u^2 is the long-run covariance of u_t and $W(r)$ is a standard Wiener process, with $\lfloor \cdot \rfloor$ denoting the integer part of $\cdot$.
4. The pair z_1, z_2 can also be random $O_p(1)$ processes, but in that case the cycle's range is random. As earlier, alternative models for u_t can be considered. Notice that if $\rho = 1$, u_t is a nonstationary process and therefore y_t itself would resemble a $I(1)$ process (the cycle z_t would not be clearly defined in the data).

5. From Nielsen (2001) and Del Barrio Castro et al. (2013, 2015), we learn that if the data does not follow our decomposition, but only includes the persistent cycles, we should at least add two lags in the VAR analysis or use information criteria for lag selection when testing for unit roots and cointegration.

6. Results are very similar for $\phi_1 = 1.6355457, \phi_2 = -0.7$ or for $\phi_1 = 1.411423, \phi_2 = -0.5$

7. The results for $T = 50{,}100$ have been left out because in these cases the cycles are not noticeable in the time series.

8. To put it in perspective, it is worth mentioning that in their empirical applications with macro variables, Müller and Watson (2018) found for fixed q only a few number of pairs of series with such a large degree of covariability. Despite the differences in terms of the observed data, it seems that climate data has a more significant long-term covariability compared to macroeconomic data.

9. This pattern of model selection criteria picking q corresponding to shorter cycles than those observed from ice-age data also happens in the next cases – Tables 5.6 to 5.8. A possible explanation for the selection of large q might be the fact that the low-frequency trigonometric series form a basis and therefore the regressors are far from being correlated.

10. It is straightforward to show that a variant of the Frisch-Waugh-Lovell also holds in the case of the MW framework (results available upon request).

11. Results for other values of q produce qualitatively and quantitatively similar results.

12. See also Müller and Watson (2016) for a discussion on long-horizon prediction intervals and Müller et al. (2020) for an interesting application about the long-run path of GDP for a list of 113 countries.

13. See Castle and Hendry (2020, pp. 254–256) for a discussion on the choice of 385 ppm for CO_2.

REFERENCES

Anderson, S. A., Brons, H. K., & Jensen, S. T. (1983). Distribution of eigenvalues in multivariate statistical analysis. *The Annals of Statistics*, *11*(2), 392–415.

Baillie, R. T., & Chung, S.-K. (2002). Modeling and forecasting from trend-stationary long memory models with applications to climatology. *International Journal of Forecasting*, *18*(2), 215–226.

Bierens, H. J. (2001). Complex unit roots and business cycles: Are they real? *Econometric Theory*, *17*(5), 962–983.

Bierens, H. J. (1994). *Topics in advanced econometrics: Estimation, testing, and specification of cross-section and time series models*. Cambridge University Press.

Blazsek, S., & Escribano, A. (2022). Robust estimation and forecasting of climate change using score-driven ice-age models. *Econometrics*, *10*(6), 9.

Blazsek, S., & Escribano, A. (2023). Score-driven threshold ice-age models: Benchmark models for long-run climate forecasts. *Energy Economics*, *118*, 106522.

Bloomfield, P. (1992). Trends in global temperature. *Climatic Change*, *21*(1), 1–16.

Bloomfield, P., & Nychka, D. (1992). Climate spectra and detecting climate change. *Climatic Change*, *21*(3), 275–287.

Castle, J. L., & Hendry, D. F. (2020). Climate econometrics: An overview. *Foundations and Trends in Econometrics*, *10*(3-4), 145–322.

Covey, C., Sloan, L. C., & Hoffert, M. I. (1996). Paleoclimate data constraints on climate sensitivity: The paleocalibration method. *Climatic Change*, *32*, 165–184.

Davidson, J. E. H., Stephenson, D. B., & Turasie, A. A. (2016). Time series modeling of paleoclimate data: Paleoclimate data. *Environmetrics*, *27*(1), 55–65.

Del Barrio Castro, T., Rodrigues, P. M. M., & Taylor, A. M. R. (2013). The impact of persistent cycles on zero frequency unit root tests. *Econometric Theory*, *29*(6), 1289–1313.

Del Barrio Castro, T., Rodrigues, P. M. M., & Taylor, A. M. R. (2015). On the behaviour of Phillips–Perron tests in the presence of persistent cycles. *Oxford Bulletin of Economics and Statistics*, *77*(4), 495–511.

Diebold, F. X., & Rudebusch, G. D. (2022). Probability assessments of an ice-free Arctic: Comparing statistical and climate model projections. *Journal of Econometrics*, *231*, 520–524.

Ditlevsen, P., Mitsui, T., & Crucifix, M. (2020). Crossover and peaks in the Pleistocene climate spectrum; understanding from simple ice age models. *Climate Dynamics*, *54*, 1801–1818.

Dou, L., & Müller, U. (2021). Generalized local-to-unity models. *Econometrica*, *89*, 1825–1854.

Duffy, J. A., & Simons, J. A. (2023). *Cointegration without unit roots*. Working paper.

Elliott, G. (1998). On the robustness of cointegration methods when regressors almost have unit roots. *Econometrica*, *66*, 149–158.

Engle, R. F., & Kozicki, S. (1993). Testing for common features. *Journal of Business and Economic Statistics*, *11*, 369–380.

Fomby, T. B., & Vogelsang, T. J. (2002). The application of size-robust trend statistics to global-warming temperature series. *Journal of Climate*, *15*(1), 117–123.

Friedrich, M., Margaritella, L., & Smeekes, S. (2023). *High-dimensional causality for climatic attribution*. Working paper.

Gordon, A. H. (1991). Global warming as a manifestation of a random walk. *Journal of Climate*, *4*(6), 589–597.

Gordon, D. C., Boudreau, P. R., Mann, K. H., Ong, J. E., Silvert, W. L., Smith, S. V., Yattayakorn, G., Wulff, F., & Yanagi, T. (1996). LOICZ Biogeochemical modelling Guidelines. *LOICZ REPORTS & STUDIES NO. 5*, 104.

Hylleberg, S., Engle, R. F., Granger, C. W. J., & Yoo, B. S. (1990). Seasonal integration and cointegration. *Journal of Econometrics*, *44*, 215–238.

Imbrie, J., & Imbrie, J. Z. (1980). Modeling the climatic response to orbital variations. *Science*, *207*, 943–953.

Jaccard, S. L., Galbraith, E. D., Martínez-García, A., & Anderson, R. F. (2016). Covariation of deep Southern Ocean oxygenation and atmospheric CO_2 through the last ice age. *Nature*, *530*(7589), 207–210.

Johansen, S. (1988). Statistical analysis of cointegration vectors. *Journal of Economic Dynamics and Control*, *12*, 231–254.

Johansen, S. (1991). Estimation and hypothesis testing of cointegration vectors in Gaussian vector autoregressive models. *Econometrica*, *59*(6), 1551–1580.

Johansen, S. (1995). *Likelihood-based inference in cointegrated vector autoregressive models*. Oxford University Press.

Jouzel, J., Masson-Delmotte, V., Cattani, O., Dreyfus, G., Falourd, S., Hoffmann, G., Minster, B., Nouet, J., Barnola, J. M., Chappellaz, J., Fischer, H., Gallet, J. C., Johnsen, S., Leuenberger, M., Loulergue, L., Luethi, D., Oerter, H., Parrenin, F., Raisbeck, G., … Wolff, E. W. (2007). Orbital and millennial Antarctic climate variability over the past 800,000 years. *Science*, *317*(5839), 793–796.

Kang, D. N., & Marmer, V. (2024). Modeling long cycles. *Journal of Econometrics*, *242*, 105751.

Kärner, O. (1996). Global temperature deviations as a random walk. *Journal of Climate*, *9*(3), 656–658.

Kaufmann, R. K., & Juselius, K. (2013). Testing hypotheses about glacial cycles against the observational record. *Paleoceanography*, *28*(1), 175–184.

Kaufmann, R. K., Kauppi, H., Mann, M. L., & Stock, J. H. (2013). Does temperature contain a stochastic trend: linking statistical results to physical mechanisms. *Climatic Change*, *118*(3-4), 729–743.

Kaufmann, R. K., & Pretis, F. (2020). *Testing hypotheses about glacial dynamics and the stage 11 paradox using a statistical model of paleo-climate*. Working Paper.

Kaufmann, R. K., & Pretis, F. (2021). Understanding glacial cycles: A multivariate disequilibrium approach. *Quaternary Science Reviews*, *251*, 106694.

Kawamura, K., Parrenin, F., Lisiecki, L. E., Uemura, R., Vimeux, F., Severinghaus, J. P., Hutterli, M. A., Nakazawa, T., Aoki, S., & Jouzel, J. (2010). Northern Hemisphere forcing of climatic cycles in Antarctica over the past 360,000 years. *Nature*, *448*, 912–916.

Knutti, R., Rugenstein, M. A. A., & Hegerl, G. C. (2017). Beyond equilibrium climate sensitivity. *Nature Geoscience*, *10*(10), 727–736.

Lea, D. W. (2004). The 100 000-year cycle in tropical SST, greenhouse forcing, and climate sensitivity. *Journal of Climate*, *17*(11), 2170–2179.

Lisiecki, L. E. (2010). Links between eccentricity forcing and the 100,000-year glacial cycle. *Nature Geoscience*, *3*, 349–352.

Lisiecki, L. E., & Raymo, M. E. (2005). A Pliocene-Pleistocene stack of 57 globally distributed benthic 18O records. *Paleoceanography*, *20*.

Lüthi, D., Le Floch, M., Bereiter, B., Blunier, T., Barnola, J., Siegenthaler, U., Raynaud, D., Jouzel, J., Fischer, H., Kawamura, K., & Stocker, T. F. (2008). High-resolution carbon dioxide concentration record 650,000–800,000 years before present. *Nature*, *453*, 379–382.

Mann, M. E., & Lees, J. M. (2019). Robust estimation of background noise and signal detection in climatic time series. *Climatic Change*, *33*, 409–445.

McMillan, D. G., & Wohar, M. E. (2013). The relationship between temperature and CO2 emissions: evidence from a short and very long dataset. *Applied Economics*, *45*(26), 3683–3690.

Meyers, S. R., Sageman, B. B., & Pagani, M. (2008). Resolving Milankovitch: Consideration of signal and noise. *American Journal of Science*, *308*, 770–786.

Miller, J. I. (2019). Testing cointegrating relationships using irregular and non-contemporaneous series with an application to paleoclimate data. *Journal of Time Series Analysis*, *40*, 936–950.

Mitchell, J. M. (1976). An overview of climatic variability and its causal mechanisms. *Quaternary Research*, *6*, 481–493.

Muller, R. A., & MacDonald, G. J. (1997). Glacial cycles and astronomical forcing. *Science*, *277*, 215–218.

Müller, U. K., Stock, J. H., & Watson, M. W. (2020). An econometric model of international growth dynamics for long-horizon forecasting. *The Review of Economics and Statistics*, 1–47.

Müller, U. K., & Watson, M. W. (2016). Measuring uncertainty about long-run predictions. *The Review of Economic Studies*, *83*(4), 1711–1740.

Müller, U. K., & Watson, M. W. (2018). Long-run covariability. *Econometrica*, *86*(3), 775–804.

Müller, U. K., & Watson, M. W. (2024). Low-Frequency analysis of economic time series. *Handbook of Econometrics*, forthcoming.

Nielsen, B. (2001). The asymptotic distribution of unit root tests of unstable autoregressive processes. *Econometrica*, *69*(1), 211–219.

Pesaran, M. H., Shin, Y., & Smith, R. J. (2001). Bounds testing approaches to the analysis of level relationships. *Journal of Applied Econometrics*, *16*, 289–326.

Phillips, P. C. B. (2021). *Estimation and inference with near unit roots*. [Cowles Foundation Discussion Paper, 10-22-2021].

Proietti, T., & Maddanu, F. (2024). Modelling cycles in climate series: The fractional sinusoidal waveform process. *Journal of Econometrics*, *239*, 105299.

Rial, J. A. (1999). Pacemaking the ice ages by frequency modulation of Earth's orbital eccentricity. *Science*, *285*, 564–568.

Vahid, F., & Engle, R. F. (1993). Common trends and common cycles. *Journal of Applied Econometrics*, *8*, 341–360.

Vahid, F., & Engle, R. F. (1997). Codependent cycles. *Journal of Econometrics*, *80*, 199–221.

Vuong, Q. H. (1989). Likelihood ratio tests for model selection and non-nested hypotheses. *Econometrica*, *57*, 307–333.

Woodward, W. A., & Gray, H. L. (1993). Global warming and the problem of testing for trend in time series data. *Journal of Climate*, *6*(5), 953–962.

Woodward, W. A., & Gray, H. L. (1995). Selecting a model for detecting the presence of a trend. *Journal of Climate*, *8*(8), 1929–1937.

Wunsch, C. (2008). The spectral description of climate change including the 100 ky energy. *Climate Dynamics*, *20*, 353–363.

APPENDIX

A.1. LEMMA A

Under Assumption 1, as $T \to \infty$,

$$\frac{1}{T}\sum_{t=1}^{T} \Delta y_t^2 \overset{p}{\to} 2\left(\sigma_x^2 + \sigma_y^2\right) \tag{30}$$

$$\frac{1}{T}\sum_{t=1}^{T} \Delta x_t^2 \overset{p}{\to} 2\sigma_x^2; \qquad \frac{1}{T}\sum_{t=1}^{T} \Delta y_t \Delta x_t \overset{p}{\to} 2\sigma_x^2 \tag{31}$$

$$\frac{1}{T}\sum_{t=1}^{T} y_{t-1}^2 \overset{p}{\to} \frac{1}{2}\delta^2\left(1+\frac{\sin(2\lambda\pi)}{2\lambda\pi}\right) + \sigma_x^2 + \sigma_y^2 \tag{32}$$

$$\frac{1}{T}\sum_{t=1}^{T} x_{t-1}^2 \overset{p}{\to} \frac{1}{2}\delta^2\left(1+\frac{\sin(2\lambda\pi)}{2\lambda\pi}\right) + \sigma_x^2 \tag{33}$$

$$\frac{1}{T}\sum_{t=1}^{T} y_{t-1}x_{t-1} \overset{p}{\to} \frac{1}{2}\delta^2\left(1+\frac{\sin(2\lambda\pi)}{2\lambda\pi}\right) + \sigma_x^2 \tag{34}$$

$$\frac{1}{T}\sum_{t=1}^{T} \Delta y_t y_{t-1} \overset{p}{\to} -\sigma_x^2 - \sigma_y^2 \tag{35}$$

$$\frac{1}{T}\sum_{t=1}^{T} \Delta x_t x_{t-1} \overset{p}{\to} -\sigma_x^2; \qquad \frac{1}{T}\sum_{t=1}^{T} \Delta x_t y_{t-1} \overset{p}{\to} -\sigma_x^2 \tag{36}$$

$$\frac{1}{T}\sum_{t=1}^{T} \Delta y_t x_{t-1} \overset{p}{\to} \frac{1}{2}\delta^2\left(1+\frac{\cos(\lambda\pi)\sin(\lambda\pi)}{\lambda\pi}\right) - \frac{1}{2}\delta^2\left(1+\frac{\sin(2\lambda\pi)}{2\lambda\pi}\right) - \sigma_x^2 \tag{37}$$

A.2. PROOF OF LEMMA A

Under Assumption 1, as $T \to \infty$, for $0 < r \le 1$, we have $\frac{1}{\sqrt{T}}\sum_{t=1}^{\lfloor rT \rfloor} x_t = \frac{1}{\sqrt{T}}\sum_{t=1}^{\lfloor rT \rfloor} y_t = \frac{1}{\sqrt{T}}\sum_{t=1}^{\lfloor rT \rfloor} u_{xt} = \frac{1}{\sqrt{T}}\sum_{t=1}^{\lfloor rT \rfloor} u_{yt} = O_p(1)$. The results in Lemma A follow from

$$\frac{1}{T}\sum_{t=1}^{T}\Delta y_t^2$$

$$=\frac{1}{T}\sum_{t=1}^{T}\left(\delta\cos\left(\lambda\pi\frac{t}{T}\right)-\delta\cos\left(\lambda\pi\frac{(t-1)}{T}\right)+\Delta u_{xt}+\Delta u_{yt}\right)^2$$

$$=\frac{1}{T}\sum_{t=1}^{T}\left[\begin{array}{l}\delta^2\cos^2\left(\lambda\pi\frac{t}{T}\right)+\delta^2\cos^2\left(\lambda\pi\frac{(t-1)}{T}\right)\\ -2\delta^2\cos\left(\lambda\pi\frac{t}{T}\right)\cos\left(\lambda\pi\frac{(t-1)}{T}\right)\end{array}\right.$$

$$+2\delta\cos\left(\lambda\pi\frac{t}{T}\right)\Delta u_{xt}+2\delta\cos\left(\lambda\pi\frac{t}{T}\right)\Delta u_{yt}-2\delta\cos\left(\lambda\pi\frac{(t-1)}{T}\right)\Delta u_{xt}$$

$$\left.-2\delta\cos\left(\lambda\pi\frac{(t-1)}{T}\right)\Delta u_{yt}+(\Delta u_{xt})^2+(\Delta u_{yt})^2+2\Delta u_{xt}\Delta u_{yt}\right]$$

$$\xrightarrow{p}\frac{1}{2}\delta^2\left(1+\frac{\cos(\lambda\pi)\sin(\lambda\pi)}{\lambda\pi}\right)+\frac{1}{2}\delta^2\left(1+\frac{\sin(2\lambda\pi)}{2\lambda\pi}\right)$$

$$-\delta^2\left(1+\frac{\cos(\lambda\pi)\sin(\lambda\pi)}{\lambda\pi}\right)+2\sigma_x^2+2\sigma_y^2$$

$$=\frac{1}{2}\delta^2\left(\frac{\sin(2\lambda\pi)-2\cos(\lambda\pi)\sin(\lambda\pi)}{2\lambda\pi}\right)+2\sigma_x^2+2\sigma_y^2=2\left(\sigma_x^2+\sigma_y^2\right);$$

$$\frac{1}{T}\sum_{t=1}^{T}\Delta x_t^2=\frac{1}{T}\sum_{t=1}^{T}\left(\delta\cos\left(\lambda\pi\frac{t}{T}\right)-\delta\cos\left(\lambda\pi\frac{(t-1)}{T}\right)+\Delta u_{xt}\right)^2$$

$$=\frac{1}{T}\sum_{t=1}^{T}\left[\delta^2\cos^2\left(\lambda\pi\frac{t}{T}\right)+\delta^2\cos^2\left(\lambda\pi\frac{(t-1)}{T}\right)\right.$$

$$-2\delta^2\cos\left(\lambda\pi\frac{t}{T}\right)\cos\left(\lambda\pi\frac{(t-1)}{T}\right)$$

$$\left.+2\delta\cos\left(\lambda\pi\frac{t}{T}\right)\Delta u_{xt}-2\delta\cos\left(\lambda\pi\frac{(t-1)}{T}\right)\Delta u_{xt}+(\Delta u_{xt})^2\right]$$

$$\xrightarrow{p}\frac{1}{2}\delta^2\left(1+\frac{\cos(\lambda\pi)\sin(\lambda\pi)}{\lambda\pi}\right)+\frac{1}{2}\delta^2\left(1+\frac{\sin(2\lambda\pi)}{2\lambda\pi}\right)$$

$$-\delta^2\left(1+\frac{\cos(\lambda\pi)\sin(\lambda\pi)}{\lambda\pi}\right)+2\sigma_x^2$$

$$=\frac{1}{2}\delta^2\left(\frac{\sin(2\lambda\pi)-2\cos(\lambda\pi)\sin(\lambda\pi)}{2\lambda\pi}\right)+2\sigma_x^2=2\sigma_x^2;$$

$$\frac{1}{T}\sum_{t=1}^{T}\Delta y_t \Delta x_t = \frac{1}{T}\sum_{t=1}^{T}\left(\delta\cos\left(\lambda\pi\frac{t}{T}\right) - \delta\cos\left(\lambda\pi\frac{(t-1)}{T}\right) + \Delta u_{xt} + \Delta u_{yt}\right)$$

$$\left(\delta\cos\left(\lambda\pi\frac{t}{T}\right) - \delta\cos\left(\lambda\pi\frac{(t-1)}{T}\right) + \Delta u_{xt}\right)$$

$$= \frac{1}{T}\sum_{t=1}^{T}\left[\delta^2\cos^2\left(\lambda\pi\frac{t}{T}\right) + \delta^2\cos^2\left(\lambda\pi\frac{(t-1)}{T}\right)\right.$$

$$-2\delta^2\cos\left(\lambda\pi\frac{t}{T}\right)\cos\left(\lambda\pi\frac{(t-1)}{T}\right)$$

$$+2\delta\cos\left(\lambda\pi\frac{t}{T}\right)\Delta u_{xt} + \delta\cos\left(\lambda\pi\frac{t}{T}\right)\Delta u_{yt}$$

$$-2\delta\cos\left(\lambda\pi\frac{(t-1)}{T}\right)\Delta u_{xt} - \delta\cos\left(\lambda\pi\frac{(t-1)}{T}\right)\Delta u_{yt}$$

$$\left. + \left(\Delta u_{xt}\right)^2 + \Delta u_{xt}\Delta u_{yt}\right]$$

$$\overset{p}{\to}\frac{1}{2}\delta^2\left(1 + \frac{\cos(\lambda\pi)\sin(\lambda\pi)}{\lambda\pi}\right) + \frac{1}{2}\delta^2\left(1 + \frac{\sin(2\lambda\pi)}{2\lambda\pi}\right)$$

$$-\delta^2\left(1 + \frac{\cos(\lambda\pi)\sin(\lambda\pi)}{\lambda\pi}\right) + 2\sigma_x^2$$

$$= \frac{1}{2}\delta^2\left(\frac{\sin(2\lambda\pi) - 2\cos(\lambda\pi)\sin(\lambda\pi)}{2\lambda\pi}\right) + 2\sigma_x^2 = 2\sigma_x^2;$$

$$\frac{1}{T}\sum_{t=1}^{T} y_{t-1}^2$$

$$= \frac{1}{T}\sum_{t=1}^{T}\left(\delta\cos\left(\lambda\pi\frac{(t-1)}{T}\right) + \left(u_{xt-1} + u_{yt-1}\right)\right)^2$$

$$= \frac{1}{T}\sum_{t=1}^{T}\left[\delta^2\cos^2\left(\lambda\pi\frac{(t-1)}{T}\right) + 2\delta\cos\left(\lambda\pi\frac{(t-1)}{T}\right)u_{xt-1} + 2\delta\cos\left(\lambda\pi\frac{(t-1)}{T}\right)u_{yt-1}\right.$$

$$\left. + u_{xt-1}^2 + u_{yt-1}^2 + 2u_{xt-1}u_{yt-1}\right]$$

$$\overset{p}{\to}\frac{1}{2}\delta^2\left(1 + \frac{\sin(2\lambda\pi)}{2\lambda\pi}\right) + \sigma_x^2 + \sigma_y^2;$$

$$
\begin{aligned}
\frac{1}{T}\sum_{t=1}^{T} x_{t-1}^2 &= \frac{1}{T}\sum_{t=1}^{T}\left(\delta\cos\left(\lambda\pi\frac{(t-1)}{T}\right)+u_{xt-1}\right)^2 \\
&= \frac{1}{T}\sum_{t=1}^{T}\delta^2\cos^2\left(\lambda\pi\frac{(t-1)}{T}\right)+2\delta\cos\left(\lambda\pi\frac{(t-1)}{T}\right)u_{xt-1}+u_{xt-1}^2 \\
&\overset{p}{\to}\frac{1}{2}\delta^2\left(1+\frac{\sin(2\lambda\pi)}{2\lambda\pi}\right)+\sigma_x^2;
\end{aligned}
$$

$$
\begin{aligned}
&\frac{1}{T}\sum_{t=1}^{T} y_{t-1}x_{t-1} \\
&= \frac{1}{T}\sum_{t=1}^{T}\left(\delta\cos\left(\lambda\pi\frac{(t-1)}{T}\right)+\left(u_{xt-1}+u_{yt-1}\right)\right)\left(\delta\cos\left(\lambda\pi\frac{(t-1)}{T}\right)+u_{xt-1}\right) \\
&= \frac{1}{T}\sum_{t=1}^{T}\left[\delta^2\cos^2\left(\lambda\pi\frac{(t-1)}{T}\right)+2\delta\cos\left(\lambda\pi\frac{(t-1)}{T}\right)u_{xt-1}+\delta\cos\left(\lambda\pi\frac{(t-1)}{T}\right)u_{yt-1}\right. \\
&\left.+u_{xt-1}^2+u_{xt-1}u_{yt-1}\right] \\
&\overset{p}{\to}\frac{1}{2}\delta^2\left(1+\frac{\sin(2\lambda\pi)}{2\lambda\pi}\right)+\sigma_x^2;
\end{aligned}
$$

$$
\begin{aligned}
&\frac{1}{T}\sum_{t=1}^{T} \Delta y_t y_{t-1} \\
&= \frac{1}{T}\sum_{t=1}^{T}\left(\delta\cos\left(\lambda\pi\frac{t}{T}\right)-\delta\cos\left(\lambda\pi\frac{(t-1)}{T}\right)+\left(\Delta u_{xt}+\Delta u_{yt}\right)\right) \\
&\qquad\left(\delta\cos\left(\lambda\pi\frac{(t-1)}{T}\right)+\left(u_{xt-1}+u_{yt-1}\right)\right) \\
&= \frac{1}{T}\sum_{t=1}^{T}\left[\delta^2\cos\left(\lambda\pi\frac{t}{T}\right)\cos\left(\lambda\pi\frac{(t-1)}{T}\right)-\delta^2\cos^2\left(\lambda\pi\frac{(t-1)}{T}\right)\right. \\
&+\delta\cos\left(\lambda\pi\frac{(t-1)}{T}\right)\Delta u_{xt}+\delta\cos\left(\lambda\pi\frac{(t-1)}{T}\right)\Delta u_{yt} \\
&+\delta\cos\left(\lambda\pi\frac{t}{T}\right)u_{xt-1}-\delta\cos\left(\lambda\pi\frac{(t-1)}{T}\right)u_{xt-1} \\
&+\delta\cos\left(\lambda\pi\frac{t}{T}\right)u_{yt-1}-\delta\cos\left(\lambda\pi\frac{(t-1)}{T}\right)u_{yt-1} \\
&\left.+\Delta u_{xt}u_{yt-1}+\Delta u_{yt}u_{yt-1}+\Delta u_{xt}u_{xt-1}+\Delta u_{yt}u_{xt-1}\right] \\
&\overset{p}{\to}\frac{1}{2}\delta^2\left(1+\frac{\cos(\lambda\pi)\sin(\lambda\pi)}{\lambda\pi}\right)-\frac{1}{2}\delta^2\left(1+\frac{\sin(2\lambda\pi)}{2\lambda\pi}\right)-\sigma_x^2-\sigma_y^2=-\sigma_x^2-\sigma_y^2;
\end{aligned}
$$

$$\frac{1}{T}\sum_{t=1}^{T}\Delta x_t x_{t-1}$$

$$=\frac{1}{T}\sum_{t=1}^{T}\left(\delta\cos\left(\lambda\pi\frac{t}{T}\right)-\delta\cos\left(\lambda\pi\frac{(t-1)}{T}\right)+\Delta u_{xt}\right)\left(\delta\cos\left(\lambda\pi\frac{(t-1)}{T}\right)+u_{xt-1}\right)$$

$$=\frac{1}{T}\sum_{t=1}^{T}\left[\delta^2\cos\left(\lambda\pi\frac{t}{T}\right)\cos\left(\lambda\pi\frac{(t-1)}{T}\right)-\delta^2\cos^2\left(\lambda\pi\frac{(t-1)}{T}\right)\right.$$

$$\left.+\delta\cos\left(\lambda\pi\frac{(t-1)}{T}\right)\Delta u_{xt}+\delta\cos\left(\lambda\pi\frac{t}{T}\right)u_{xt-1}-\delta\cos\left(\lambda\pi\frac{(t-1)}{T}\right)u_{xt-1}+\Delta u_{xt}u_{xt-1}\right]$$

$$\xrightarrow{p}\frac{1}{2}\delta^2\left(1+\frac{\cos(\lambda\pi)\sin(\lambda\pi)}{\lambda\pi}\right)-\frac{1}{2}\delta^2\left(1+\frac{\sin(2\lambda\pi)}{2\lambda\pi}\right)-\sigma_x^2=-\sigma_x^2;$$

$$\frac{1}{T}\sum_{t=1}^{T}\Delta y_t x_{t-1}$$

$$=\frac{1}{T}\sum_{t=1}^{T}\left(\delta\cos\left(\lambda\pi\frac{t}{T}\right)-\delta\cos\left(\lambda\pi\frac{(t-1)}{T}\right)+\left(\Delta u_{xt}+\Delta u_{yt}\right)\right)$$

$$\left(\delta\cos\left(\lambda\pi\frac{(t-1)}{T}\right)+u_{xt-1}\right)$$

$$=\frac{1}{T}\sum_{t=1}^{T}\left[\delta^2\cos\left(\lambda\pi\frac{t}{T}\right)\cos\left(\lambda\pi\frac{(t-1)}{T}\right)-\delta^2\cos^2\left(\lambda\pi\frac{(t-1)}{T}\right)\right.$$

$$+\delta\cos\left(\lambda\pi\frac{(t-1)}{T}\right)\Delta u_{xt}+\delta\cos\left(\lambda\pi\frac{(t-1)}{T}\right)\Delta u_{yt}$$

$$\left.\delta\cos\left(\lambda\pi\frac{t}{T}\right)u_{xt-1}-\delta\cos\left(\lambda\pi\frac{(t-1)}{T}\right)u_{xt-1}+\Delta u_{xt}u_{xt-1}+\Delta u_{yt}u_{xt-1}\right]$$

$$\xrightarrow{p}\frac{1}{2}\delta^2\left(1+\frac{\cos(\lambda\pi)\sin(\lambda\pi)}{\lambda\pi}\right)-\frac{1}{2}\delta^2\left(1+\frac{\sin(2\lambda\pi)}{2\lambda\pi}\right)-\sigma_x^2;$$

and

$$\frac{1}{T}\sum_{t=1}^{T}\Delta x_t y_{t-1}$$

$$=\frac{1}{T}\sum_{t=1}^{T}\left(\delta\cos\left(\lambda\pi\frac{t}{T}\right)-\delta\cos\left(\lambda\pi\frac{(t-1)}{T}\right)+\Delta u_{xt}\right)$$

$$\left(\delta\cos\left(\lambda\pi\frac{(t-1)}{T}\right)+\left(u_{xt-1}+u_{yt-1}\right)\right)$$

$$=\frac{1}{T}\sum_{t=1}^{T}\left[\delta^2\cos\left(\lambda\pi\frac{t}{T}\right)\cos\left(\lambda\pi\frac{(t-1)}{T}\right)-\delta^2\cos^2\left(\lambda\pi\frac{(t-1)}{T}\right)\right.$$

$$+\delta\cos\left(\lambda\pi\frac{(t-1)}{T}\right)\Delta u_{xt}+\delta\cos\left(\lambda\pi\frac{t}{T}\right)u_{xt-1}-\delta\cos\left(\lambda\pi\frac{(t-1)}{T}\right)u_{xt-1}$$

$$\left.+\delta\cos\left(\lambda\pi\frac{t}{T}\right)u_{yt-1}-\delta\cos\left(\lambda\pi\frac{(t-1)}{T}\right)u_{yt-1}+\Delta u_{xt}u_{yt-1}+\Delta u_{xt}u_{xt-1}\right]$$

$$\xrightarrow{p}\frac{1}{2}\delta^2\left(1+\frac{\cos(\lambda\pi)\sin(\lambda\pi)}{\lambda\pi}\right)-\frac{1}{2}\delta^2\left(1+\frac{\sin(2\lambda\pi)}{2\lambda\pi}\right)-\sigma_x^2=-\sigma_x^2.$$

These results follow from simple convergence of moments. Namely, as $T\to\infty$,

$$\frac{1}{T}\sum_{t=1}^{T}u_{xt-1}^2\xrightarrow{p}V\left(u_{xt-1}\right)=\sigma_x^2;\frac{1}{T}\sum_{t=1}^{T}\left(\Delta u_{xt}\right)^2\xrightarrow{p}V\left(\Delta u_{xt}\right)=2\sigma_x^2$$

$$\frac{1}{T}\sum_{t=1}^{T}\Delta u_{xt}\Delta u_{yt}\xrightarrow{p}Cov\left(\Delta u_{xt},\Delta u_{yt}\right)=0;\frac{1}{T}\sum_{t=1}^{T}u_{xt-1}u_{yt-1}\xrightarrow{p}Cov\left(u_{xt-1},u_{yt-1}\right)=0$$

$$\frac{1}{T}\sum_{t=1}^{T}\Delta u_{xt}u_{xt-1}\xrightarrow{p}Cov\left(\Delta u_{xt},u_{xt-1}\right)=-\sigma_x^2;\frac{1}{T}\sum_{t=1}^{T}\Delta u_{xt}u_{yt-1}\xrightarrow{p}Cov\left(\Delta u_{xt},u_{yt-1}\right)=0.$$

Those involving the trigonometric functions are cumbersome but trivial. For example,

$$\frac{1}{T}\sum_{t=1}^{T}\delta^2\cos^2\left(\lambda\pi\frac{t}{T}\right)$$

$$=\delta^2\frac{1}{T}\left(\frac{T}{2}+\frac{\cos\left((T+1)\frac{\lambda\pi}{T}\right)\sin\left(T\frac{\lambda\pi}{T}\right)}{2\sin\left(\frac{\lambda\pi}{T}\right)}\right)=\delta^2\left(\frac{1}{2}+\frac{\cos\left(\lambda\pi+\frac{\lambda\pi}{T}\right)\sin(\lambda\pi)}{2\sin\left(\frac{1}{T}\lambda\pi\right)/(1/T)}\right)$$

$$\to\ \frac{1}{2}\delta^2\left(1+\frac{\cos(\lambda\pi)\sin(\lambda\pi)}{\lambda\pi}\right)$$

because $\sin\left(\lambda\pi\frac{1}{T}\right)/(1/T)\to\lambda\pi$ as $T\to\infty$. Similar results are obtained for $\frac{1}{T}\sum_{t=1}^{T}\delta^2\cos^2\left(\lambda\pi\frac{(t-1)}{T}\right)$ and $\frac{1}{T}\sum_{t=1}^{T}2\delta^2\cos\left(\lambda\pi\frac{t}{T}\right)\cos\left(\lambda\pi\frac{(t-1)}{T}\right)$. Moreover,

$$
\begin{aligned}
&\frac{1}{T}\sum_{t=1}^{T}2\delta\cos\left(\lambda\pi\frac{t}{T}\right)\Delta u_{xt}\\
&=2\delta\left(\frac{1}{T}\sum_{t=1}^{T}\cos\left(\lambda\pi\frac{t}{T}\right)u_{xt}-\frac{1}{T}\sum_{t=1}^{T}\cos\left(\lambda\pi\frac{(t-1)}{T}+\lambda\pi\frac{1}{T}\right)u_{xt-1}\right)\\
&=2\delta\begin{pmatrix}\frac{1}{T}\sum_{t=1}^{T}\cos\left(\lambda\pi\frac{t}{T}\right)u_{xt}-\cos\left(\lambda\pi\frac{1}{T}\right)\frac{1}{T}\sum_{t=1}^{T}\cos\left(\lambda\pi\frac{(t-1)}{T}\right)u_{xt-1}\\
+\sin\left(\lambda\pi\frac{1}{T}\right)\frac{1}{T}\sum_{t=1}^{T}\sin\left(\lambda\pi\frac{(t-1)}{T}\right)u_{xt-1}\end{pmatrix}\\
&=2\delta\begin{pmatrix}\frac{1}{T}\sum_{t=1}^{T}\cos\left(\lambda\pi\frac{t}{T}\right)u_{xt}\\
-\cos\left(\lambda\pi\frac{1}{T}\right)\left(\frac{1}{T}\sum_{t=1}^{T}\cos\left(\lambda\pi\frac{t}{T}\right)u_{xt}+\frac{1}{T}\cos(0)u_{x0}-\frac{1}{T}\cos(\lambda\pi)u_{xT}\right)\\
+\sin\left(\lambda\pi\frac{1}{T}\right)\left(\frac{1}{T}\sum_{t=1}^{T}\sin\left(\lambda\pi\frac{t}{T}\right)u_{xt}+\frac{1}{T}\sin(0)u_{x0}-\frac{1}{T}\sin(\lambda\pi)u_{xT}\right)\end{pmatrix}\\
&=2\delta\begin{pmatrix}\frac{1}{T}\sum_{t=1}^{T}\cos\left(\lambda\pi\frac{t}{T}\right)u_{xt}\\
-\cos\left(\lambda\pi\frac{1}{T}\right)\left(\frac{1}{T}\sum_{t=1}^{T}\cos\left(\lambda\pi\frac{t}{T}\right)u_{xt}+\frac{1}{T}u_{x0}-\frac{1}{T}\cos(\lambda\pi)u_{xT}\right)\\
+\sin\left(\lambda\pi\frac{1}{T}\right)\left(\frac{1}{T}\sum_{t=1}^{T}\sin\left(\lambda\pi\frac{t}{T}\right)u_{xt}-\frac{1}{T}\sin(\lambda\pi)u_{xT}\right)\end{pmatrix}
\end{aligned}
$$

$$
= 2\delta \left(\begin{array}{l} \cos(\lambda\pi)\frac{1}{T}\sum_{t=1}^{T} u_{xt} + (\lambda\pi)\int_0^1 \sin(\lambda\pi r)\left(\frac{1}{T}\sum_{t=1}^{\lfloor rT \rfloor} u_{xt}\right)dr \\ -\cos\left(\lambda\pi\frac{1}{T}\right)\left(\begin{array}{c} \cos(\lambda\pi)\frac{1}{T}\sum_{t=1}^{T} u_{xt} + (\lambda\pi)\int_0^1 \sin(\lambda\pi r) \\ \left(\frac{1}{T}\sum_{t=1}^{\lfloor rT \rfloor} u_{xt}\right)dr + \frac{1}{T}u_{x0} - \frac{1}{T}\cos(\lambda\pi)u_{xT} \end{array} \right) \\ +\sin\left(\lambda\pi\frac{1}{T}\right)\left(\begin{array}{c} \sin(\lambda\pi)\frac{1}{T}\sum_{t=1}^{T} u_{xt} - (\lambda\pi)\int_0^1 \cos(\lambda\pi r) \\ \left(\frac{1}{T}\sum_{t=1}^{\lfloor rT \rfloor} u_{xt}\right)dr - \frac{1}{T}\sin(\lambda\pi)u_{xT} \end{array} \right) \end{array} \right)
$$

$$\to 0.$$

See Bierens (1994, Lem 9.6.3, p. 200). A similar proof is done for $\frac{1}{T}\sum_{t=1}^{T} 2\delta\cos\left(\lambda\pi\frac{(t-1)}{T}\right)\Delta u_{xt}$, $\frac{1}{T}\sum_{t=1}^{T} \delta\cos\left(\lambda\pi\frac{t}{T}\right)u_{xt-1}$, and $\frac{1}{T}\sum_{t=1}^{T} \delta\cos\left(\lambda\pi\frac{(t-1)}{T}\right)u_{xt-1}$.

A.3. PROOF OF LEMMA 1

From Lemma A,

$$
S_{00,T} = \frac{1}{T}\sum_{t=1}^{T} \Delta z_t \Delta z_t' = \frac{1}{T}\sum_{t=1}^{T} \begin{bmatrix} \Delta y_t^2 & \Delta y_t \Delta x_t \\ \Delta x_t \Delta y_t & \Delta x_t^2 \end{bmatrix}
$$

$$
\overset{p}{\to} 2\begin{bmatrix} (\sigma_x^2 + \sigma_y^2) & \sigma_x^2 \\ \sigma_x^2 & \sigma_x^2 \end{bmatrix} = 2\Upsilon;
$$

$$S_{11,T} = \frac{1}{T}\sum_{t=1}^{T} z_{t-1}z_{t-1}^{'} = \frac{1}{T}\sum_{t=1}^{T}\begin{bmatrix} y_{t-1}^2 & y_{t-1}x_{t-1} \\ x_{t-1}y_{t-1} & x_{t-1}^2 \end{bmatrix}$$

$$\xrightarrow{p}\begin{bmatrix} \frac{1}{2}\delta^2\left(1+\frac{\sin(2\lambda\pi)}{2\lambda\pi}\right)+\sigma_x^2+\sigma_y^2 & \frac{1}{2}\delta^2\left(1+\frac{\sin(2\lambda\pi)}{2\lambda\pi}\right)+\sigma_x^2 \\ \frac{1}{2}\delta^2\left(1+\frac{\sin(2\lambda\pi)}{2\lambda\pi}\right)+\sigma_x^2 & \frac{1}{2}\delta^2\left(1+\frac{\sin(2\lambda\pi)}{2\lambda\pi}\right)+\sigma_x^2 \end{bmatrix}$$

$$= \frac{1}{2}\delta^2\left(1+\frac{\sin(2\lambda\pi)}{2\lambda\pi}\right)\iota + \Upsilon;$$

and

$$S_{01,T} = \frac{1}{T}\sum_{t=1}^{T}\Delta z_t z_{t-1}^{'} = \frac{1}{T}\sum_{t=1}^{T}\begin{bmatrix} \Delta y_t y_{t-1} & \Delta y_t x_{t-1} \\ \Delta x_t y_{t-1} & \Delta x_t x_{t-1} \end{bmatrix}$$

$$\xrightarrow{p}\begin{bmatrix} -\sigma_x^2-\sigma_y^2 & -\sigma_x^2 \\ -\sigma_x^2 & -\sigma_x^2 \end{bmatrix} = -\Upsilon,$$

where $\Upsilon = \begin{bmatrix} (\sigma_x^2+\sigma_y^2) & \sigma_x^2 \\ \sigma_x^2 & \sigma_x^2 \end{bmatrix}$ and $\iota = \begin{bmatrix} 1 & 1 \\ 1 & 1 \end{bmatrix}$.

A.4. PROOF OF THEOREM 2

We start by sketching the proof of Theorem 1. Following the Lemma 2 in Anderson et al. (1983) and our Lemma 1, the ordered solutions $\hat{\theta}_1 \geq \hat{\theta}_2$ of the generalized eigenvalue problem

$$\det\left[\theta S_{11,T} - S_{10,T}S_{00,T}^{-1}S_{01,T}\right] = 0$$

converge in probability to the ordered solutions $\theta_1 \geq \theta_2$ of

$$\det\left[\theta\left(\frac{1}{2}\delta^2\left(1+\frac{\sin(2\lambda\pi)}{2\lambda\pi}\right)\iota+\Upsilon\right) - \Upsilon'(2\Upsilon)^{-1}\Upsilon\right] = 0 \Leftrightarrow$$

$$\det\begin{bmatrix} \theta\left(\frac{1}{2}\delta^2\left(1+\frac{\sin(2\lambda\pi)}{2\lambda\pi}\right)+(\sigma_x^2+\sigma_y^2)\right)-\frac{1}{2}(\sigma_x^2+\sigma_y^2) & \theta\left(\frac{1}{2}\delta^2\left(1+\frac{\sin(2\lambda\pi)}{2\lambda\pi}\right)+\sigma_x^2\right)-\frac{1}{2}\sigma_x^2 \\ \theta\left(\frac{1}{2}\delta^2\left(1+\frac{\sin(2\lambda\pi)}{2\lambda\pi}\right)+\sigma_x^2\right)-\frac{1}{2}\sigma_x^2 & \theta\left(\frac{1}{2}\delta^2\left(1+\frac{\sin(2\lambda\pi)}{2\lambda\pi}\right)+\sigma_x^2\right)-\frac{1}{2}\sigma_x^2 \end{bmatrix} = 0 \Leftrightarrow$$

$$\det\begin{bmatrix} \theta\left(\frac{1}{2}\delta^2\left(1+\frac{\sin(2\lambda\pi)}{2\lambda\pi}\right)+\sigma_x^2\right)-\frac{1}{2}\sigma_x^2+\left(\theta\sigma_y^2-\frac{1}{2}\sigma_y^2\right) & \theta\left(\frac{1}{2}\delta^2\left(1+\frac{\sin(2\lambda\pi)}{2\lambda\pi}\right)+\sigma_x^2\right)-\frac{1}{2}\sigma_x^2 \\ \theta\left(\frac{1}{2}\delta^2\left(1+\frac{\sin(2\lambda\pi)}{2\lambda\pi}\right)+\sigma_x^2\right)-\frac{1}{2}\sigma_x^2 & \theta\left(\frac{1}{2}\delta^2\left(1+\frac{\sin(2\lambda\pi)}{2\lambda\pi}\right)+\sigma_x^2\right)-\frac{1}{2}\sigma_x^2 \end{bmatrix}=0\Leftrightarrow$$

$$\det\begin{bmatrix} \Delta+\left(\theta\sigma_y^2-\frac{1}{2}\sigma_y^2\right) & \Delta \\ \Delta & \Delta \end{bmatrix}=0$$

where $\Delta=\theta\left(\frac{1}{2}\delta^2\left(1+\frac{\sin(2\lambda\pi)}{2\lambda\pi}\right)+\sigma_x^2\right)-\frac{1}{2}\sigma_x^2$. This is clearly very different to the standard Johansen's cointegration results. The determinant equals $\Delta^2+\left(\theta\sigma_y^2-\frac{1}{2}\sigma_y^2\right)\Delta-\Delta^2=\left(\theta\sigma_y^2-\frac{1}{2}\sigma_y^2\right)\Delta$. The two roots do not depend on the parameter σ_y^2 nd are given by

$$\theta_1=\frac{1}{2} \text{ and } \theta_2=\frac{1}{\frac{\delta^2}{\sigma_x^2}\left(1+\frac{\sin(2\lambda\pi)}{2\lambda\pi}\right)+2}<\frac{1}{2}=\theta_1,$$

for all admissible $\sigma_x^2,\lambda,\delta$ because $\frac{\delta^2}{\sigma_x^2}\left(1+\frac{\sin(2\lambda\pi)}{2\lambda\pi}\right)>0$. For any λ such that $\frac{\sin(2\lambda\pi)}{2\lambda\pi}=0$ we have $\theta_2=\frac{1}{\frac{\delta^2}{\sigma_x^2}+2}$. That is true for integer $\lambda>2$. Again, contrary to the standard cointegration approach, there are no zero solutions and, in particular, the largest $\hat{\theta}$ converges in probability to $\frac{1}{2}$. Moreover, since $\theta_2\neq 0$, $T\hat{\theta}_2$ will not converge in distribution to a random variable, but rather tends to infinity and therefore the Johansen's tests will also diverge to infinity as $T\to\infty$.

Now, we can discuss the limiting properties of the estimator (Theorem 2). The ML estimator for β is the eigenvector associated with the largest eigenvalue $\hat{\theta}$:

$$S_{10,T}S_{00,T}^{-1}S_{01,T}\,\hat{\beta}=\hat{\theta}S_{11,T}\hat{\beta}.$$

The estimator $\hat{\beta}$ converges in probability to the eigenvector associated with the largest eigenvalue $\theta_1 = \frac{1}{2}$ and therefore $p\lim_{T\to\infty} \hat{\beta} = b$ where b is the solution to

$$p\lim_{T\to\infty} S_{10,T} S_{00,T}^{-1} S_{01,T} b = \theta\, p\lim_{T\to\infty} S_{11,T} b.$$

It can be easily shown that the normalized b is given by $b = (1,-1)'$, which is the true coefficient in the misspecified bivariate cointegrated ECM. To prove this, we find that the solution b for $\theta_1 = \frac{1}{2}$ satisfies

$$\frac{1}{2}\delta^2\left(1+\frac{\sin(2\lambda\pi)}{2\lambda\pi}\right)(b_1+b_2)=0,$$

so that for the normalized $b_1 = 1$, we obtain $b_2 = -1$

For the estimator $\tilde{\alpha}$ we have

$$\tilde{\alpha} = S_{01,T}\tilde{\beta}\left(\tilde{\beta}' S_{11,T}\tilde{\beta}\right)^{-1},$$

where $\tilde{\beta}$ is the normalized MLE of $\hat{\beta}$ (defined below), which converges to

$$-\Upsilon b\left(b'\left(\frac{1}{2}\delta^2\left(1+\frac{\sin(2\lambda\pi)}{2\lambda\pi}\right)\iota+\Upsilon\right)b\right)^{-1} = \begin{pmatrix}-1\\0\end{pmatrix} = \alpha.$$

For

$$\hat{\Omega} = S_{00,T} - \tilde{\alpha}\tilde{\beta}' S_{10,T},$$

it converges to

$$2\Upsilon + \alpha b'\Upsilon = \begin{bmatrix} 2\sigma_x^2+\sigma_y^2 & 2\sigma_x^2 \\ 2\sigma_x^2 & 2\sigma_x^2 \end{bmatrix} \neq \begin{bmatrix} \sigma_y^2 & 0 \\ 0 & \sigma_x^2 \end{bmatrix}.$$

In terms of the limiting distribution of $\hat{\beta}$, notice first that the matrix $S_{11,T} = \frac{1}{T}\sum_{t=1}^{T} z_{t-1}z_{t-1}'$ is $O_p(1)$, something distinct from the $I(1)$ case where $\frac{1}{T}S_{11,T} = O_p(1)$. In standard cointegration, the MLE $\hat{\beta}$ of β is normalized as $\tilde{\beta} = \hat{\beta}\left(\beta'\hat{\beta}\right)^{-1}\beta'\beta$ and one can write $\tilde{\beta} - \beta = \beta_\perp U_T$, where $\beta_\perp'\beta = 0$ and $U_T = \left(\beta_\perp'\beta_\perp\right)^{-1}\left(\beta_\perp'\hat{\beta}\right)\left(\beta'\hat{\beta}\right)^{-1}\left(\beta'\beta\right)$, with an expansion

$$T.U_T = \left(T^{-1}\beta_\perp' S_{11,T}\beta_\perp\right)^{-1}\beta_\perp'\left(S_{10,T} - S_{11,T}\beta\alpha'\right)\Omega^{-1}\alpha\left(\alpha'\Omega^{-1}\alpha\right)^{-1} + o_p(1)$$

from which the distribution is derived. However, in our setup, this cannot be done this way because $S_{11,T}$ has a different order of integration. From the previous results, as $T \to \infty$,

$$\left(\tilde{\beta}' S_{11,T} \tilde{\beta}\right)^{-1} \xrightarrow{p} \left(b' \left(\frac{1}{2}\delta^2 \left(1 + \frac{\sin(2\lambda\pi)}{2\lambda\pi}\right)\iota + \Upsilon\right) b\right)^{-1} = \frac{1}{\sigma_y^2}$$

and

$$S_{11,T}\tilde{\beta} \xrightarrow{p} \left[\frac{1}{2}\delta^2 \left(1 + \frac{\sin(2\lambda\pi)}{2\lambda\pi}\right)\iota + \Upsilon\right]\beta = -\sigma_y^2 \alpha.$$

Thus, $\tilde{\beta}$ converges in distribution at a rate $\sqrt{T}$ instead of T. Deriving the expression of the limiting distribution for constant or time-varying δ_t is a very complicated exercise and, for that reason, we rest on the results we find in the Monte Carlo section.